'THE MOST DREADFUL VISITATION': MALE MADNESS IN VICTORIAN FICTION

LIVERPOOL ENGLISH TEXTS AND STUDIES, 46

'THE MOST DREADFUL VISITATION': MALE MADNESS IN VICTORIAN FICTION

VALERIE PEDLAR

LIVERPOOL UNIVERSITY PRESS

First published 2006 by
Liverpool University Press
4 Cambridge Street
Liverpool L69 7ZU

British Library Cataloguing-in-Publication data
A British Library CIP record is available

ISBN 0-85323-839-1 cased

ISBN-13 978-0-85323-839-3 cased

Typeset in Garamond by Servis Filmsetting Ltd, Manchester
Printed and bound in the European Union by Biddles Ltd, King's Lynn,
Norfolk

To the memory of my parents,
Geoffrey and Marjorie Robinson

Contents

Acknowledgements

During the many years it has taken me to produce this book, which started life as a PhD thesis at the University of Liverpool, I have received help and encouragement from many friends and colleagues. I owe thanks to the anonymous reader for Liverpool University Press whose report suggested the focus on male insanity, and also to Robin Bloxsidge and Andrew Kirk for help and encouragement at critical points along the path to publication. I am particularly grateful to Simon Dentith, Brean Hammond and David Seed (my PhD supervisor), who at various times read and commented on parts of my manuscript and I should like to express my appreciation of the stimulating and supportive conferences run by the British Association for Victorian Studies. Needless to say, I alone am responsible for the shortcomings of the book. Friends and family have sustained me when the going got tough, though there must have been times when I tested their patience with my complaints and anxieties. My greatest debt, as always, is to Arthur, my ever-supportive husband.

Introduction

In 1842, whilst he was staying in New York, Charles Dickens visited a lunatic asylum on Long Island or Rhode Island ('I forget which'). He depicts the scene graphically:

> The moping idiot, cowering down with long, dishevelled hair; the gibbering maniac, with his hideous laugh and pointed finger; the vacant eye, the fierce wild face, the gloomy picking of the hands and lips, and munching of the nails; there they were all, without disguise, in naked ugliness and horror.[1]

In part his horror at the sight of these mad people is inspired by the dreary, dirty, ill-ordered conditions in which they are kept. These inmates are people on whose minds has fallen 'the most dreadful visitation to which our nature is exposed',[2] and they need and deserve a wholesome and stimulating environment if they are to be restored to full humanity. Madness for nineteenth-century writers was both an alien state of mind and something that could afflict 'our nature' at any time. Imaginatively, therefore, it offered opportunities to explore the extremities of human mental and emotional suffering, uniting the fascination of the strange and the abnormal with the familiarity of the known and the shared. Since madness denotes a dissonance between the individual and society, it provides a channel for the exploration of moral dilemmas, focusing on the issues of egoism and self-control. But since it also denotes individual suffering, moral judgement must be qualified by sympathy, respect and understanding. 'Madness' is a term more common in literary than in medical usage, but the conditions it describes are not simply literary conditions. Imaginative representations of madness are inevitably influenced by cultural conceptions of insanity, whether they are medical, juridical, philosophical, or a composite that has entered into popular currency. In this book I shall be looking at a variety of fictional texts which figure mad men. My main focus is on the way that madness functions in the texts and on what the representation of madness in men reveals about contemporary fears, insecurities and ambiguities concerning the state of manhood. This introductory chapter provides the background for that investigation, summarising the changes in nineteenth-century concepts and treatments of insanity, the gendering of madness and the way in which the representation of madness is related to fictional genres.

Nineteenth-century conceptions of insanity

In 1823 John Haslam, who had been apothecary at the famous Bethlem Hospital, in London, published *A Letter to the Right Honourable, the Lord Chancellor, on the Nature and Interpretation of Unsoundness of Mind, and Imbecility of Intellect* in which he defined three types of insanity: idiocy, lunacy and unsoundness of mind. This threefold definition was given legal recognition in the important Lunatics Act of 1845, the three classes being subsumed under the generic term '*non compos mentis*'. An idiot was described as a person 'whose mind from his birth by a perpetual infirmity is so deficient as to be incapable of directing him in any matter which requires thought or judgement'. A lunatic was someone who enjoyed lucid intervals and sound memory, but sometimes was *non compos mentis*. A person of unsound mind was 'every person, who, by reason of a morbid condition of intellect is incapable of managing himself and his affairs, not being an idiot or lunatic, or a person merely of weak mind'.[3] Although there was a recognition by the early 1840s of the need for specialist provision for 'idiots', they were still being classed as 'insane' in, for instance, Forbes Winslow's *On Obscure Diseases of the Brain* in 1860.[4] I shall be saying more about conceptions of idiocy (or idiotcy) in Chapter 1, but the main distinction between idiocy and other types of insanity was that it was a condition from birth and it was a perpetual infirmity. Although the other types of insanity may be the result of heredity, and may in fact show early signs in childhood, they only became established later in life and could, in theory at any rate, be cured. Different types of mental disorder might be classified according to symptoms or causes. Basing his nosology on symptoms, Jean Etienne Esquirol, the influential French physician, recognises four categories in addition to idiocy: 'lypemania' or melancholy, 'mania', 'dementia' and 'monomania'.[5] Monomania, 'in which delirium is limited to one or a small number of objects, with excitement, and predominance of a gay, and expansive passion', was an important addition to the lexicon of madness and became a term that entered the general vocabulary.[6] It describes obsessive behaviour and thinking, such as could be seen in people who were otherwise conducting a normal life, and, since it was also described as 'partial insanity', it raises the endlessly difficult question of the borderline between madness and sanity. Nor is this question evaded in a nosology based on causes. Here, as Esquirol recognises, the situation is complex: 'The causes of mental alienation are as numerous, as its forms are varied. They are general or special, physical or moral, primitive or secondary, predisposing or exciting.'[7] They included climate, the seasons, age, sex, temperament, profession and mode of life. I should like to focus particularly on the distinction between physical and moral causes, which was adopted by many clinical writers in their taxonomies of mental disease. Moral causes had to do with the passions, which could be excited by unrequited love, domestic troubles and grief, as well as economic hardship; madness lay in excessive response, in fact, to the trials of life. But the notion of excess already involved an appeal to normative standards and thus undermines any idea of diagnosis as a straightforward assessment of facts. The physical causes listed by early nineteenth century writers might encompass disease to the brain, but would also include drink, fever, masturbation, injury to the head and even over-study. Moral causes, therefore, did not cover all the behaviour that might have been registered as ethically suspect, but they do incorporate eighteenth-century ideas about the need for passion to be regulated by reason. The madnesses that feature in the novels discussed in Chapters 2–4 fall into this category of insanity excited by moral causes.

The link between madness and morality became still more complex with the introduction of the concept of 'moral insanity'. James Prichard is commonly credited as being, and indeed was concerned to establish himself as the inventor of this term and with popularising it in his influential *Treatise on Insanity* (1835).[8] In fact the term was also used by Thomas Mayo in 1834. Mayo distinguishes moral insanity from intellectual insanity, though he maintains both types of insanity lack the conflict which the sane experience by having standards of judgement: 'Many a sane person indeed, may envy the contented and self-satisfied lunatic.'[9] In thus explicitly linking madness and morality, Mayo recognises the existence in the human mind of a 'moral sense' analogous to the 'intellectual sense'; it is not the case that insanity simply 'unseats the moral principle'.[10] Prichard's nosology recognises four types of insanity, three of which constitute 'intellectual insanity', whilst the fourth was designated 'moral insanity', which was defined as 'a morbid perversion of the feelings, affections, inclinations, temper, habits, moral dispositions, and natural impulses, without any remarkable disorder or defect of the intellect or knowing and reasoning faculties, and particularly without any insane illusion or hallucination'.[11] Like monomania this is a partial insanity and by removing from diagnosis the defining necessity of delusion or hallucinations, the idea of moral insanity opens up for *medical* inspection a range of behaviour that would previously have been subject to official or unofficial *moral* judgement only. Once again the result is a blurring of the boundaries between diagnosis and judgement. But in any case the concept of diagnosis implies judgement, since it involves the measuring of an individual's physical or mental state against some standard of health or normality. Where madness was concerned, opinion and practice fluctuated between appeal to a standard conceived in the abstract, that is, some sort of ideal state, and a standard established through common patterns of behaviour, or an amalgam of these two things. But it was also recognised by some writers (for instance, Forbes Winslow) that the question of aberrancy concerned only the comparison of an individual's behaviour and emotional state with what it had been previously. Once it had been accepted by the medical profession, enshrined in law and acknowledged by the public at large that confinement in an institution of one kind or another was the appropriate way of handling madness, the question of diagnosis became crucial, and imaginative literature was not slow in exposing its juridical nature and the difficulties and ambiguities this involved. *Hard Cash* was only one of a rash of novels concerned with wrongful confinement and the correlative problems of diagnosing insanity or defining sanity, which will be discussed in Chapter 3.

As the first chapter will show, the idea of madness being imprinted on the body, manifest in physiognomy or posture, was widely accepted. That 'there is an art to find the mind's construction in the face' is a tradition going back to Aristotle, as Jenny Bourne Taylor points out in her excellent brief history of nineteenth-century psychology.[12] Sander Gilman's fascinating survey of the visual representations of madness from the Middle Ages to the end of the nineteenth century traces the shifts in such perceptions and, illustrating the thesis expounded by Ernst Gombrich in *Art and Illusion*, explores the degree to which they were influenced by traditional conventions.[13] But, whereas physiognomy conceived of the face and body as the outward expression of internal processes, phrenology, interested in cranial formation, regarded the shape of the skull as indicative of the particular organs it contained. Roger Cooter has isolated four key tenets in phrenology: the brain was seen as the organ of the mind; the brain was a congeries of organs; each cerebral part corresponded to a particular moral or intellectual quality; since the cranium was ossified over the shape of the brain its shape could be used to determine the state of the internal parts.[14] These ideas, which were linked to the physiognomic studies of Lavater, whose work will be examined in more detail in Chapter 1, and originated in the observations of Franz Joseph Gall, were popularised in England by J.G. Spurzheim and George Combe, and, as Cooter explains, were used to give moral therapy scientific status. Since mental health, it was thought, depended on the equal development of all the organs of the brain, the treatment for those who showed over- or under-development of one particular faculty was precisely along the lines of contemporary morality: sobriety, chastity, self-improvement and moderation in all things. So, on the one hand, phrenology commandeered the sphere of morality, and on the other hand, it instituted a physiological justification of practices which had previously relied on religious sanctions.

In yet another confusion of the mental and the bodily, the idea of nervous breakdown relied on the structural conception of the body's nervous system, though there was no clear idea how this worked. Skirting the charge of insanity, psychological symptoms were given greater respectability, for the image of a somatic breakdown absolved the sufferer from moral blame. The terminology might vary: breakdown, shattered nerves, broken health, nervous collapse, exhaustion, prostration, or, towards the end of the century, neurasthenia, could all indicate some sort of mental breakdown. Whatever the terminology used, however, it could be difficult, in fact, to distinguish nervous breakdown from actual insanity; like the partial insanities, monomania and moral insanity, it designated an awkward borderline state. As Janet Oppenheim shows in her comprehensive book, 'Shattered Nerves', although there was a tendency to diagnose nervous breakdown if the patient was middle class and insanity if the patient was working class, in practice such class differentials were not hard and fast.[15] In Wilkie Collins's novel *Basil*, which I discuss in Chapter 2, Basil hears himself charged with madness by passing strangers, describes his feverish hallucinations, and is diagnosed as suffering from brain fever. Like nervous breakdown, brain fever was another of those capacious categories in the taxonomies of mental and physical suffering that blurred the boundaries between body and mind. More specific understanding of how the relationship between the brain and the rest of the body developed in the latter decades of the nineteenth century as the separate discipline of neurology emerged, and neurologists such as Hughlings Jackson and

David Ferrier were able to give substance to the tenets of phrenology. Chapter 5 will look at *Dracula's* imaginative engagement with David Ferrier's experiments in cerebral localisation.

By the end of the century phrenology itself had fallen from favour, and doctors who were interested in the mind rather than the brain were anxiously searching for the causes of madness in other ways, though the belief in physical causes of psychological symptoms seemed impossible to avoid. During the latter part of the century, the influence of Darwinism had encouraged belief in the hereditary aspect of madness, and two French writers, B.A. Morel and Jacques Moreau, had introduced ideas of degeneracy that were to be taken up by the most influential psychiatrist of the late nineteenth century, Henry Maudsley, who presented a bleak vision not just of madness, but of life in general. Basing his analysis on an assurance that mental illness had a physical basis as well as being inherited, he saw madness as an inevitable destiny, in which the lunatic, unable to escape the 'tyranny of his organization', was ill-adapted to cope with the harshness of life. Despite his reliance on a somatic aetiology, Maudsley castigated madness as moral degeneracy and projected a gloomy future of racial decline. The opening of *The Pathology of Mind* (1879) incorporates several of the motifs that have already been touched on in this introductory chapter and which will be explored further in the discussions of the novels:

> By insanity of mind is meant such derangement of the leading functions of thought, feeling, and will, together or separately, as disable the person from thinking the thoughts, feeling the feelings, and doing the duties of the social body in, for, and by which he lives. Alienated from his normal self and from his kind, he is in the social organisation that which a morbid growth is in the physiological organism: something which, being a law unto itself, in the body but not of it, is an alien there, a morbid kind, and ought in the interests of the whole either to be got rid out of it or sequestrated and rendered harmless in it. However it has come about, whether by fate or fault, he is now so self-regarding a self as to be incapable of right regard to the notself; altruism has been swallowed up in a morbid egoism.[16]

The ideas of alienation and egoism expressed in this extract will be seen to resurface in the discussion of *Dracula*, but what I should particularly like to comment on here is the strong moralistic tone, which, by comparing the deranged person with 'a morbid growth', denies him or her the sensibilities of humanity as effectively as the eighteenth-century insistence on the animality of the insane. Maudsley links the mad with the bad: 'It is not possible to draw a distinct line of demarcation between insanity and crime ... There are criminals who are more mad than bad, insane persons who are more bad than mad,' but in both cases 'a man's nature is essentially a recompense or a retribution'.[17] Like Dickens earlier in the period, Maudsley sees the sins of the fathers being visited upon the children, but he promotes a more judgemental attitude by suggesting that a person will not only have a 'tendency' to 'perform the function pre-ordained in his structure', but it will also be his 'pleasure'.[18] By amalgamating the basic principle of utilitarianism with strict determinism, Maudsley illogically manages to blame people for what they cannot help. The penultimate sentence of his book indicates the pessimism of his thinking:

> Nor would the scientific interest of his [a physician's] studies compensate entirely for the practical uncertainties, since their revelation of the structure of human nature might inspire a doubt whether, notwithstanding impassioned aims, paeans of progress, endless pageants of self-illusions, its capacity of degeneration did not equal, and might some day exceed, its capacity of development.[19]

Andrew Wynter was obviously indebted to Maudsley's ideas, but writes in a more humane spirit, concerned to remove the 'moral stigma' from madness, but he, too, fosters the fear of inherited insanity; even when it has not become apparent, there are 'latent seeds' which only require 'some exciting cause to force them into vigorous growth'.[20] Wynter called his collection of essays published in 1875 *The Borderlands of Insanity*, and it might be thought that his concern was with the way sanity can so easily shade into insanity. And in a way it is, but it is not a case of insanity lying in wait for the unwary, something that can happen to anyone, as is recognised by the narrator of *Lady Audley's Secret*: 'Who has not been, or is not to be, mad in some lonely hour of life? Who is quite safe from the trembling of the balance?'[21] When this narrator talks about the 'the narrow boundary between reason and unreason' she is thinking more democratically than is Wynter.[22] For the physician, madness does not strike indiscriminately; it is those who are harbouring the latent seeds of madness, those who are hovering in the borderlands, where it is difficult to distinguish true madness from 'mere eccentricity' or 'moral perversity', who are in danger of one day becoming insane.[23] Wynter conceptualises madness as a 'brain disease', but the 'changes that take place are of too delicate a nature for our science to reach in its present condition',[24] therefore the physician is driven back on the usual moral treatment in which the true principle of cure and support is 'an association with healthy minds'.[25]

The treatment of madness

The question of treatment was much discussed. The Lunatics Act of 1845 made the provision of county asylums compulsory, and in the years that followed there was a huge growth in what became huge institutions; nine county asylums existed in 1827, sixty-six in 1890. Wynter was one of the many Whiggish commentators who saw the eighteenth century as a back-ward period of cruel treatment of the insane, compared with the human-itarian efforts of the nineteenth century. Nevertheless, in his volume of 1875 he is critical of the growth in the size of asylums and of their dubious use: 'The county asylum is the mental lumber-room of the surrounding district; friends are only too willing, in their poverty, to place away the human encumbrance of the family in a palatial building, at the county expense.'[26] These 'museums of madness', to use Andrew Scull's resonant phrase, housed hundreds of patients; indeed, by the 1850s the two largest, Hanwell and Colney Hatch, both serving Middlesex, each contained well over a thousand inmates.[27] The county asylum, however, figures relatively rarely in Victorian fiction. The unfortunate Richard Marwood, the hero of Braddon's *The Trail of the Serpent*, is unusually cast into a public asylum as a result of his successful acting of madness in a court of law, but for most of those who are consigned to custodial care in fiction it is the private madhouse that receives them, despite the fact that the number of such establishments steadily decreased after the act of 1845.[28] Here the wrong that most exercised public opinion was not the use of public resources for 'warehousing the unwanted', but the wrongful confinement of people who were not necessarily mad for the convenience or economic advantage of unscrupulous family members, as well of course to the profit of madhouse proprietors. The theme of wrongful confinement is the subject of Chapter 3. The novels that are discussed in this chapter show that the concern was not only dubiety over the grounds for confining people of unsound mind, but fears of the treatment to which they were subjected once they had been shut up in a place that inevitably became a place of secrets. One of the most sustained attacks on two well-known private madhouses is John Perceval's *Narrative*, published in 1840. Not only does he castigate members of his family for having him certified in the first place, but he is virulent in his criticism of the treatment he received at both Brislington and Ticehurst, two of the best-known private madhouses. He complains of the violence, cruel treatment, deprivation and lack of privacy he faced at Brislington:

Nothing did I require but wholesome diet, moderate and healthy exercise, and pure air; instead of which I was drenched with the most nauseous medicines against my will and against my conscience: I was fastened in a strait-waistcoat, or huge, hot leathern arm-cases, and compelled to lie day and night in the same bed, and in the same room, and fed on slops of bread in broth.[29]

A contrasting image is drawn in *What Asylums Were, Are, and Ought to be*, published in 1837, where Dr W.A.F. Browne describes an idyllic picture of the ideal asylum. Instead of the whips, chains, darkness and filth associated with Bedlam and eighteenth-century disgust at the animality of madness, Browne envisages sun and air, gardens and workshops, busyness and contentment. The inmates are denizens of an idealised community of spontaneous cooperation, where productivity is achieved without compulsion and there is no threat to the social order. Roy Porter in particular has done much to disabuse twentieth-century readers of the notion that the eighteenth century offered an unremittingly bleak environment for madness, and that there is a clear divide between eighteenth-century and nineteenth-century thinking and practice.[30] Nevertheless the dominant image of the asylum in the age of reason was that of Bedlam, and in general it stood as a warning, as in Hogarth's *Rake's Progress* or as a criticism of society, as in Swift's *Tale of a Tub*. Browne, on the other hand, associates the asylum with the ideal; it presents an ideal picture not only of life in an asylum, but of life in society. The architecture and surroundings are those of a 'palace', which is also a 'vast emporium of manufacture', where the division of labour accommodates individual interest as well as ability. But it is a labouring world governed by middle-class values, giving the tending of flowers higher status than the preparation of vegetables for the table, and whilst men and women 'toil incessantly' for no other recompense than 'being kept from disagreeable thoughts and the pains of illness', ladies and gentlemen engage in the familiar occupations of the leisured classes: music, reading, painting, walking, riding, sick-visiting (for the ladies) and billiards (for the gentlemen). The occupations for both classes are carefully gendered in conventional ways and the insistence on work, which brings its own reward, on order, and on tranquillity anticipates the dominant ideology of the Victorian period, based on the 'gospel of work' and showing faith in the social and natural order.

It is noteworthy that there is no mention in his vision of treatment as such, but in fact for Browne treatment meant 'moral treatment' and that, for him, meant 'kindness and occupation'. It is this concept that informs Perceval's request for 'wholesome diet, moderate and healthy exercise, and pure air'. It is also incorporated into many of the contemporary fictional discussions of the treatment of madness. There is also an interestingly explicit account of moral treatment in Wilkie Collins's *Jezebel's Daughter*, for instance, which features Jack Straw, an inmate of Bedlam, whom Mrs Wagner wants to 'rescue'. Her husband, a governor of Bedlam who has recently died, 'held the torturing of the poor mad patients by whips and chains to be an outrage on humanity'.[31] To honour his memory, Mrs Wagner arranges for Jack's release and proves, by taking him into her own home and treating him kindly, that a humane approach can restore to a reasonable state of normality someone who has been considered 'incurable'. The narrative, written from the perspective of 1878, refers to 1828, when Mr Wagner, the narrator tells us, would have been considered to have revolutionary views. In fact the 'moral treatment' which the Wagners advocate had already received much attention from the end of the eighteenth century. It was associated particularly with the work of Philippe Pinel at Bicêtre and Salpêtrière in Paris and Samuel Tuke at the York Retreat. Operating from rather different starting points, but sharing a belief in the need to treat symptoms rather than search for causes, both men recommended firmness, kindness, fresh air and exercise, discussion and occupation, although neither entirely abolished the use of physical restraint. The term 'moral' in the context of nineteenth-century psychiatry can be seen as embodying two meanings: psychological, mental, or emotional, as opposed to physical, on the one hand; and, on the other hand, ethical, and the relationship between these two meanings is extremely complex.[32]

Freeing the insane from their chains was for Pinel a symbolic act given the climate of liberation fostered by the French Revolution. Acutely aware of his revolutionary surroundings, he saw madness as caused by disappointed or ungovernable ambition and religious fanaticism, as well as by the revolution itself. He writes in a tone whose humanitarianism contrasts strikingly with the tracts of earlier writers; nevertheless, his belief in his own authority is manifest and, given the fundamental importance of observation in his epistemology, there is inevitably a conceptualisation of the mad as specimens. Of equal eminence was the reformist approach of William Tuke, which, unlike the secularist stance of Pinel, was informed by religious tenets. The Retreat was founded in response to what were felt to be unsuitable conditions at York Asylum. These conditions were indeed spectacularly exposed in the Report of 1815–16, but in 1792 it was the fate of a Quaker woman that was in question and the matter remained for the time being simply one of the Quaker mad being better cared for by their own kind. Quaker beliefs, like those of the revolutionaries, rested on the assumption of the equality of mankind, with modifications, however, that were almost inescapable in the late eighteenth and early nineteenth century; the Retreat, for instance, offered higher-quality accommodation to 'higher'-class inmates. And informing Samuel Tuke's description of how things were done there, for all the concern and compassion he projects, is an understanding of the mad as intrinsically different, possessed of an 'opposite' state of mind.[33]

Under both regimes, then, madness meant otherness, and the system of moral treatment was intended to restore sufferers to the community of mankind. It is significant in this context that the term 'alienist' was coined around the middle of the nineteenth century as an alternative to the older term 'mad-doctor', and the insane were conceived as being alienated, not simply from ordinary life, but from their 'right' minds. In medical thinking of the Victorian period the loss of reason no longer entailed demotion to animal status and the surrender of rights to humane treatment, but the reconditioning process that was moral treatment implied inhumanity of a psychological complexion. This has been spelt out most famously by Michel Foucault, who sees the asylum as a place of perpetual judgement under Pinel's regime. It is not

> a free realm of observational diagnosis, and therapeutics; it is a juridical space where one is accused, judged, and condemned, and from which one is never released except by the version of this trial in psychological depth – that is, by remorse. Madness will be punished in the asylum, even if it is innocent outside of it. For a long time to come, and until our own day at least, it is imprisoned in a moral world.[34]

This is strong language and clearly spells out the way in which moral treatment was moral in the ethical sense. It might seem that the benevolent regime operated by the Tukes at the Retreat, with its emphasis on the community of the 'family', offered a better chance of reducing the *threat* of madness and of removing the burden of blame, but Foucault is as critical of the Tukes as he is of Pinel. The rigorous Quakerism of their approach, he maintains, merely shifted guilt from the fact of being mad to the interiority of the disease; the madman must now assume responsibility for that within him that is likely to disturb morality and society. His confinement is effected through a system of rewards and punishments, a conditioning process that, in the end, recognises only the outer face of madness: 'It is judged only by its acts; it is not accused of intentions, nor are its secrets to be fathomed. Madness is responsible only for that part of itself which is visible. All the rest is reduced to silence. Madness no longer exists except as *seen*.'[35] Within the asylum the madman is confronted with authority rather than repression; the community imitates the patriarchal, bourgeois family, with the mad instituted as children. In Samuel Tuke's words: 'The principle of fear, which is rarely decreased by insanity, is considered as of great importance in the management of the patients. But it is not allowed to be excited, beyond that degree which naturally arises from the necessary regulations of the family.'[36] Here madness is domesticated, and the important lesson of self-control is taught. Andrew Scull, in his article 'The Domestication of Madness', distinguishes two senses of 'domestic', one defining the opposite of wild or untamed, the other the opposite of public.[37] He re-examines the changing concepts of madness from the end of the eighteenth century to the beginning of the nineteenth century in terms of the metaphor of domestication. It is, again, the transition from 'efforts to tame the wildly asocial to attempts to transform the company of the deranged into at least a facsimile of bourgeois family life' that is being commented on.[38] But, I would suggest, it is still the outer forms of behaviour that are prioritised and in this, as in the continued conceptualisation of the mad as 'other', there is a continuity with the past. Nevertheless, Scull is surely right to focus on the 'domestication' of madness as a salient characteristic of Victorian ways of handling lunacy. The family and home were viewed with veneration in this period, despite glaring instances of their failure to provide comfort, safety and support. Freud's essay 'The "Uncanny"', however, draws attention to the ambiguity that is inseparable from the concept of home, and if medical writers were anxious to represent the asylum as a 'home', the fictional writers whose work I discuss give an alarming picture of home as not simply harbouring, but fostering madness, and of the family, not as the supportive community of Victorian ideology, but as a potentially and actually antagonistic group of people, whose conflicts could nurture madness and whose blood could transmit it.

Madness and gender

In his novel *The Man of Feeling* (1771), Henry Mackenzie describes the visit of Harley, the 'man of feeling', to Bedlam. There he meets a young mad woman: 'Her face, though pale and wasted, was less squalid than those of the others, and showed a dejection of that decent kind, which moves our pity unmixed with horror.'[39] There is a comparable incident in Henry Cockton's *The Life and Adventures of Valentine Vox, the Ventriloquist* (1840). Goodman and Whiteley, two sane inmates of an asylum, beg a keeper to let them see a 'poor lost creature' whose screams have aroused their curiosity:

> from the harsh screams and bitter imprecations which preceded from this den, Goodman was led to imagine that its inmate was an old withered, wretched-looking creature, whose intemperance had reduced her to a raving maniac, and whose former life had been spent among the vilest and most degraded. Conceive, then, his astonishment when, instead of a miserable, wasted, haggard being, he beheld a fair girl, whose skin was as pure as alabaster, and whose hair hung luxuriantly down her back in flaxen ringlets, running round, shouting, screaming, and uttering the most dreadful imprecations that ever preceded from the lips of the most vicious of her sex.[40]

Playing on the contrast between expectation and actuality, Cockton makes all the more striking the contrast between appearance and voice, almost as though we are witnessing yet another ventriloqual feat, such as Valentine has been displaying throughout the novel. Both these examples rely on the pathos of the conventional situation of a beautiful young woman who has lost her wits, but the later piece lacks the romantic sentimentality of the earlier one. In Mackenzie's novel madness is represented as the result of thwarted love; in Cockton's novel it is the result of sexual frustration or what was generally known as erotomania. Responding to Whiteley's observation that her disease must be 'very dreadful', the keeper replies: 'No, there ain't much the matter with her. She only wants a husband.'[41] As if to give substance to his words, her behaviour presents a parody of matrimonial embraces: 'At this moment the poor girl saw them at the window and her shrieks were truly awful. She raved, and spat at them, and flew round the den, and endeavoured to clutch them and folded her arms as if she had one of them in her embrace, and then she shrieked again horribly.'[42] The mad woman in *The Man of Feeling* is pathetic and proper, never losing sight of her 'poor Billy', and her discourse has the lyricism of one of the mad songs that were so popular, but the woman in *Valentine Vox* has lost the attributes of womanhood and is condemned to an animal existence. It is a pattern that is repeated in Bertha Rochester, where the moral implications are made still clearer.

Feminist critics have drawn attention to the way in which the connection between madness and morality has wrought madness into yet another weapon in patriarchy's defensive armoury. During the eighteenth century the private nature of the madhouse trade meant that some proprietors were women, since the business tended to be handled by families and passed on from one generation to the next, and there was no question of professional qualifications. With increasing regulation and the growth of public asylums, the medical profession gradually established its hegemony in the field of madness and, since until the end of the nineteenth century doctors were invariably male, women were squeezed out of positions of authority in the private asylums, except that of matron, responsible of course to the physician. Elaine Showalter in *The Female Malady* quotes statistics to show that women have formed the larger proportion of lunatics since the 1850s.[43] Breaking new ground by specifically addressing the gender issue, she draws attention to the two assumptions usually made to explain this predominance. The first assumption is that there is a real difference in the rate at which the two sexes succumb to madness and that women's madness is the product of their social situation, 'their confining roles as wives, and mothers and their mistreatment by a male-dominated and possibly misogynistic profession.'[44] Showalter cites Richard Napier in this context, but the Victorians, too, recognised the particular risks posed in women's lives. Andrew Wynter, for instance, notes the deleterious results of leaving girls with 'imperfectly educated minds', especially when the developments of a railway network left wives stranded for long days in the suburbs whilst their husbands were at work.[45]

The other assumption has to do with the difficulties of diagnosis that I have already commented on, and suggests that madness is attributed to women on the basis of qualities and aspects of behaviour that are simply not-male. There is a 'fundamental alliance' between women and madness, the argument runs, with women being 'typically situated on the side of irrationality, silence, nature, and body, while men are situated on the side of reason, discourse, culture and mind'.[46] Given these underlying homologies, madness as a cultural or discursive construct belongs in the female domain with the power of definition resting inevitably in the hands of men. Whether they manifested exaggeratedly female traits, then, or behaved in unfemale ways, Victorian women were, in Showalter's analysis, being punished for sexual rebellion. Furthermore, the alliance between women and madness is reflected in a changing iconography. When Caius Gabriel Cibber sculpted his two figures of 'Raving Madness' and 'Melancholy Madness' as symbolic guardians at the gate of Bethlehem Hospital in 1677, he chose the male form. In 1887 the figure chosen by Tony Robert-Fleury, in his painting that represented the insanity that Pinel set free from chains, was that of a woman. Bethlem, or Bedlam, as it was popularly known, housed female as well as male lunatics, just as Pinel's liberation of the insane in the Parisian asylums, authorised by the Commune in 1793, affected men and women alike. But, from the end of the eighteenth century, the shift in the iconography of madness from an emphasis on the male to a greater focus on the female, was so marked that, in Showalter's opinion, madness could change its designation from 'the English malady' to 'the female malady'.

However, the amount of attention that the madness of women has received has tended to obscure the fact that men still formed a considerable proportion of the numbers classified as insane in the nineteenth century.[47] Esquirol, writing in 1838, for instance, notes that in England insane men bear a more equal proportion to women than they do in France, and the figures that Showalter quotes show that even as late as 1871, the census returns record a ratio of 1,182 female lunatics for every 1,000 male lunatics. These figures concerned lunatics who were confined in various public institutions, the county asylums, licensed houses, workhouses, and in single care. Men still predominated in private madhouses, asylums for the criminally insane, military hospitals and idiot schools.[48] Insane men, whether or not they were confined in institutions of one kind or another, continued to be the concern of clinicians; indeed, as Helen Small points out, even as late as the 1860s medical literature dealt with madness in general, rather than showing a bias towards hysteria and other disorders associated with women.[49] Men published their own accounts of what it was like to be insane or confined in an asylum, and, above all, mad men featured extensively in the imaginative writings of the period.

In *Victorian Masculinities* Herbert Sussman discusses the conflict in the poetry of Browning and Tennyson between entrepreneurial manhood, which is defined by success in the market-place, and the poetic ideal, which valorises the opposing qualities of emotional openness, imaginative inwardness, passivity and even the drive towards dissolution and death, and concludes that for the Victorians 'the opposite of manliness is madness'.[50] This is a bold and suggestive statement, but the discussion in the chapters to follow will show how often the failure to establish a manly identity nudges a man into insanity. In an earlier article, 'The Study of Victorian Masculinities', Sussman emphasises the importance of recognising the plurality of constructions: manliness is not innate, unitary or unquestioned.[51] Rather, boys were brought up to a version of masculinity that depended on a variety of social variables, and having achieved it had then the task of maintaining what might often be an unstable equilibrium. Emphasising the importance of domestic life in the formation of masculinity, John Tosh, too, has drawn attention to the need to look at changes over time. In his essay 'What Should Historians Do with Masculinity?' he defines three areas in which a Victorian man had to assert his masculinity within society: home, work and all-male associations.[52] The balance struck between these three components will vary between individual men, between social classes and over time. For instance, towards the end of the century there was a cultural shift in which all-male associations became proportionally more important than they had been earlier in the century. In *A Man's Place: Masculinity and the Middle-Class Home in Victorian England,* Tosh shows, through detailed reference to diaries, journals, letters and other unofficial papers of Victorian families of varied social status, how central domesticity was both in the forming of masculinity in boys and young men, and also in defining a man's sense of his gender through his role as householder, husband and father.[53]

The words 'masculinity' and 'manliness' are frequently used interchangeably, but in fact the latter term had particular connotations in the nineteenth century. In *Sinews of the Spirit* Norman Vance discusses manliness as the opposite of childishness, beastliness and effeminacy.[54] This opposition reiterates Sussman's opposition of manliness and madness, since, as the following chapters will show, mad men have been variously characterised as childish, beastly and feminised. More positively, Vance associates manliness with physical prowess, which would combine strength and courage and was linked with a valorisation of sport. The importance of sport in the manly ideal is discussed in more detail by Roberta Park, in her article 'Biological Thought, Athletics and the Formation of a "Man of Character": 1830–1900'.[55] She points to the cult of games-playing that became so popular by the 1860s, inspired by the belief that exercise not only promoted health but helped with character development. Such ideas can be seen underlying *Hard Cash* and its particular brand of adventure sensationalism. Vance also discusses how the concept of manliness included chivalric ideals of protecting the weak and innocent, particularly as they were domesticated in the idea of the gentleman who would show loyalty, courage and unselfish devotion. Finally he emphasises the importance of moral qualities deriving from Christianity. This is particularly noticeable in the work of Thomas Hughes and Charles Kingsley, who wanted to get the message across that Christianity was manly without allying themselves to the narrower ideals of the Evangelicals or the

Tractarians, both of whom tended to encourage notions of saintliness and estrangement from the everyday world. Kingsley in particular was strongly opposed to celibacy, holding to a Christian ideal of healthiness, social commitment and domesticity. Hughes's meditation on the meaning of manliness, *The Manliness of Christ* (1879), describes the ideals in detail.[56] Whilst acknowledging the traditional virtues Christ displayed in his life (charity, meekness, purity, long-suffering), he wants to show that he also displayed courage. He distinguishes between 'animal' and 'manly' courage, the latter of course being the ideal, since it embraced tenderness and thoughtfulness for others. Whether a man is facing the more dramatic demands on his courage, such as a battlefield, a sinking ship, a mining disaster or a blazing house, or the more likely moral challenges of falsehood, disease, wrong and misery, he is required to show his courage and manfulness. Such ideals run not only through Reade's sensation fiction, but can be seen in the gothic fantasy *Dracula*, where even the lunatic shows chivalrous feelings towards Mina.

Madness and genre

An article on the subject of madness in novels in *The Spectator* in 1866 draws attention to the advantages of making the heroine mad.[57] For Miss Braddon's purpose, according to this anonymous writer, 'it was necessary to strengthen the old machinery of novel-writing, to introduce changes more frequent, acts more unaccountable, catastrophes more violent and appalling'.[58] Mary Braddon is credited with hitting upon madness as a way of introducing and explaining such effects: 'Madness may intensify any quality, courage, or hate, or jealousy, or wickedness', and once introduced, 'probability became unnecessary, vraisemblance a burden, naturalness a mistake in art, everything was possible, and the less possible the emotion the greater the surprise and pleasure.'[59] Looked at in this way, madness is a narrative device, a dramatic mediator between realism and sensationalism; it is the locus of the sensational in the real world. Unlike the legislative view of insanity that demanded its confinement in municipal institutions, or the medical view that saw it as a disease of the brain, or the moralistic view that condemned the loss of self-control, the concept projected in this article is apparently 'carnivalesque', a celebration of the loosening of bonds. In murder one may recognise, it is suggested, 'the undeveloped wild beast in one's own heart'.[60] But for this to happen, the murder must be presented 'artistically'. This can be accomplished, it is implied, by making it the result of insanity. As far as Braddon is concerned insanity can be exploited not simply because, as the *Spectator* suggests, it makes the improbable probable, but because the web of societal attitudes and expectations, and the ways in which madness was conceptualised allow for its inclusion in the secret areas of life.

The frequency with which the theme of madness occurs in sensation and gothic fiction is noted by several commentators.[61] To those writers whose literary imagination was fired by the desire to arouse horror and terror, madness presented a ready-made locus of the horrible and the terrifying in human existence, and the reasons for this are not hard to find. Given the eighteenth-century conception of the asylum as a repository for those who have broken their tie with humanity and are therefore to some extent regarded as exotic beings, and given its prison-like status, it is unsurprising to find the madhouse favoured by gothic writers. Like the monastery it stands as a threat, a place for the removal of unwanted members of society, or those who had transgressed social codes. This attitude can be seen to persist in the some of nineteenth-century texts that I shall be analysing, particularly *Dracula*, but it is given a contemporary slant in the concern with wrongful confinement that is the topic in Chapter 3. Sensation and gothic novelists tend to look at madness from outside, and in this the conventions of genre coalesce with the conventions of representing madness in clinical literature, which frequently include case studies accompanied by illustrations of cranial formation or facial expression. Moreover, as I have already pointed out, the interest in the appearance of madness had its scientific counterpart in the disciplines of physiognomy and phrenology. The texts that I discuss in Chapters 1, 3 and 5 show a strong bias towards the visual and the representation of external characteristics, but they subtly undermine any simple-minded reliance on the cognitive possibilities of sight: neither people, nor places are always quite what they seem to be.

For sensationalist and gothic writers alike, madness and the madhouse represented sources of secrecy and mystery. The possibilities of the madhouse as a repository for an inconvenient or unruly member of the family is exploited in a 'matter-of-fact' way by the sensation writer Charles Reade, who insists on the factual basis of his plot. Sensationalism prioritises plot, which in conjunction with the interest in deviant and abnormal figures, functions to present a vision of existence where people have little control over their destinies or even identities. This was recognised by E.S. Dallas, the literary critic of the *Times*, who wrote a lively and original book, *The Gay Science* (1866), in which he distinguishes between the novel of plot and the novel of character.[62] In the novel of plot, generally taken to be a sensation novel, character is subordinate to plot and 'man is represented as made and ruled by circumstance', whereas in the novel of character, which we might call a 'realist' novel, man is 'supreme over incident and plot', master of his destiny.[63] As Dallas recognises, most novelists combine these two approaches, but his point is that the world-view projected by the sensation novelists is not necessarily any less true than that of the realists. In his *Autobiography* (1883) Anthony Trollope discusses the distinction between realism and sensationalism, which he sees as artificial and not altogether helpful, and it is interesting that, of the generally recognised realist writers, he provides possibly the most sustained analysis of madness in *He Knew He Was Right* (1869).[64] Starting with an obstinate man and a self-willed woman, Trollope traces, with painful detail, the breakdown of their marriage and the husband's descent into insanity and death because of an unreasonable jealousy. Following the psychological manoeuvres by which reasonable people find themselves in unreasonable positions, the drama of the text is predominantly internal, with little violence and none of the trappings of the madhouse, with the narrator maintaining the relatively objective pose of analyst and commentator. Mary Braddon's novel, *The Fatal Three*, written nearly twenty years later, combines acute psychological analysis with the secrecy of sensationalism. As philosophy merged into the new discipline of psychology and doctors authoritatively produced 'explanations' of insanity, these might be incorporated into the discourse of fictional characters, or acknowledged in authorial comment, yet the depiction of madness and its contribution to plot relies upon a continued belief in the mystery of the mind. Braddon shows a respect for such mystery, and at the same time recognises the way in which people swing between a fatalistic sense of being at the mercy of circumstances and an alternative conviction that action must follow the dictates of their own conscience.

In what might appear to be an exception to the general reluctance of nineteenth-century alienists to invite patients to talk about their condition, Forbes Winslow's study of insanity has a chapter which is devoted to the 'confessions' of patients who have recovered. However, the purpose of including such autobiographies is, it seems, the help they can give in the classification of mental diseases; they are not an early instance of the 'talking cure', since the 'talking' happens after recovery. Wilkie Collins's

Basil, on the other hand, offers itself as a confession, which the narrator hopes 'may do good'.[65] Unusually for the time, Collins uses a first-person narrator who suffers and describes in great detail a mental breakdown. In this case, unlike those in Winslow's book, writing the 'confession' can be read as a therapeutic exercise. *Basil* comes close to the psychological drama of *Maud*, but the novel is inevitably a less intense form than the dramatic monologue, and the psychological drama of Basil's breakdown is clearly set against the events and inhabitants of a world that is recognisably external, and drawn in terms that allow the reader to recognise it as her or his world too. The dramatic monologue, on the other hand, is suited to a direct exploration of the inner experience of insanity far more intense than is usually to be found in prose fiction, and events and people other than the speaker can seem insubstantial, figments almost of the protagonist's imagination. Through the dramatic monologue, Tennyson and Browning, for example, voiced internal processes, leaving the symptomatic behaviour to be deduced and relying on the reader's complicity with the implied author's rather than the protagonist's moral standards to communicate criticism. In *Maud*, perhaps the most extended analysis of mental pathology, the protagonist's fragile mental balance both determines and is reflected in the fragmentary plot. The characteristic romantic preoccupation with emotion and states of being is here pushed to extremes so that the external world seems a projection of the speaker's obsessions rather than as having its own objective reality. Both social and literary conventions are pushed to limits that take the poem to the verge of modernism and question the stability of standards of judgement. In Browning's 'Porphyria's Lover', the technique is rather different. Outrageous behaviour is made to seem almost normal because of the reasonable tone of voice; it is only the disparity between the description of Porphyria's behaviour and her lover's reaction to it that allows the reader to deduce insanity. Browning, in fact, gives a particular instance of Locke's theoretical statement that madmen, 'having taken their fancies for realities', 'argue right from wrong principles'.

The distinction between fantasy and reality is one of the themes of *Barnaby Rudge*, the first text I shall examine, and the only example in this book of an historical novel. In it documentary 'fact' is recounted with Dickens's unique imaginative power and combined with fiction to produce a sensational text whose insights reach beyond the particular circumstances of the historical event described. *Dracula*, on the other hand, has a more combative relationship with realism. Despite an almost neurotic insistence by the various characters on the truth and accuracy of their accounts, the phenomena they describe take the text into the realm of fantasy. Rosemary Jackson in her book *Fantasy*, makes the point that the 'fantastic exists as the inside or underside, of realism'. At the same time the 'fantastic is predicated on the category of the "real", and it introduces areas which can be conceptualised only by negative terms according to the categories of nineteenth century realism: thus, the im-possible, the un-real, the nameless, formless, shapeless, un-known, in-visible' – and, I would add, the un-dead.[66] I shall be returning to this question of fantasy more fully in the discussion of *Dracula* in Chapter 5.

My focus in this book will be on the madness of men as it is represented in literary texts. As Lillian Feder points out, literary depictions both reflect and question current medical, cultural, political and religious as well as psychological assumptions.[67] Like many other studies which have appeared recently, I shall be drawing on the relationship between the ideas and images that appear in imaginative writings and the ideas and images expressed in the writings of medical men and psychologists. I do not see this relationship as one in which fiction simply adopts the latest psychological or medical thinking and, as it were, makes up case studies to illustrate types of madness or to exemplify the latest theory in causation. I shall also be looking at imaginative writing as an element in the culture of Victorian Britain, and therefore as ideologically linked (whether in consensus or in conflict) with other elements in that culture. But this is primarily a literary study, and the emphasis is on the way that the madness of men functions in fictional texts, what this tells us about the meaning of masculinity and about the difficulties men may face in living up to the ideals of masculine behaviour. The texts that will receive detailed readings are, with the exception of Tennyson's *Maud* and Bram Stoker's *Dracula*, the less-discussed novels of well-known writers: Charles Dickens, *Barnaby Rudge*; Wilkie Collins, *Basil*; Charles Reade, *Hard Cash*; Anthony Trollope, *He Knew He Was Right*; and Mary Braddon, *The Fatal Three*.

The chapters will follow a broad chronological sequence, dictated by the focal text or texts, but each chapter will be devoted to a different aspect of insanity and will not therefore be confined to the precise period of that text. This does not mean that I shall be bound by clinical categories; rather, I shall concentrate on those issues to do with the understanding and treatment of insanity which seem to offer a particularly fertile field for the imaginative writer. Thus in Chapter 1 I will pursue the question of idiocy, its apparent undermining of male autonomy, its association with violence, and its worrying relation with the creative imagination. As Herbert Sussman shows, the poetic writer must struggle with the tension between the isolation and inwardness that is traditionally associated both with writing poetry and with femininity. A writer like Browning might seek to resolve the tension by grounding his poetry in the recognised masculine qualities of commercial engagement, warfare, male bonding, phallic sexuality and imperialism. But Dickens foregrounds the role of wayward imagination in political processes. Chapter 2 will be concerned with mental breakdown following thwarted or disappointed love, a common convention in the representation of female madness, but here seen from the male point of view. Stereotypically, the feminine is associated with emotion, sensitivity and passivity; as a disappointed lover, a man who loses his reason risks losing his masculinity. *Basil* and *Maud* show different strategies by which the sensitive man can construct for himself a role in a world where he is temperamentally out of place. In Chapter 3 I will look at some of the extensive literature to do with wrongful confinement, its implications for power relationships, and its particular appeal for the sensation novelist. These novels show the way in which masculine power can be eroded and the man put in a feminised position once he is labelled mad and put in an asylum. Chapter 4 will discuss psychological realism, marital relationships and madness as a response to the breakdown of the relationship. The question of power and the source of authority within marriage is a crucial issue here. Chapter 5 will focus on madness and ideas about degeneracy. By the end of the century conceptions of gender were becoming increasingly problematic; there was concern about manly women and feminised men, and these concerns were further implicated in fears of racial degeneration. *Dracula* exemplifies two ways in which literature attempted to contain these fears and establish some form of control.

In *The Female Malady*, Elaine Showalter says that 'madness, even when experienced by men, is metaphorically and symbolically represented as feminine: a female malady'.[68] What I hope this volume will show is that the representation of insanity in men is too various and its significance in the texts under discussion too complex to be confined within the rhetoric of feminism. Lillian Feder, on the other hand, is not concerned with gender, nor is she thinking particularly of the nineteenth century when she writes in *Madness in Literature*: 'Imaginative writers ... have always been concerned with madness as a revelation of the processes of the human mind.'[69] This is as true of the Victorian texts which I shall be discussing, as it is of the eighteenth-century literature which is the basis of her study.

The ensuing chapters will see madness as a revelation of fears and desires, of alternative ways of seeing the world and its inhabitants, and of the irrational processes of the unconscious – and as leading to further understanding of the human condition.

Notes

1 Charles Dicken, *American Notes* [1842] (Harmondsworth: Penguin, 1972), p. 140.
2 Dickens, *American Notes*, p. 141.
3 Quoted in David Wright, *Mental Disability in Victorian England: The Earlswood Asylum, 1847–1901* (Oxford: Oxford University Press, 2001), p. 16.
4 Forbes B. Winslow, *On Obscure Diseases of the Brain and Disorders of the Mind* (London: John Churchill, 1860).
5 Jean Etienne Esquirol, *Mental Maladies. A Treatise on Insanity*, trans. E.K. Hunt (Philadelphia: Lea & Blanchard, 1845), p. 29.
6 I have taken the quoted definition from the 1845 translation (Esquirol, *Mental Maladies*, p. 29), but the term had been in circulation since the 1820s.
7 Esquirol, *Mental Maladies*, p. 30.
8 The concept of moral insanity is discussed by Eric T. Carlson and Norman Dain, 'The Meaning of Moral Insanity', *Bulletin of the History of Medicine*, 36 (1962), pp. 130–40; Vieda Skultans, *Madness and Morals* (London: Routledge & Kegan Paul, 1975); Jenny Bourne Taylor, *In the Secret Theatre of Home: Wilkie Collins, Sensation Narrative and Nineteenth Century Psychology* (London: Routledge, 1988). Richard Hunter and Ida MacAlpine give a brief discussion of the controversy surrounding the category in *Three Hundred Years of Psychiatry, 1535–1860. A History Presented in Selected English Texts* (London: Oxford University Press, 1963), pp. 837–38.
9 Thomas Mayo, *An Essay on the Relation of the Theory of Morals to Insanity* (London, 1834), p. 15.
10 Mayo, *Essay*, p. 22.
11 James Cowles Prichard, *A Treatise on Insanity and Other Disorders Affecting the Mind* (London: Sherwood, Gilbert & Piper, 1835), p. 6.
12 Taylor, *Secret Theatre*.
13 Sander Gilman, *Seeing the Insane* (New York: John Wiley & Sons, 1982); Ernst Gombrich, *Art and Illusion* (Oxford: Phaidon Press, 1960).
14 Roger Cooter, 'Phrenology and British Alienists, ca.1825–45', in Andrew Scull (ed.), *Madhouses, Mad-Doctors and Madmen* (London: Athlone Press), pp. 58–104.
15 Janet Oppenheim, *'Shattered Nerves': Doctors, Patients, and Depression in Victorian England* (Oxford: Oxford University Press, 1991), pp. 9–10.
16 Henry Maudsley, *The Pathology of Mind: A Study of Its Distempers, Deformities and Disorders* [1895] (London: Friedman, 1979), p. 1.
17 Maudsley, *Pathology of Mind*, p. 82.
18 Maudsley, *Pathology of Mind*, p. 83.
19 Maudsley, *Pathology of Mind*, p. 563.
20 Andrew Wynter, *The Borderlands of Insanity* (London: Robert Hardwicke, 1875), p. 45.

21 M.E. Braddon, *Lady Audley's Secret* [1862] (Oxford: Oxford University Press, 1987), p. 404.

22 Braddon, *Lady Audley's Secret*, p. 205.

23 Wynter, *Borderlands of Insanity*, p. 45.

24 Wynter, *Borderlands of Insanity*, p. 14.

25 Wynter, *Borderlands of Insanity*, p. 129.

26 Wynter, *Borderlands of Insanity*, p. 110.

27 Andrew T. Scull, *Museums of Madness: The Organization of Insanity in Nineteenth-Century England* (Harmondsworth: Penguin), p. 197.

28 M.E. Braddon, *The Trail of the Serpent* [1861], ed. Chris Willis (New York: The Modern Library, 2003).

29 John Perceval, *A Narrative of the treatment experienced by a gentleman during a state of mental derangement; designed to explain the causes and the nature of insanity, and to expose the injudicious conduct pursued towards many unfortunate sufferers under that calamity* (London: Effingham Wilson, 1840), p. 14.

30 See particularly Roy Porter, *Mind-Forg'd Manacles: A History of Madness in England from the Restoration to the Regency* (Harmondsworth: Penguin, 1990).

31 Wilkie Collins, *Jezebel's Daughter* [1888], Pocket Classics (Stroud: Alan Sutton Publishing Ltd, 1995), p. 7.

32 The question of moral treatment has been much discussed in, for instance, Alexander Walk, 'Some Aspects of the "Moral Treatment" of the Insane up to 1854', *Journal of Mental Science*, 100 (1954), pp. 807–37; Andrew Scull, 'Moral Treatment Reconsidered: Some Sociological Comments on an Episode in the History of British Psychiatry', in Andrew Scull (ed.), *Madhouses, Mad-Doctors and Madmen* (London: Athlone Press, 1981), pp. 105–18; Taylor, *Secret Theatre*.

33 Samuel Tuke, grandson of William, the founder of the Retreat, gave the history of the foundation and a comprehensive survey of the conditions at the asylum, the treatment it offered and the degree to which it was able to help patients in his *Description of the Retreat* (York: Alexander, 1813).

34 Michel Foucault, *Madness and Civilization: A History of Insanity in the Age of Reason*, trans. R. Howard (London: Tavistock, 1971), p. 269.

35 Foucault, *Madness and Civilization*, p. 250.

36 Tuke, *Description*, p. 141. Walk, 'Some Aspects', maintains that Samuel Tuke, when he wrote the *Description*, understated the part played by fear in actual practice at the Retreat.

37 Andrew Scull, 'The Domestication of Madness', *Medical History*, 27 (1983), pp. 233–48.

38 Scull, 'Domestication of Madness', p. 233.

39 Henry Mackenzie, *The Man of Feeling* [1771], Oxford English Novels (Oxford: Oxford University Press, 1967), p. 33.

40 Henry Cockton, *The Life and Adventures of Valentine Vox, the Ventriloquist* [1840] (London: Robert Tyas, 1840), pp. 173–74.

41 Cockton, *Valentine Vox*, p. 175. Interestingly, this exchange between Whiteley and the keeper is omitted from some of the later editions of the novel.

42 Cockton, *Valentine Vox*, p. 175.

43 Elaine Showalter, *The Female Malady: Women, Madness and English Culture, 1830–1980* (London: Virago, 1987), p. 52.

44 Showalter, *Female Malady*, p. 3.

45 Wynter, *Borderlands of Insanity*, p. 62.

46 Showalter, *Female Malady*, pp. 3–4.

47 In recent years much has been written on the subject of madness by cultural historians and by literary critics. As far as nineteenth-century literature is concerned some critics have concentrated on studies of single authors: Natalie McKnight, *Idiots, Madmen, and Other Prisoners in Dickens* (London: Macmillan, 1993); Ann Colley, *Tennyson and Madness* (Atlanta, GA: University of Georgia Press, 1983); Jenny Bourne Taylor, *Secret Theatre*; and Sally Shuttleworth, *Charlotte Brontë and Victorian Psychology* (Cambridge: Cambridge University Press, 1996). Alternatively, inspired by Elaine Showalter's *The Female Malady* and Sandra M. Gilbert and Susan Gubar's *The Madwoman in the Attic: The Woman Writer and the Nineteenth-Century Literary Imagination* (New Haven and London: Yale University Press, 1979), there have been studies of female madness by Philip Martin (*Mad Women in Romantic Literature* [Brighton: Harvester, 1987]), and Helen Small (*Love's Madness: Medicine, the Novel, and Female Insanity, 1800–1865* [Oxford: Clarendon Press, 1996]). More recently Jane Wood's *Passion and Pathology in Victorian Fiction* (Oxford: Oxford University Press, 2001) analyses the discourses of medicine and of imaginative literature in relation to mental disorders depicted in fiction, looking at both men and women. Similarly, Chris Wiesenthal's, *Figuring Madness in Nineteenth-Century Fiction* (Basingstoke: Macmillan, 1997), analysing the semiotics of madness, covers male and female examples.

48 Showalter, *Female Malady*, p. 52.

49 Small, *Love's Madness*, pp. 44–45.

50 Herbert Sussman, *Victorian Masculinities: Manhood and Masculine Politics in Early Victorian Literature and Art* (Cambridge: Cambridge University Press, 1995), p. 48.

51 Herbert Sussman, 'The Study of Victorian Masculinities', *Victorian Literature and Culture*, 20 (1992), 366–77.

52 John Tosh, 'What Should Historians Do with Masculinity? Reflections on Nineteenth-Century Britain', *History Workshop Journal*, 38 (Autumn 1994), pp. 179–202.

53 John Tosh, *A Man's Place: Masculinity and the Middle-Class Home in Victorian England* (New Haven and London: Yale University Press, 1999).

54 Norman Vance, *The Sinews of the Spirit: The Ideal of Christian Manliness in Victorian Literature and Religious Thought* (Cambridge: Cambridge University Press, 1985).

55 Roberta J. Park, 'Biological Thought, Athletics and the Formation of a "Man of Character": 1830–1900', in J.A. Mangan and James Walvin (eds), *Manliness and Morality: Middle-Class Masculinity in Britain and America, 1800–1940* (Manchester: Manchester University Press, 1987).

56 Thomas Hughes, *The Manliness of Christ* (London: Macmillan, 1879).

57 Anon., 'Madness in Novels', *The Spectator*, 3 February 1866, pp. 134–35.

58 Anon., 'Madness in Novels', p. 134.

59 Anon., 'Madness in Novels', p. 135.

60 Anon., 'Madness in Novels', p. 135.

61 See in particular Elizabeth MacAndrew, *The Gothic Tradition in Fiction* (New York: Columbia University Press, 1979); Winifred Hughes, *The Maniac in the Cellar. Sensation Novels of the 1860s* (Princeton, NJ: Princeton University Press, 1980); Rosemary Jackson, *Fantasy: The Literature of Subversion* (London, 1984); Eve Kosovsky

Sedgwick, *The Coherence of Gothic Conventions* (London: Methuen, 1986); Taylor, *Secret Theatre*.

62 E.S. Dallas, *The Gay Science*, 2 vols (London: Chapman & Hall, 1866).

63 Dallas, *Gay Science*, vol. II, p. 293.

64 Anthony Trollope, *An Autobiography* (Harmondsworth: Penguin, 1996).

65 Wilkie Collins, *Basil* [1852], ed. Dorothy Goldman, The World's Classics (Oxford: Oxford Univeristy Press, 1990), p. 1.

66 Jackson, *Fantasy*, p. 26.

67 Lillian Feder, *Madness in Literature* (Princeton, NJ: Princeton University Press, 1980).

68 Showalter, *Female Malady*, p. 4.

69 Feder, *Madness in Literature*, p. xi.

Insurrection and Imagination: Idiocy and *Barnaby Rudge*

'It is something to look upon enjoyment, so that it be free and wild and in the face of nature, though it is but the enjoyment of an idiot,' says the narrator of *Barnaby Rudge*. 'Who would not rather see a poor idiot happy in the sunlight, than a wise man pining in a darkened jail!'[1] Dickens's representations of idiocy and insanity are permeated by images of light and darkness, confinement and liberty. Although his fictional work makes little reference to the institutions of madness, a range of mad and eccentric men and women contribute their individuality to the panorama of human types in the Dickens world. Some are confined, voluntarily or involuntarily – the madman in *Pickwick Papers* in a cell, Miss Flite in the debtors' prison, Miss Havisham in Satis House – but they are not in madhouses. Others, such as Mr Dick in *David Copperfield*, roam freely. How far the gentleman next door to Mrs. Nickleby is constrained is not made clear. In many of these instances madness is not explicitly acknowledged and in some cases, for example Miss Havisham, it is arguable. Indeed, one of Dickens's contributions to the fictional exploration of human nature is precisely his recognition of the variety of quirks and eccentricities that blur the distinction between sanity and insanity. The novel, however, that does deal explicitly with madness is *Barnaby Rudge*, an early work, published in 1841, ten years before the first of the journalistic pieces on insanity published in *Household Words*. Here madness is not only explicit but a central theme.

Although its unusually long gestation took place during years when madness was a subject of popular and official interest, in which two of Dickens's friends, John Forster and John Conolly, were deeply involved, the novel is set at a time well before the main period of legislative interest in insanity, and one of the aims of this chapter will be to assess the ways in which the historical context allows Dickens to preserve a critical distance from the madness he depicts. *Barnaby Rudge* is remarkable for its foregrounding of madness, not only in the eponymous character of an idiot, but in the insistence on the madness of the mob in the riot scenes surrounding the historical figure of the 'half-crazy' Lord George Gordon. Madness, then, operates in three different ways in this text: there is the fictional construction of what might count as a case study of an idiot, there is the retrospective glance at an historical example, and there is the metaphorical or quasi-metaphorical appeal to madness to describe, explain and criticise the behaviour of the mob. In this chapter I shall looking at some of the articles on madness and idiocy by Dickens himself, and others that appeared in *Household Words* and were, therefore, thoroughly scrutinised and sanctioned by him. Returning to *Barnaby Rudge*, I hope, by comparing the representations of madness and idiocy within the novel with the concepts and images running through contemporary non-fiction writing, to show that it draws on conventional and sometimes rather punitive conceptions at the same time as revealing preoccupations in common with the later, 'reformist' writing by Dickens and others. In this way Dickens criticises the idiocy of political uprising, whilst at the same time rescuing the idiot from blame. I shall, further, be discussing how the concept of idiocy allows Dickens to explore concerns about the power of the creative imagination and the dangers that ensue when male authority is divorced from responsibility.

Dickens was familiar with the Bedlam of 1815, which he mentions in *Sketches by Boz* (1836), drawing an analogy with Newgate prison:

> If Bedlam could be suddenly removed like another Aladdin's palace, and set down on the space now occupied by Newgate, scarcely one man out of a hundred, whose road to business every morning lies through Newgate Street or the Old Bailey, would pass the building without bestowing a hasty glance on its small, grated windows, and a transient thought upon the condition of the unhappy beings immured in its dismal cells.[2]

Both Newgate and Bedlam stand as representatives of a confinement that may be just but is certainly inimical to human dignity, and will probably corrode rather than restore the soul. *Barnaby Rudge* allows Dickens to vent his spleen against Newgate, but Bedlam is a less concrete presence in this novel. This cannot be explained as the consequence of unfamiliarity, for his involvement with the treatment of insanity was intimate and long-lived, and Barnaby is certainly not the first lunatic to appear in his fiction. However, the non-fictional writing on madness and its treatment started shortly after the completion of *Barnaby Rudge*, when Dickens paid his first visit to America and recorded his visits to three asylums in *American Notes* (1842). This was followed by the articles that appeared frequently in

Household Words that, even if they were not written by Dickens, were included in the periodical only with his approval. Running through all these pieces is a steady concern for society's unfortunates, belief in the possibility of cure, or at least improvement, and the advantages of sufferers being cared for in a well-run institution. But the discussions of their plight and treatment reveal continuity of feeling also in the frequent observation of the alienation of the insane, which is persistently expressed in terms of internal darkness. It is the insane's lack of ability to relate to others that can be seen as a variation of the typical nineteenth century castigation of egotism, while at the same time it relates to the mystery of the imagination.

Dickens shows great faith in the need for confinement if insanity is to be cured, but the asylum must offer appropriate conditions. At Long Island or Rhode Island ('I forget which'), he criticises the dreary asylum with 'a lounging, listless, madhouse air, which was very painful' and deplores the effect of party politics on the organisation of 'this sad refuge of afflicted and degraded humanity'.[3] Ten years later *Household Words* included the article 'A Curious Dance Round a Curious Tree', in the first part of which the inhumane practices of the eighteenth century when St Luke's was founded are outlined, re-fuelling, incidentally, the myth of the eighteenth century as a period of exclusive torture of the mad. Madness is seen in the workings of the asylum in those days, as much as in the inmates. The doctors themselves are said to suffer from monomania in their belief in the efficacy of 'wildly extravagant' and 'monstrously cruel' devices for the 'coercion of the outward man', and 'rabid physicking' of the inward man, whilst the hospital's consequent resemblance to 'a collection of chambers of horrors' is a sight likely to ensure the loss of reason in even 'the least irrational new patient'.[4]

A favourite theme is the parsimony of the local authorities or the misguided belief that the county asylums can expand *ad infinitum*, which sit uncomfortably with nineteenth-century pride in its the more enlightened attitude towards madness. The first of the *Household Words* articles, published in 1851, is a severely documentary piece on 'The Treatment of the Insane', written in the aftermath of the 1845 Act which compelled local authorities to provide for the insane.[5] Backing up his argument with official statistics on the one hand and, on the other hand, two individual cases, the writer draws attention to the continuing ills the pauper class may still have to endure because of the parsimony that frequently attends public provision, and to the lack of suitable public provision for private patients. The latter point may have less humanitarian force for readers who are out of sympathy with Victorian fine tuning to considerations of class, but the article's concern for the plight of the insane is undeniable. Reviewing the statistics, the author unhesitatingly attributes the cause of insanity to 'poverty and its attendant evils'. Since, however, those attendant evils include not only 'defective education', but 'the unrestrained sway of appetites and passions', it is clear that we are not far from the prevailing moralistic attitude to madness.[6] The last of the *Household Words* articles, written in 1859, returns to the question of county asylums and abhors the possibility of an increase in the size of the already large Middlesex asylums, Hanwell and Colney Hatch.[7]

If these pieces recommend the confinement of the mad, it is not because confinement as such is considered desirable, though it might sometimes be necessary, but because the asylum is considered better able to provide the right environment and treatment than the home, offering, in particular, the help of practitioners experienced in the handling of lunacy. But confinement does not mean for the writers of these articles that it is right to shut people away out of sight and out of mind. The first piece about idiots, published in 1853, includes a Sterne-like address to the reader (assumed unfortunately to be a female) to castigate the 'class of persons ... who are so desperately careful to receive no uncomfortable emotions from sad realities or pictures of sad realities, that they become the incarnation of the demon selfishness'.[8] The perennial concern for egocentricity impels the writer to the conclusion that people have no right to be so 'sensitive' that they require 'the putting away of these unfortunates in past years, and ... the putting away of many kinds of unfortunates at any time'.[9] The periodical itself is testimony to the desire to make public the plight of the insane and other unfortunates. In doing so the articles expose another type of confinement that seems to be the worst aspect of insanity for Dickens. Time and again they return to the idea of the mad confined by their inability to interact, trapped in an inner life. In the 1852 piece about St Luke's, he conveys his depression at the solitude of the women and men in their separate sitting rooms, caged within their own preoccupations as the fires are caged for security. Paying tribute to the resident matron, Dickens sees her shining 'like a star in a dark spot' amongst the afflicted people she regards as her children.[10] The conceit of a star shining in the darkness is picked up again and elaborated in an article called 'The Star of Bethlehem', which *Household Words* published in 1857.[11] Here the star is Bethlehem Hospital itself, whose history is traced up to the prevailing supervision of Dr Hood, when the unenlightened methods of the past having been abandoned, it is able to lighten the darkness of the insane.

The first asylum that Dickens had visited in America, an institution in Boston, had struck him as similarly enlightened, but it is worth noting also the preceding account of his visit to the Perkins Institution and Massachusetts Asylum for the Blind.[12] Like the mad, the blind and especially those, such as Laura Bridgman, who lack also hearing and a sense of smell, are shut off from the outside world, imprisoned in the limited world of their own being. Dickens is impressed by the kindliness with which workers at both establishments seek to integrate the inmates into some sort of social network, to break down their isolation. 'It is obvious', he writes of the hospital for the insane, 'that one great feature of the system is the inculcation and encouragement, even among such unhappy persons, of a decent self-respect.'[13] A post-Foucauldian reader, however, is likely to be more critical of the methods he describes. The treatment detailed falls into the familiar pattern of moral treatment: lack of physical restraint, occupation, fresh air and exercise, dances and friendly informal contact with the staff, which sounds humanitarian. But in giving a detailed study of one of the patients whom, with literary self-consciousness, he describes as a sort of Madge Wildfire in appearance, Dickens reveals the cruel irony that results from taking literally the woman's delusions. As in the examples Foucault gives in *Madness and Civilization* under the heading 'recognition by mirror', the physician talks to the woman as though she were indeed as important as she thinks she is, thus establishing, according to Dickens, 'a thorough confidence' with the patient and, incidentally providing amusement for the other patients, who 'seemed to understand the joke perfectly (not only in this case, but in all the others, except their own), and to be highly amused by it'.[14] As Foucault puts it: 'Madness is made to observe itself, but in others: it appears in them as a baseless pretense – in other words, as absurd.'[15] At the Boston asylum, 'opportunities are afforded for seizing any moment of reason, to startle them [the mad] by placing their own delusion before them in its most incongruous and ridiculous light'.[16] Dickens provides no example of how this volte-face is effected, but his reference to 'any moment of reason', like Foucault's reference to approaches made when the patient is 'calmer', suggests that disabusing a madman of his delusions relies upon the operation of reason, of pouncing on moments of sanity and using them to break up the carapace of madness and pull the patient back into the 'real' world. By 'moral influence' the inmates are re-trained in the ways of respectable society.

The belief in the possibility of cure persists, provided, according to the article of 1859, the patient is caught soon enough, and great emphasis is placed on the need for good physical health and well-being. Cure is not supposed to be possible, however, in the case of idiots, the subject of two articles in *Household Words*. The first, written in 1853, extols new efforts at caring for idiots, which means stimulating their defective faculties at the same time as developing their idiosyncratic talents:

> a closer study of the subject has now demonstrated that the cultivation of such senses and instincts as the idiot is seen to possess, will, besides frequently developing others that are latent within him but obscured, so brighten those glimmering lights, as immensely to improve his condition, both with reference to himself and to society.[17]

Drawing on the contrast between light and darkness yet again, this piece seems to me to spring from genuine humanitarian concern, whatever may be said about the way it is informed by bourgeois ideology. The article offers a distinction between insanity and idiocy: '... in the Insane certain faculties which once existed have become obliterated or impaired ... in Idiots, they either never existed or exist imperfectly.'[18] A quotation from Dr Voisin is added, specifying the faculties in his definition of idiocy as 'that particular state in which the instincts of reproduction and preservation, the moral sentiments, and the intellectual and perceptive powers are never manifested, or that particular state in which the different essentials of our being are only imperfectly developed'.[19] This is a variation on the distinction presented by John Locke, which influenced not only nineteenth century thinking, but is still quoted in medico-legal texts:

> The defect in *Naturals*, seems to proceed from want of quickness, activity, and motion, in the intellectual Faculties, whereby they are deprived of Reason: whereas *mad Men*, on the other side, seem to suffer by the other Extream. For they do not appear to me to have lost the Faculty of Reasoning: but having joined together some *Ideas* very wrongly, they mistake them for Truths; and they err, as Men do, that argue right from wrong Principles. For by the violence of their Imaginations, having taken their Fansies for Realities, they make right deductions from them.[20]

The word 'natural', which was a common enough synonym for idiot, underlines the relationship with the natural rather than the man-made scheme of things and emphasises the concept of idiocy as inborn rather than acquired. Locke's discussion concentrates on the idiot's inability to grasp, remember and connect ideas, which in turn impairs their ability to handle language, to make judgements and to reason. Since these qualities were stereotypically associated with the masculine gender in the nineteenth century, their absence in the male idiot implies a diminished masculinity.

A further threat to masculinity is entailed in one of the traditional indices of idiocy, the inability to beget a child. But the other tests (the abilities to count to twenty, to measure a yard of cloth, to name the days of the week, to give the age and name of parents and to read) in aggregate provided an assessment of an individual's ability to function in society and to manage their own affairs. Where those affairs were of some significance the matter could be brought to court, but, as Sir William Blackstone points out in his *Commentaries on the Laws of England* (1765–69), there were few instances of juries convicting anyone of idiocy; they were more likely to bring in a verdict of *non compos mentis*, which had different legal consequences. The distinction drawn in the *Household Words* article is close to the legal definition of an idiot *a nativitate*, who 'hath had no understanding from his nativity, and therefore is by law presumed never likely to attain any', whereas 'a lunatic, or *non compos mentis*, is one who hath had understanding, but by disease, grief, or other accident hath lost the use of his reason'.[21] Also classed as an idiot in law was anyone born deaf, dumb and blind, 'he being supposed incapable of understanding, as wanting those senses which furnish the human mind with ideas'.[22]

By the beginning of the nineteenth century recognition was dawning that not all those classified as idiots had the same problems. John Thelwall, in *Imperfect Developements of the Faculties, Mental and Moral* (1810), drawing on his experience of working with handicapped children, repudiated the notion that all idiocy was incurable, having learned that in some cases the child's mind 'is contracted in its sphere of activity by physical privation', thus producing the impression of 'supposed Deficiency of general Faculty'.[23] Such children could, he maintained, be helped with care and training. Not all writers on idiocy were as enlightened. Dickens owned an 1840 edition of John Abercrombie's *Inquiries Concerning the Intellectual Powers and the Investigation of Truth* (1830) and in 'Idiots' quotes with disapproval the old-fashioned ideas about idiocy expressed therein. But the discussions of Dr Howe's institution in Boston and the efforts of Drs Reed and Conolly in England indicate the more general awareness by the middle of the century of what could be done in this direction. It is the 1848 report of the Massachusetts Commissioners led by Dr Howe that is drawn on for the second article on idiots in *Household Words*, 'Idiots Again', written in 1854.[24] Attention is drawn to one particular statistic: that 44 out of the 95 children born into 17 families where the mother and father were related by blood were idiots. Repeating the injunction of the earlier article to care for idiots and develop what abilities they have, this article reads as a warning against intermarriage, one serious and common consequence of which is said to be the production of idiot offspring. There are implications here that relate to the meaning of idiocy in *Barnaby Rudge*, for the situation reads as one where the sins of the fathers are being visited upon their children. Once begotten, however, idiots must be properly treated and the article ends by recommending that we 'act upon the medium view ... neither to cast out our idiots, like the savages who leave their helpless ones to perish, nor to worship them, as the pious Egyptians did'.[25]

In the interests, presumably, of encouraging a humane domestic attitude to idiots, neither casting them out, nor worshipping them, this article presents a lengthy anecdotal exploration of the consequences for a household of having an idiot member. As the author vividly unrolls the process of discovery of this idiocy, she or he adopts a rhetoric that idealises the 'normal' business of the expectation and arrival of a new baby, thus increasing the horror of the disclosure of abnormality; painstakingly tracing the signs by which a mother gradually grows to awareness of her child's idiocy, the writer communicates his own feeling that this is the most terrible thing that can happen to her:

> How sweet was the prospect of the little one coming ... And when it came, how amiable, and helpful, and happy everybody was ... Perhaps there was a wager that baby would 'take notice' ... at the end of ten days or a fortnight, and the wager was lost. Here, perhaps, was the first faint indication. But it would not be thought much of, the child was so very young! ... Time goes on; and the singularity is apparent that the baby makes *no response* to anything ... His mother longs to feel the clasp of his arms round her neck; but her fondlings receive no return.[26]

Similarly, in *Barnaby Rudge*, as Barnaby and his mother come within sight of the Warren, the narrator conveys the mother's thoughts and memories of the years in which the 'conviction forced itself upon her' of his 'darkened intellect' (p. 250). Like Tommy, 'the favourite' at St Luke's, a 'harmless old man ... at once so childish and so dreadfully un-childlike', Barnaby is childish in his early years, but gives tokens of something 'unchildlike in its cunning' (p. 250).[27] The whole of this description, as Michael Hollington notes in his investigation of the importance of physiognomy in *Barnaby Rudge*, appears to confirm 'a traditional association of idiot children with demonic changelings'.[28] But, Hollington's argument runs, Dickens's 'grotesque art' comes close to a 'physiognomical paradox' by which 'the most apparently monstrous creatures are innocent and harmless, whilst those with the most apparently attractive surfaces are the most terrifying monsters'.[29] Barnaby, lacking the ability or even the intent to control his features, stands at the opposite end of the moral spectrum from Sir John Chester, whose mastery over his features allows him to deceive Mrs Varden and (at least temporarily) the waiter at the Covent Garden coffee house into thinking him saintly. I shall return to the question of Barnaby's moral status, but first I should like to discuss the importance of the visual element in Barnaby's representation.

In examining the way Barnaby is represented I am not concerned with the issue of realism so much as with the degree to which that representation draws on the contemporary concept of an idiot. In many ways he stands as a convincing enough idiot in nineteenth-century terms; his lack of memory, his disjointed utterances, his seemingly irrational fears can all be accommodated within the contemporary understanding of the simpleminded, as can his attachment to and integration with the world of nature where he roams freely and unharmed, and his alienation from the social world where his simplicity is a source of danger. Nevertheless, there are also extraneous elements in his representation that need to be accounted for otherwise. On the whole, Barnaby is presented externally and much emphasis is placed on his appearance. Not only is this typical of Dickens's narrative method generally, but it can be related to the interest in physiognomy which developed into the phrenology that was so popular in the first half of the nineteenth century. In *Barnaby Rudge*, furthermore, the illustrations by George Cattermole and Hablot K. Browne (Phiz) play a particularly important role.[30] It is worth looking, therefore, at the relation between the illustrations of Barnaby and those of idiots in the studies of the late eighteenth and early nineteenth century.

Probably the most influential study of idiocy for the nineteenth century was that of Johann Caspar Lavater, which was based on the tradition of classical physiognomy, the main source of his influence being the four-volume illustrated study of human physiognomy which appeared between 1774 and 1778. In this he characterises the idiotic thus: 'Indolent distortion, animalistic obtuseness, convulsive attitude, crooked smiles, inconstancy, indifferentiatedness, vacancy, looseness – the usual, most common, most evident signs of inherent and natural stupidity.'[31] Publishing his *Ideas toward a Mimetic Theory* (1785) partly in response to Lavater, Johann Jakob Engel concentrated less on facial structure and more on the role of movement and gesture 'as a reflection of the intrinsic relationship between soul and body'.[32] His portrait of an idiot shows dropped head, unclosed lips, hanging chin, half-open eyes and hands in the pockets, and has an accompanying comment:

> Who does not recognize at first glance the weak inactive mind incapable of attention or interest; a mind, which never can bring even the limited energy to create a tension in his muscles so that the body carries itself correctly, that the limbs are held correctly. Only the most stupid and lazy can assume such a meaningless, mindless position.[33]

By moving outside those aspects of appearance that are beyond an individual's control, for instance bone structure, Engel might seem to legitimate the harsh moralistic attitude which lay behind the eighteenth century treatment of idiots and of which Dickens patently disapproved. And the depiction of the whole of an idiot's person was unusual at a time when attention was usually concentrated on the face and cranium.[34]

There is some similarity between this depiction and that of Barnaby, most obviously in the late-eighteenth-century style of dress, but also in the drooping stockings and the long hair hanging in jagged clumps. But whereas Engel's idiot has his coat and waistcoat unbuttoned, Barnaby's is always done up, except in the third illustration of his sojourn in prison, and never is he represented, even in the prison scenes, in the posture of torpidity. On the contrary, his stance always demonstrates vigour and emotional alertness; even in the third prison scene, it is his mother who droops on his shoulder in the pose of the idiot, whilst Barnaby's arms are raised, occupied with decorating the hat he holds almost unnaturally high. Pictorially, then, Barnaby's idiocy is represented in the conventional drooped stocking and lanky hair, but otherwise he lacks the torpor of the Engel figure. That Dickens was well aware of the conventions of idiocy is made clear, not only in the opening paragraph of 'Idiots', which surveys the several types of representation he sees as belonging to different countries, but also in the section of *American Notes* that deals with the asylum on one of the New York islands. Here the inmates are described as types and include the 'moping idiot, cowering down with long, dishevelled hair'.[35] However, when Dickens describes Barnaby's first appearance in the novel (pp. 73–74) it is not the iconography of idiocy that is most noticeable. Rather than 'moping' or 'cowering', Barnaby has an ambivalent posture, 'half shrinking back and half bending forward'; his hair is profuse, hanging in disorder about his face and shoulders, and his eyes are 'protuberant'. There are signs of the maniac here. But Barnaby's feeble-mindedness is given away by his 'wan and haggard' aspect, which for Dickens indicates 'the absence of soul', by the broken sword, which might be symbolic of an idiot's supposed impotence, and by the limpness of the peacock's feathers that ornament his hat. The illustration at this point incorporates other signs of mania: splayed legs, waving arms, wild clothing and the fool's staff as represented by the flaming torch. Once Barnaby has become involved with the rioters, however, it is his care of his person rather than the neglect and apathy of the idiot or the wild dishevelment of the maniac that is remarked upon; Barnaby as the sentry outside The Boot has an 'erect and lofty bearing' and his 'poor dress' shows signs of 'careful arrangement' (p. 478). There is no illustration of Barnaby at this point, but there *is* one of him defending himself against the Foot Guards who have come for his arrest, and this shows an almost heroic pose, Barnaby's person dominating the composition and only the somewhat anguished expression on the face giving him away. Equally significant is the first illustration showing him in Newgate. Although his body huddles in the typical posture of the melancholic, his face looks up and catches the sunlight that is streaming through the grated window. The image here is of one who is especially favoured by heaven. What I am suggesting is that both in the illustrations and the verbal descriptions, Barnaby is more alert than the conventional idiot of documentary accounts; that, in fact, his representation combines elements of both mania and idiocy, as well as aspects that are characteristic of neither but might be attributed to a Holy Fool.

Ascribing the appellation of Holy Fool to Barnaby rescues him from potential charges of evil in his enthusiastic support of the rioters and installs him in the fold of Christianity. Penelope Doob has discussed the conventions of madness in Middle English literature, paying particular attention to the dramatic portrayals of Herod where he is opposed to all that Christ stands for, thus representing 'the spiritual madness of those who reject Christ' as opposed to 'the madness of Christianity as seen by the worldly wise'.[36] Though he clearly lacks worldly wisdom, there are signs that Barnaby possesses especial grace in, for example, the scene when he stands as sentry before The Boot (p. 478).[37] And it is clear that in his almost heroic indifference to intrigue and personal safety, and in his essential innocence, Barnaby does indeed stand above his companions. The passage where Dickens tells of his condemnation to death, like the description of the death of Little Nell, employs the device of a simple repeated phrase ('Barnaby was to die') to drive home the fate of a character who, a victim of circumstances beyond his control, has risen to heights of dignified acceptance of his plight.

And the illustration I commented on earlier casts the same, rather senti-
mental aura about the idiot. Unlike Little Nell, however, Barnaby's innocence is not combined with understanding; he has already shown the 'taint'
of his inheritance and been swayed by the forces of corruption, and he
therefore lacks true heroism. Similarly, he falls short of the status of Holy
Fool, I think, in that he cannot really be said to possess the 'madness of
Christianity'. There are indeed scenes where Barnaby is shown as being
endowed with the grace of Christianity, but it is a gift outside his own
sphere of action, undeserved by behaviour that is especially meritorious. In
Chapter 73, for instance, when, captured for the second time, Barnaby lies
'caged in his narrow cell', the moon shines in and he 'was as much lifted up
to God, while gazing on the mild light, as the freest and most favoured man
in all the spacious city' (p. 658). If there is a sense of epiphany here,
however, it seems to be gratuitous. There is no particular reason why
Barnaby should be especially favoured at this point, nor has his mother
acted with unusual merit. The suggestion of virtue is, in fact, slipped in by
means of simile: 'But the moon came slowly up in all her gentle glory, and
the stars looked out, and through the small compass of the grated window,
as through the narrow crevice of one good deed in a murky life of guilt, the
face of Heaven shone bright and merciful' (p. 658).

The association of natural phenomena with God is common enough,
not only in Dickens's work but in that of many other writers, but here the
further association with a 'natural' and his mother puts Dickens in the
Wordsworthian camp, elevating the socially downtrodden and neglected.
Comparing *Barnaby Rudge* with Wordsworth's 'The Idiot Boy', Iain
Crawford suggests that, although Dickens was not as interested as
Wordsworth in revising attitudes to idiots and savages, he was perhaps
more concerned than has usually been recognised.[38] My survey of the non-
fictional writing by Dickens and the contributors to *Household Words* on
idiocy and madness suggests that he certainly was, in one area of his work,
involved in reforming public attitudes to those who were mentally defective, but I do not think that this was particularly part of his aim in writing
Barnaby Rudge. In the absence of any justification of this position in terms
of actual deeds, though, this passage is representative of the retreat into a
rather sentimentalised Christianity that seems designed to reduce the
blame that must otherwise attach to Barnaby's behaviour. It is only possible to accept Barnaby as a Holy Fool, in fact, if one also accepts that imagination is equivalent in its mediations in the world of personal, social and
political intrigue to those of Christianity. This is a proposition that

Dickens develops more fully in *Hard Times*, but which is only fitfully suggested in *Barnaby Rudge*.

What is particularly striking about this earlier novel is the insight it provides into the mind of someone who is a liminal member of society. In this Dickens makes a striking departure from Wordsworth's poem. 'The Idiot Boy' is narrated from the point of view of the boy's mother, and as Crawford has pointed out, the focus is on the relationship between these two characters. But not even Betty Foy can reach into her son's mind. After a night of frantic anxiety, the only answer to her question about what he has been up to is: 'The cocks did crow to-whoo, to-whoo, / And the sun did shine so cold!' The poem's narrator laconically observes that Johnny had heard the owls and 'No doubt' seen the moon, but to the more pressing questions about where he has been and why he has failed in the important mission he had been entrusted with, there is no answer. Focusing on the emotions of Betty Foy, the narrator can only confess ignorance as to the feelings of her son:

> And Johnny burrs, and laughs aloud;
> Whether in cunning or in joy
> I cannot tell ... (*ll.* 377–79)[39]

For the mind of the idiot is alienated from normal human understanding and its workings a mystery. This sense of alienation, combined with a sense of wonder and an opposing sense of criticism, is incorporated in the representation of Barnaby, but it is complicated by the way in which alienation is entwined with the representation of a creative imagination. Barnaby is more articulate than Wordsworth's idiot boy, as for instance when he describes what he sees from the window in John Willet's inn:

> Look down there ... do you mark how they whisper in each other's ears; then dance and leap, to make believe they are in sport? Do you see how they stop for a moment, when they think there is no one looking, and mutter among themselves again; and then how they roll and gambol, delighted with the mischief they've been plotting? (p. 133)

As Willet points out, 'They are only clothes,' but Barnaby's vivid imagination, like that of Dickens, endows the inanimate with life and foresees in the washing blowing on the line, the activity of the rebellious crowd.

In 1909 the *Dickensian* published a two-part rhapsody by John MacLeod on 'The Personality of Barnaby Rudge', praising his innocent, childlike qualities and denying that he is either mad or bad: 'His life was blameless and pure, and his record was never so much as once smudged by an unfair or dastardly action.'[40] It is perhaps the writer's appreciation, shared with a number of other critics, that Barnaby 'possessed many characteristics which were Dickens's most poignant and noticeable characteristics' that inhibits him from allowing that Barnaby is mad.[41] Ernest Polack, equally inclined to panegyric, does not make the comparison between Dickens and his creation explicitly, but it is implicit in the view that the character is 'blessed with the boundless, overflowing imagination of the poet'.[42] There is, though, a slippage in this essay to try to accommodate the question of idiocy. Instead of the sort of distinctions that MacLeod draws, Polack denies that Barnaby is a serious study of an idiot at all: 'Barnaby is no more than a poetic and artistic creation' and 'his life is one long poem'.[43] But this writer, too, concludes that Barnaby is a child-like character, kept 'pure and undefiled amid the bloody horrors of the Gordon riots' because of his 'simple love of right and truth', 'his unquestioned trustfulness in everyone' and 'his innocent self-pride'.[44]

However, I do not think that Barnaby, however child-like, can be seen simply as pure and innocent, because of the way in which, by making Barnaby an idiot, Dickens coalesces in symbolic form a number of motifs that run throughout the text. As an innate deficiency, idiocy dramatises the tyrannical hold the past has over the present and, what is more, the deforming influence of a past that consists of greed, violence and fear. Significantly, this theme, so important in the novel, is expressed through the parallel father-and-son relationships, which of course include Barnaby and Rudge. In this case the stigmatising power of past evil is made still more emphatic by the literal stain on Barnaby's skin. This is an acute example of the materialism that Dickens embraces and that underpins the physiognomic tendency both of his fictional method and of so many of the studies of idiocy. It is not surprising to find that Lavater was persuaded of every person's uniqueness: he was, after all, a pastor, but his equally firm belief in the correspondence between outward and inner being has little to do with religious belief:

> For everything, because it is itself and not something else, has something in it with which it can be distinguished from everything else. Does this not tell us that an exact relationship exists between the soul and the body, between the internal and the external of man, that the infinite variety of the souls or the internal nature of man creates an infinite variety in his body or externality.[45]

But, given the infinite variety of souls and the infinite variety of bodies, there still remains the problem of pinning down the correspondences between states of the soul and their external expression. In his attempt to find the mind's construction in this face, Dickens plunges into superlatives and negatives when it comes to the difficult task of rendering the suggestion, merely, of horror:

> One thing about this face was very strange and startling. You could not look upon it in its most cheerful mood without feeling that it had some extraordinary capacity of expressing terror. It was not on the surface. It was in no one feature that it lingered. You could not take the eyes or mouth, or lines upon the cheek, and say, if this or that were otherwise, it would not be so. Yet there it always lurked – something for ever dimly seen, but ever there, and never absent for a moment. It was the faintest, palest shadow of some look, to which an instant of intense and most unutterable horror only could have given birth, but indistinct and feeble as it was, it did suggest what that look must have been, and fixed it in the mind as if it had had existence in a dream. (p. 87)

I have quoted at length this description of Barnaby's mother to show how Dickens lingers over the mysterious blend of the physical and the psychological. Obviously the creation of mystery is one of the objects of this passage and equally obviously taking time over a description is one way of giving it importance, but the expression of the mother's face is important not only in itself and for clues it sets for the plot, but, as the subsequent paragraph makes clear, it is also significant in the way it is imprinted on Barnaby: 'More faintly imaged, and wanting force and purpose, as it were, because of his darkened intellect, there was this same stamp upon the son' (p. 87). It is as if Barnaby, whilst still in the womb, had suffered the same terror as his mother. However telling facial expression is, though, it cannot tell the whole story: 'Seen in a picture, it must have had some legend with it, and would have haunted those who looked upon the canvas' (p. 87). Born on the very day the murder became known, his body and mind marked by the deed, Barnaby carries an overloading of signifiers indicative of the horror of Rudge's murder of his master and indicative, also, of the dire results attendant upon such actions.

Making Barnaby stand as mute testimony to his father's evil deeds is one way in which Dickens draws on conventional beliefs about idiocy. As I have already argued, though, the representation of idiocy in this case is not whole-hearted, and there are features of the way that Barnaby is presented that are more usually associated with mania. But there is one aspect of both idiocy and insanity that, striking Dickens the journalist most forcibly, is rendered imagistically in terms of darkness and light. Barnaby is said to be

of 'darkened intellect', and later the narrator, in the summary description
of the time spent in the country retreat, says: 'The daily suns of years had
shed no brighter gleam of reason on his mind; no dawn had broken on his
long, dark night' (p. 416). Leaving aside the evidence of the later writing,
what might be a *façon de parler* receives additional significance when it is
remembered that so much of the action of the novel takes place in the dark.
Furthermore, Barnaby's inseparable companion is a black raven who
repeatedly insists, 'I'm a devil.' There is a sense in which Grip functions as
Barnaby's other self, hovering about him like a familiar, or like the shadow
of the past as represented by his father.[46] There is also the suggestion that
Barnaby has inherited his father's guilt, which is reinforced in the scene of
recognition when, at the height of the disturbances, the three are united in
prison. In the dark cell Barnaby hugs his father, questioning him about his
mother: 'Not a word was said in answer; but Grip croaked loudly, and
hopped about them, round and round, as if enclosing them in a magic
circle, and invoking all the powers of mischief' (p. 567). The tableau crys-
tallises symbolically what is happening in society at large, but Grip is too
much of a comic creation to be taken seriously as a representative of evil.
He is a *reductio ad absurdum* of Barnaby, who is himself an extreme
instance in so many way. Grip's parody of human speech emphasises the
unthinking parroting that is really all that Barnaby's involvement in the
riots amounts to, just as his discovery of the plunder hidden in Hugh's bed,
the result of a more successful effort than Barnaby's to find gold in London,
is ultimately just as fruitless.

Grip is, as it were, an externalisation of Barnaby's inner darkness, the
'blindness of the intellect', as Stagg the evil blind man puts it (p. 422),
which alienates him from normal human life and, in some of the text's for-
mulations, denies him a soul. The narratorial comment on his first appearance makes a harsh judgement: '… the absence of the soul is far more
terrible in a living man than in a dead one; and in this unfortunate being
its noblest powers were wanting' (p. 74). Analogous with this observation
is John Willet's facile dismissal of Hugh's claim to consideration as a
human being and the verdict that if he has a soul 'it must be such a very
small one' that it does not signify what he does in the way of praying
(p. 150). Willet's attitude to Hugh, in fact, is very similar to the eighteenth-
century attitude to lunatics that Dickens the reformer so abhorred; considered to be 'quite an animal', the youth is indeed treated like an animal.
The narrator does not otherwise align himself with Willet of whom the
novel is clearly critical, but this early comment on Barnaby does betray

conservative thinking about madness that is to become still more manifest in the second part of the book. But if Barnaby, especially at the opening, is depicted like one of the living dead in the emphasis on his vacant stare, the paleness of his complexion and his unfathomable appearances and disappearances, this is countered by his wild disorder and consternation at the sight of blood. And in later episodes there is little in Barnaby's conduct or the narratorial comment on him to support the theory that he lacks a soul. Having been captured at The Boot and confined at the barracks, for instance, he is described as behaving and feeling in a way that would be quite appropriate for any man of normal intellect; his speech is totally coherent and the narrator ventures to represent the scene through the idiot's perceptions. One may feel that his attachment to Grip would be better directed towards his mother, but in the latter important relationship, the son is again not consistently lacking in sensitivity. When, Rudge hidden in the closet of their London home, Mrs Rudge listens as Barnaby gives an account of his day's activities, he notices her fear, and a little later, in the dialogue about his birthday (pp. 191–92), he shows not only remarkable perception, but greater powers of memory than were generally attributed to idiots or are attributed to Barnaby elsewhere in the novel.

In choosing a species of madman as the eponymous protagonist rather than, as was originally proposed, Gabriel Varden, the leading (though not unflawed) representative of virtue, Dickens gives importance to that element of society which demands wise guidance if it is not to be corrupted by those self-seekers against whose wily machinations naivety is no protection. For innocence, which might have been a defence, is no part of this materialistic world; Barnaby, literally tainted by the past, shares his father's and society's longing for wealth, which leads him into the centre of corruption. As another example of naivety manipulated by opportunists, Lord George Gordon stands as Barnaby's historical counterpart, as Gashford is Sir John Chesters's and Grueby is Varden's. But whereas Gashford and Grueby are semi-fictionalised, Gordon is not. It is perhaps for this reason that he is not strongly delineated and his madness not fully explored. The first description of him, again focusing on externals, indicates insanity in comparatively subtle ways: his dress is remarkable only for its sobriety, but the lack of vitality is discernible also in the 'sallow' complexion, 'a certain lankness of cheek and stiffness of deportment' (p. 336). In striking contrast, however, is his 'very bright large eye, which betrayed a restlessness of thought and purpose, singularly at variance with the studied composure and sobriety of his mien, and with his quaint and sad apparel' (p. 336). It is the restlessness signalled in the eyes that associates Gordon with Barnaby. Dickens goes to some trouble to explain the expression of the nobleman's eye and face:

> It had nothing harsh or cruel in its expression; neither had his face, which was thin and mild, and wore an air of melancholy; but it was suggestive of an indefinable uneasiness, which infected those who looked upon him, and filled them with a kind of pity for the man: though why it did so, they would have had some trouble to explain. (p. 336)

For all Dickens's mockery of religious extremism in general, he here seems concerned to treat Lord George with some sympathy, but at the same time to reveal him as a source of danger. The dialogue after their arrival at the inn shows how his deficiency of wit permits a stronger man to work on the 'something wild and ungovernable' that lies beneath his puritan demeanour (p. 340). In this he is allied with Barnaby, who has similar outbreaks, and with the crowd, which also can be manipulated into becoming wild and ungovernable. Later we see Gashford pouring poison into his lord's ear and Lord George responding like one who is hypnotised. Dickens then makes explicit his assessment of the nobleman's state of mind:

> This lord was sincere in his violence and in his wavering. A nature prone to false enthusiasm, and the vanity of being a leader, were the worst qualities apparent in his composition. All the rest was weakness – sheer weakness; and it is the unhappy lot of thoroughly weak men, that their very sympathies, affections, confidences – all dwindle into foibles, or turn into downright vices. (p. 346)

The final picture of Lord George before he rides off to London, is of a Don Quixote, grotesquely ill-suited to his situation and totally oblivious to the eccentricity of the effect he is creating. Like Barnaby, Gordon lives largely in a world of his own imagination, but unlike Barnaby his social position allows his sway to extend beyond his immediate circle and his qualities of mind are therefore of importance in the world at large.

Having established Gordon as the nominal leader of the riots, Dickens allows him to remain as a fairly shadowy figure. In part this is no doubt to be explained by the exigencies of historical fact; changing the names of the secretary of the association and Lord George's personal servant allows him some latitude for invention with respect to those two figures, but this is not possible with Lord George himself, and presumably an absence of relevant material precluded a fuller investigation of the causes of his 'weakness'. But it is also appropriate in a text that is heavily symbolic that the 'leader' of the riots should remain pretty well hidden behind his henchman and the new recruits: Hugh, Dennis, Tappertit and Barnaby. Gordon does, however, appear centre-stage again for the important scene when he and Barnaby come face-to-face. This is one of those coincidences that can perhaps be accommodated, as Stignant and Widdowson suggest, by the 'random detailing of the "world"', but it is obviously crucial that these two men should meet.[47] The striking feature of the accompanying illustration is the contrast between Barnaby's fantastically ornamented clothing and the dour simplicity of Lord George's, but their stance and their holding of staffs gives the effect of a mirror image. Lord George's involuntary recognition of their affinity is indicated by the blush which twice rises to his face, belying his confidence in his own words, as he tries to protest against the widow's representation of her son as 'not in his right senses' (p. 444). Like the episode in *American Notes*, this scene schematically represents the belief in the ability of madness to recognise itself in others. Lord George recognises madness, but does not acknowledge it. To do so would, of course, have necessitated acknowledging the feeble-minded among his own supporters, if not his own weakness, and to do so would have required greater independence of Gashford's evil promptings than is at any time conceivable. This scene underlines, then, the degree to which the riots are the responsibility of the maliciously self-seeking. It also differentiates between the suppressed awareness and implicit rejection of moral responsibility on the part of the insane Gordon, as opposed to the oblivion of Barnaby, who, as an idiot, is absolved from such responsibility.

Lord George confronts Barnaby a second time in Chapter 57, whilst he is holding the fort at The Boot. On this occasion their companions are Grip and John Grueby instead of Gashford and Mrs Rudge. Grueby's uncompromising answer to Lord George's question about Barnaby brings madness to the foreground:

> 'Did – did it seem to you that his manner was at all wild or strange?' Lord George demanded, faltering.
> 'Mad', said John, with emphatic brevity. (p. 520)

In response to his master's request for the signs of madness, Grueby draws attention to Barnaby's dress, his eyes, his restlessness, his cries of 'No Popery!' Gordon recognises the signifiers of his own madness, but when his rephrasing of the particular in general terms ('So because one man dresses unlike another ... and happens to differ from other men in his carriage and manner, and to advocate a great cause which the corrupt and irreligious desert, he is to be accounted mad, is he?') is answered by

Grueby's 'Stark, staring, raving, roaring mad, my lord,' he refuses to acknowledge what is signified and arranges to part company with his one true adviser (p. 520). Gordon by now seems to have surpassed the need for Gashford's tutelage and to be confirmed in his fanatical madness beyond the control of reason, and in this he is representative of the mob, for by this time the crowd, too, has become excited beyond the control of reason, so that, interpolated between the scenes of riot and destruction, the meeting becomes emblematic of the state of things generally, a counterpart to the scene between Barnaby and his father I commented on earlier.

The riots, then, can be seen as the result of manipulative, vengeful and greedy power-seekers working on the gullible and the oppressed so that they lose the defining attribute of humanity and become bestial; like the Gadarene swine, the crowd rushes into the arms of the unholy in the name of religion and, forgetting their higher purpose in the satisfaction of their appetites, become, like the mad, immersed in their own desires. The word 'mad', which has been avoided in the descriptions of Barnaby and Lord George, is hammered out in scene after scene, as the crowd becomes a mob, and significantly, as he defends himself after Gordon's departure, even Barnaby is said to be dealing blows 'like a madman' (p. 525). As an idiot, he is not really mad; as a rioter, it is as if the metaphorical madness through which Dickens criticises the behaviour of the mob ('a moral plague ... whose contagion spread like a dread fever: an infectious madness', p. 484) has infected him too. Sometimes, though, the description of the madness of the crowd slips its metaphorical moorings and appears real enough. Describing the frenzy of the rioters as they lay siege to Newgate, whose door, 'although a sheet of flame, was still a door fast locked and barred' (p. 582), the narrator conveys the madness of the throng by describing the tremendous energy and senseless activity of the scene:

> The women who were looking on, shrieked loudly, beat their hands together, stopped their ears; and many fainted: the men who were not near the walls and active in the siege, rather than do nothing, tore up the pavements of the street, and did so with a haste and fury they could not have surpassed if that had been the jail, and they were near their object. Not one living creature in the throng was for an instant still. The whole great mass were mad. (p. 583)

The madness of a crowd is something that Hobbes, in *Leviathan* (1651), treats very seriously:

> Though the effect of folly in them that are possessed of an opinion of being inspired, be not visible alwayes in one man, by any very extravagant action,

that proceedeth from such Passion; yet when many of them conspire together, the Rage of the whole multitude is visible enough. For what argument of Madnesse can there be greater, than to clamour, strike, and throw stones at our best friends? Yet this is somewhat lesse than such a multitude will do. For they will clamour, fight against, and destroy those, by whom all their life-time before, they have been protected, and secured from injury. And if this be Madnesse in the multitude, it is the same in every particular man.[48]

In Hobbes's thinking, Rage of Madnesse is caused by 'excessive desire of Revenge' or 'Vehement opinion of the truth of any thing, contradicted by others'; madness is, in effect, excessive passion.

Thus far, Dickens would seem to be in agreement with Hobbes, and his depiction of the riots might well be a visualisation of the concept of the 'Madnesse of the multitude' quoted above, but for the novel's ambiguity towards the lower classes and their relationship with authority. Insofar as they are seen in the mass, they are damned by the narrator as 'the scum and refuse of London, whose growth was fostered by bad criminal laws, bad prison regulations, and the worst conceivable police' (p. 453); but the treatment of the representative figures indicates a more complex set of attitudes. The long article by Paul Stignant and Peter Widdowson referred to earlier discusses in detail the novel's historical credentials and particularly the received opinion that Dickens was sticking close to the facts of the Gordon riots. They make out a strong case for bias on the novelist's part, in that he ignores any possibility that riot might be the result of genuine working-class agitation and not the goadings of evil-minded leaders. Certainly there is no part allowed to rational debate or working-class initiative on ideological grounds and, although Dickens did abandon the original plan of having as leaders of the riots three lunatics escaped from Bedlam, the persistent references to madness harness old-fashioned notions of insanity to a nineteenth-century preoccupation with the possibility of losing social control. The writing of these episodes, however, has an excitement and an intensity that indicate more than simple criticism; in common with many Victorian writers, Dickens shows a voyeuristic enjoyment of the depravity of the 'low' life he outwardly condemns. Inspired by Bakhtin's conception of carnival and the grotesque, Peter Stallybrass and Allon White in *The Politics and Poetics of Transgression* look at the high/low opposition as it cuts across four 'symbolic domains' at various times. Those symbolic domains they identify as 'psychic forms, the human body, geographical space and the social order'.[49] Unlike the wholehearted enjoyment of the carnivalesque in earlier periods, the nineteenth century, they maintain, in its documentary as well as its fictional writing, displays a fascination and a disgust with the low and the dirty, but allows mention of the 'low' of the bourgeois body only when it is transcribed in terms of the topography of the city which already inscribes relations of class, gender, and race.[50] In *Barnaby Rudge* Sir John Chester represents the extremity of bourgeois rejection and fear of contamination by the low, and through him Dickens exposes the hypocrisy of Victorian attitudes. But at the same time the very way the mob is reduced to 'a mad monster' and seen 'for the most part' as the detritus of the city (p. 453), yet described with such exultation indicates an ambiguity of response on the part of the author.

The inconsistencies and contradictions of this novel, which have been remarked on by Stignant and Widdowson amongst other critics, extend to the way madness and idiocy are treated in the book, as I have already shown, and yet another element is added to an already complex situation with the mention of Bedlam in the latter part of the book. As I pointed out at the beginning, Dickens does not appear to be concerned with the reproduction of an historically accurate picture of the institutional treatment of insanity in his fictional writing, and the evocation of Bedlam in *Barnaby Rudge* has less to do with the concrete presence of the asylum and more to do with the author's attitude to the rioting Londoners. In the description of the attack on the Warren (Chapter 55) when similes of madness abound, the climactic point is signalled by the comparison of the frenzy of the attackers with the image of opening the gates of Bedlam and the issuing forth of the maniacs. This is a fairly commonplace device, drawing on popular conceptions of the lunatic hospital, but it is given a new twist, when, in Chapter 67, as the riots gather in fury, we are told that there was a rumour that the rioters meant to throw open the gates of Bedlam:

> This suggested such dreadful images to the people's minds, and was indeed an act so fraught with new and unimaginable horrors in the contemplation, that it beset them more than any loss or cruelty of which they could foresee the worst, and drove many sane men nearly mad themselves. (pp. 604–05)

But this 'dreadful image' is, of course, the one that the narrator has already employed to describe the behaviour of the people. It is as though the 'mirror of recognition' has been brought before the mob and not only do they, like Lord George, fail to acknowledge the resemblance, but they do not even recognise themselves in the mirror. Drawing on the hyperbole of traditional fears of madness rather than a humanitarian understanding, Dickens conveys his own fear and detestation of the mob.

This quotation, furthermore, indicates why a mad mob should be so fearsome, for if the freeing of lunatics should suggest 'unimaginable horrors', more troubling than the worst of foreseeable consequences, then the madness of the mob, too, can lead them to act in ways that are disturbingly unpredictable. The fear of the unknown is surely a contributory factor in Dickens's much-remarked conservatism. Unlike Carlyle, who saw the mob as an agent of necessary historical progress, Dickens, a sympathiser with 'moral force' rather than 'physical force' Chartism, had a horror of the loss of order and control that was implied when a crowd turned into a mob.[51] But it is a cruel irony that in *Barnaby Rudge*, the public authority that he sees as necessary to preserve law and order, perpetually threatens to 'resolve itself into nothing more than the violence at its disposal … [and] thus … presents the threat of becoming as savage as the savagery it was instituted to civilize'.[52] As Barnaby and his mother journey to London they meet, or rather are accosted by 'a fine old country gentlemen', a magistrate. It is a picaresque episode unnecessary in terms of the plot, but important in terms of theme. As a representative of law and order, he stands for harsh punishment and a total inability to understand the hardships of the poor. He is a character that Fielding would have recognised and his attitude to idiocy is one that nineteenth-century reformists felt belonged to the eighteenth century: 'It's an excuse not to work. There's nothing like flogging to cure that disorder' (p. 435). The other suggestion he makes is that the widow should shut Barnaby up. It is interesting that here Dickens falls into an anachronism, since the 'county institutions' which the 'gentleman' refers to belong to the time of the novel's composition rather than the time in which it is set. The slip is a minor one, but betrays, I think, the way in which Dickens was in fact writing about his own society.

The widow does not have Barnaby confined, but the legal system does. As a leading rioter he must take his share of the guilt. By having him imprisoned and threatened with hanging, Dickens is making the point that even an idiot must be held responsible for such dangerous behaviour. But his subsequent last-minute release and pardon is achieved on the grounds of his idiocy, which indicates a less severe attitude. There is, though, some difficulty about allowing an exception to be made of Barnaby. His state of mind, it is made clear, is the result of his heritage, yet he is not alone in being thus at the mercy of the past. All the young men in the novel are, in one way or another oppressed by paternal authority, and Hugh, in particular, is shown to be one of society's unfortunates. By having Barnaby rescued from the fate that the other rioters suffer, Dickens seems to be exonerating him on the grounds of diminished responsibility, but his consciousness of wrong is reflected in the break-down and amnesia he suffers after his rescue. The shadow that the past has exerted over the present thickens into 'a dark cloud' which effectively cuts him off from all that has happened previous to his recovery (p. 737). Barnaby is allowed to survive, but only on the condition of temporal and geographical severance; not only does he lose contact with his past, except insofar as he conceives of his condemnation and escape as 'a terrific dream', but 'he never could be tempted into London' (p. 737). Having learned his lesson, he is rewarded by the bestowal of greater rationality; he is said to have 'a better memory and greater steadiness of purpose'. Restored to the rural community, he presents no threat to society. The nostalgia of this ending is reflected in the fate of the other leading characters. Tappertit alone, 'Shorn of his graceful limbs', finds a modest prosperity in the urban environment (p. 734). Barnaby, thus excluded from the site of his crime and mentally divorced from it by reason of his breakdown and loss of memory, is a reformed character and the moral slate is wiped clean.

Part of the ambiguity in the representation of idiocy in the novel, I suggest, is to do with the link that Dickens makes between the disordered intellect and the creative imagination. Impressed by the impenetrability of the mind, especially that of an idiot, Dickens focuses his representation of madness on external appearances, drawing on traditional iconography. In the convention of the wandering madman, the geographical movement both stands for the mind that wanders out of control, and in this novel represents the idiocy that can crop up anywhere at any time. At the same time he allows his own creative imagination to expose the creativity of an idiot's wayward thoughts, in a way that both throws doubt on the responsibility of imaginative fantasies and imbues them with significance. Barnaby is not a realist character; he stands as a symbolic character, symbolic of the weaker element in society, which has the potential for good or evil depending on the quality of the leadership of that society, but which can still not be absolved from all responsibility for its own actions. Through Barnaby's mirror image, Lord George, Dickens shows the disastrous consequences when the leadership is as weak as the weakest members of society, when there is a split between authority, power and responsibility. The novel implies a paternalistic vision of the way society should be governed; madness becomes a metaphor for the violence that ensues when the 'fathers' are unable or unconcerned to fulfil their responsibilities, leaving the mob susceptible to the manipulations of evil-minded leaders.

In the next chapter I shall discuss two texts that explore madness at a domestic level, as sons break away from paternal jurisdiction and attempt to assert an autonomous manhood through union with a woman.

Notes

1 Charles Dickens, *Barnaby Rudge* [1841], ed. Gordon Spence (Harmondsworth: Penguin, 1973), p. 249. All subsequent references are incorporated into the text and are to this edition.
2 Charles Dickens, *Sketches by Boz*, The New Oxford Illustrated Dickens (London: Oxford University Press, 1957), p. 201. Bethlem had been moved from Moorfields to St George's Fields (its third building) in 1815. That building is now the Imperial War Museum.
3 Dickens, *American Notes*, pp. 140–41.
4 Charles Dickens with W.H. Wills, 'A Curious Dance Round a Curious Tree', *Household Words*, 4 (1852), pp. 385–89 (385).
5 Anon., 'The Treatment of the Insane', *Household Words*, 3 (1851), pp. 572–76.
6 Anon., 'Treatment', p. 575.
7 Anon., 'The Cure of Sick Minds', *Household Words*, 19 (1859), pp. 415–18.
8 Charles Dickens with W.H. Wills, 'Idiots', *Household Words*, 7 (1853), pp. 313–17 (316).
9 Dickens with Wills, 'Idiots', p. 316.
10 Dickens and Wills, 'Curious Dance', p. 388.
11 Anon., 'The Star of Bethlehem', *Household Words*, 16 (1857), pp. 145–50.
12 Dickens, *American Notes*, pp. 79–94.
13 Dickens, *American Notes*, p. 97.
14 Dickens, *American Notes*, p. 96.
15 Foucault, *Madness and Civilization*, p. 263.
16 Dickens, *American Notes*, p. 96.
17 Dickens with Wills, 'Idiots', p. 313.
18 Dickens with Wills, 'Idiots', p. 313.
19 Dickens with Wills, 'Idiots', p. 313.
20 John Locke, *An Essay Concerning Human Understanding* (1690), quoted with commentary in Hunter and MacAlpine, *Psychiatry*, pp. 36–37.
21 Sir William Blackstone, *Commentaries on the Laws of England* (1765–9), quoted in Hunter and MacAlpine, *Psychiatry*, pp. 434, 435.
22 Hunter and MacAlpine, *Psychiatry*, p. 435.
23 John Thelwall, *Imperfect Developments of the Faculties, Mental and Moral* (1810), quoted in Hunter and MacAlpine, *Psychiatry*, p. 657.
24 Anon., 'Idiots Again', *Household Words*, 10 (1854), pp. 197–200, refers to the case of Laura Bridgman, whom Dickens had seen and commented on at length in *American Notes*.
25 Anon., 'Idiots Again', p. 200.
26 Anon., 'Idiots Again', p. 197.
27 Dickens and W.H. Wills met Tommy during their visit to St Luke's Hospital for the insane ('A Curious Dance', p. 388).

28 Michael Hollington, 'Monstrous Faces: Physiognomy in *Barnaby Rudge*', *Dickens Quarterly*, 9 (1991), pp. 6–15 (12).

29 Hollington, 'Monstrous Faces', p. 7.

30 The illustrations in *Barnaby Rudge* are discussed by Michael Steig in *Dickens and Phiz* (Bloomington, IN: Indiana University Press, 1978) and by Joan Stevens in ' "Woodcuts Dropped into the Text": The Illustrations in *The Old Curiosity Shop* and *Barnaby Rudge*', *Studies in Bibliography*, 20 (1967), pp. 113–34.

31 Quoted in Gilman, *Seeing the Insane*, p. 63.

32 Gilman, *Seeing the Insane*, p. 66.

33 Gilman, *Seeing the Insane*, p. 67.

34 The work of Lavater and Engel was well known in England, appearing in adaptations by Thomas Holcroft amongst others, and contributing to handbooks of theatrical gestures and expressions.

35 Dickens, *American Notes*, p. 140.

36 Penelope B.R. Doob, *Nebuchadnezzar's Children: Conventions of Madness in Middle English Literature* (New Haven, CT: Yale University Press, 1974), p. 110.

37 See particularly Jack Lindsay, '*Barnaby Rudge*', in John Gross and Gabriel Pearson (eds), *Dickens and the Twentieth Century* (London: Routledge & Kegan Paul, 1962), and Juliet McMaster, 'Better to Be Silly': From Vision to Reality in *Barnaby Rudge*', *Dickens Studies Annual*, 13 (1984), pp. 1–17. A more critical attitude is adopted by Steven Marcus, *Dickens: From Pickwick to Dombey* (London: Chatto & Windus, 1965); John Lucas, *The Melancholy Man: A Study of Dickens's Novels* (London: Methuen, 1970); and A.E. Dyson, *The Inimitable Dickens: A Reading of the Novels* (London: Macmillan, 1970).

38 Iain Crawford, ' "Nature…Drenched in Blood": *Barnaby Rudge* and Wordsworth's "Idiot Boy" ', *Dickens Quarterly*, 9 (1991), pp. 28–47.

39 William Wordsworth, 'Idiot Boy'.

40 John A. MacLeod, 'The Personality of Barnaby Rudge', *Dickensian*, 5 (1909), pp. 262–66, 291–93 (293).

41 MacLeod, 'Barnaby Rudge', p. 262.

42 Ernest E. Polack, 'Was Barnaby Rudge Mad?', *Dickensian*, 12 (1911), pp. 298–99 (299).

43 Polack, 'Was Barnaby Rudge Mad?', p. 298.

44 Polack, 'Was Barnaby Rudge Mad?', p. 299.

45 Quoted in Gilman, *Seeing the Insane*, p. 62.

46 The suggestion has been made that it is Hugh who is Barnaby's *doppelgänger* by Crawford, ' "Drenched in Blood" ', pp. 28–47.

47 Paul Stignant and Peter Widdowson, '*Barnaby Rudge* – a Historical Novel?', *Literature and History*, 2 (1975), pp. 2–44 (25).

48 Thomas Hobbes, *Leviathan* [1651] (Harmondsworth: Penguin, 1985), pp. 140–41.

49 Peter Stallybrass and Allon White, *The Politics and Poetics of Transgression* (London: Methuen, 1986), p. 3.

50 Stallybrass and White, *Transgression*, p. 145.

51 Dickens's attitude to revolution is compared with that of Carlyle by William Oddie, *Dickens and Carlyle: The Question of Influence* (London: Centenary Press, 1972), ch. 7.

52 Myron Magnet, *Dickens and the Social Order* (Philadelphia: University of Pennsylvania Press, 1985), p. 6.

2

Thwarted Lovers: *Basil* and *Maud*

And ah for a man to arise in me,
That the man I am may cease to be! (*Maud* I.X.vi)

And yet, the time was soon to arrive when that lost thought of inquiry into Mannion's fate, was to become the one master-thought that possessed me – the thought that gave back its vigilance to my intellect, and its manhood to my heart. (*Basil*, p. 178)

Both the despairing protagonist (significantly unnamed) of Tennyson's *Maud* and the eponymous protagonist of Wilkie Collins's *Basil* are acutely aware of their shaky masculinity.[1] Narrated with the particular intensity and intimacy of a first-person perspective, both novel and poem are able to convey vividly the psychic dimension of identity as well as the material circumstances of its construction. The two texts that form the basis for this chapter focus on young men who admire a woman from a distance, fall in love with her, find themselves fighting a rival, suffer a breakdown and finally, arguably, recover.[2] As Helen Small has shown, madness resulting from disappointment in love is a theme that predominantly figures women in the role of the disappointed lover.[3] This is as much as anything a matter of literary convention; there are no statistics to prove or disprove the fact that women were more likely than men to go mad when a love affair went wrong. The convention of the love-mad woman conforms to the idea of females as the weaker sex, the sex that is ruled by the heart rather than the head, the sex that is passive rather than active, the sex that lacks power. Paradoxically, as Small shows, when the love-forsaken woman turns mad, she is liberated and takes on a significance beyond that of the female stereotype. In the case of *Basil* and *Maud*, the situation is different; the disappointment in love is not simply to do with rejection, but with some sort of conflict with another man, and the mental breakdown is associated with the relationships that are formative in the search for masculinity.

Basil is an extraordinary story in which the younger son of a family of ancient lineage falls in love with a girl he sees on an omnibus. Some minor detective work enables him to discover that she is Margaret Sherwin, the daughter of a shop-keeper. Trapped between his desire for her and his recognition of the impossibility of gaining his father's approval of a liaison with a girl from such a social class, Basil allows himself to be inveigled by her father into a marriage which must remain secret and unconsummated for a year. On the last night of this year she is seduced by her father's clerk and right-hand man, Robert Mannion. Basil, who has been spying on them, attacks and badly injures Mannion, but himself suffers a serious mental breakdown. Whilst visiting Mannion in hospital Margaret is infected with the typhus fever from which she dies. In the final stages of the novel, Mannion, intent on revenge, follows Basil to Cornwall, and at the end of a dramatic encounter on the wild rocky coastline Mannion falls to his death, a shocking event that causes Basil to suffer a second break-down. Again he recovers and resolves to live in peace and retirement with his sister. The novel falls into three parts: the first ends with Basil's marriage to Margaret, the second with his first breakdown, so there is a clear demarcation of the stages in his life. Jenny Bourne Taylor, in her acute analysis of *Basil* in terms of contemporary psychological thinking and the language of moral management, remarks that generically it combines many of the conventions of the tale of terror within the framework of a serious contemporary novel.[4] It is also, in part, a romance and, as Bourne Taylor points out, a confession. As a confession it is retrospective, but its forward trajectory is that of a *Bildungsroman*; this is a novel about a young man struggling towards maturity, striving for masculine independence and to be master of his own fate. The family plays an essential part in this narrative, so I shall begin my analysis with a discussion of the way in which family relationships impact on the construction of masculinity.

The historian, John Tosh, has usefully differentiated between masculinity as a social construct and masculinity as a subjective identity. In his essay 'What Should Historians Do with Masculinity?' he draws attention to three areas in which a Victorian man had to assert his masculinity within society: home, work and all-male associations.[5] In referring to home as an arena for the assertion of masculinity, he has in mind man as a householder, financially responsible for family and servants and the source of authority. Setting up a home was an important *rite de passage*, for it marked the end of dependency, but the home from which a man came was important in another sense, since it was here that the psychic sense of masculine identity was formed. In *A Man's Place: Masculinity and the Middle-Class Home in Victorian England,* Tosh shows, through detailed reference to diaries, journals, letters and other unofficial papers of Victorian families of varied social status, how central domesticity was to the formation and conception of masculinity in the period: it was 'the place both where the boy was disciplined by dependence, and where the man attained full adult status as householder'.[6] The key qualities that were generally considered desirable in men were energy, will, straightforwardness, courage and above all independence. Independence, in the sense of autonomy of action and opinion, entailed competition with one's peers; such competition might take the form of conflict where there was a valorising of physical prowess and defence of one's honour. Evangelical influence had long drawn attention to the crucial part played by women (mothers and sisters) in providing moral education and example, but during what Tosh calls 'the heyday of masculine domesticity from the 1830s to the 1860s' the role of fathers was less easily characterised; there is no stereotypic image of 'the Victorian father'.[7] However, from his examination of family documents Tosh does draw up a typology of mid-Victorian fathers: the 'absent' father, 'the tyrannical' father, 'the intimate' father and the 'distant' father. Even if there was no one style of fathering, it was nevertheless recognised that a father had an important role to play in preparing his son for independence and for performing a creditable part in society: 'Fatherhood embodies hopes and fears about the future, in the sense that a man's place in posterity depends on leaving sons behind him who can carry forward his name and lineage.'[8]

After a prefatory section, Basil starts his narrative by defining himself in terms of his family, describing its various members and the relationships between them in some detail. Since he is the younger son of a wealthy family of impressively long heritage, the issue of lineage is crucial in his relationship with his father. Basil's father is, in Tosh's classification, a 'distant' father, who is characterised as being psychologically though not physically distant, a man who withholds intimacy from his children: 'It may seem incomprehensible, even ridiculous, to some persons, but it is nevertheless true, that we were none of us ever on intimate terms with him. I mean by this, that he was a father to us, but never a companion' (p. 8). He is shown as being thoroughly dutiful, performing 'his duties towards his family honourably, delicately, and kindly', but his children are 'his household property as well as his children'. In this man, the desire to leave behind sons who will carry on the name and lineage of the family is exaggerated to an almost pathological degree; he has an inordinate pride in the

56 THE MOST DREADFUL VISITATION

length of his ancestry, and 'we were taught', says Basil, 'that to disgrace our family either by word or action, was the one fatal crime which could never be forgotten and never be pardoned' (p. 8). In describing his father, Basil specifically notes certain 'feminine' features:

> In person, my father was of not more than middle height. He was very slenderly and delicately made; his head small and well set on his shoulders – his forehead more broad than lofty – his complexion singularly pale, except in moments of agitation when I have already noted its tendency to flush all over in an instant. His eyes, large and gray, had something commanding in their look; they gave a certain unchanging firmness and dignity to his expression, not often met with … It required, indeed, all the masculine energy of look about the upper part of his face, to redeem the lower part from an appearance of effeminacy, so delicately was it moulded in its fine Norman outline. His smile was remarkable for its sweetness – it was almost like a woman's smile. In speaking, too, his lips often trembled as women's do. (p. 10)

Collins's fiction is notable for the way in which he questions gender stereotypes and the way in which external appearance can confuse the characteristics of both sexes; particularly exciting are his portraits of men who combine the mastery of masculinity with feminine nervous sensitivity.

In *The Law and the Lady*, the extraordinary character of 'mad' Miserrimus Dexter, for instance, occupies a liminal area.[9] Having been born without legs he is seen as physically, literally, only 'half of a man', but metaphorically he is only half a man too; he has the face and body of 'an unusually handsome, and an unusually well-made man', but his 'large clear blue eyes, and his long delicate white hands, were like the eyes and hands of a beautiful woman'.[10] The danger of effeminacy is averted, however, by his 'manly proportions' of throat and chest, and by his 'flowing beard and long moustache'. Yet another twist of the narratorial exposition reveals the assumption that 'a magnificent head and body' are wasted on a man who lacks legs. Later, Dexter's gender ambiguity is represented in terms of dress when he appears in a jacket of 'pink quilted silk', with a matching covelid to his wheelchair of 'pale sea-green satin', and wearing 'massive bracelets of gold'.[11] He explains to his visitor, the novel's protagonist, Valeria, that he despises the nineteenth-century fashion for gentlemen to dress in black: 'I like to be bright and beautiful, especially when brightness and beauty come to see me.'[12] Dexter's feminine qualities do not align him with the virtue expected of women (he is a malign influence in the novel), but he does lead a womanish life sequestered from society, employing himself in embroidery to calm his nerves.[13]

Similarly, Mr Fairlie, the languid hypochondriac of *The Woman in White* shuts himself up in 'profound seclusion' at Limmeridge House.[14] The effeminate nature of his attire lacks the flamboyance of Dexter's appearance and Hartright emphasises that his demeanour takes him beyond sensitivity to morbidity:

> Upon the whole, he had a frail, languidly-fretful, over-refined look – something singularly and unpleasantly delicate in its association with a man, and, at the same time, something which could by no possibility have looked natural and appropriate if it had been transferred to the personal appearance of a woman.[15]

Mr Fairlie, it is made clear, is an impostor, his nervous frailty assumed as an excuse for his reluctance to engage with his responsibilities as guardian of his vulnerable niece, Laura. He is not just a feminised, but a degenerate man. Basil's father, on the other hand, does not shirk his responsibilities towards his children, however limited his conception of those responsibilities, but he does shrink from involvement in the modern world. As a landowner, he lives the life of a country gentleman, devoting himself to his estates, and in London performing 'his parliamentary functions', but otherwise avoiding social engagements; there is the suggestion that he represents the attenuation of a long heritage, and that his values are no longer appropriate in the modern world. But neither he, nor any of the other 'feminised' characters I have just described, attract the imputation of madness.

Since Basil's mother died giving birth to his sister, that sister, Clara, is the only female member of the family and represents, conventionally enough, traditional moral values. She is introduced in obliquely negative terms: there is an 'absence of any colour in her complexion', the 'lower part of her face is rather too small for the upper', 'she would not fix attention and admiration in a box at the opera' (pp. 18–19). But these negatives are converted to a positive: 'The greatest charms that my sister has on the surface, come from beneath it.' He goes on: 'When you really knew her, when she spoke to you freely, as to a friend – then, the attraction of her voice, her smile, her manner impressed you indescribably' (p. 19). This stress on the importance of looking beneath the surface is absorbed, I shall be arguing, into the moral message of the narrative. Furthermore, Basil emphasises his sister's exceptional moral qualities by contrasting her with modern women, who 'appear to be ambitious of morally unsexing themselves before society, by aping the language and the manners of men'

(p. 20). She, on the other hand, is 'fresh, innocent, gentle, sincere' (p. 20), 'conquering by no other weapon than the purely feminine charm of everything she said, and everything she did' (p. 21). The way she is described, though, conjures up an ideal rather than an individual. In his later phenomenally successful sensation novel, *The Woman in White*, Collins has Walter Hartright (addressing a male-implied reader) describe Laura Fairlie as a generalised ideal of feminine beauty.[16] Similarly, Basil sums up his sister's qualities in an image which he asserts will present itself to men in 'their secret moments of deep feeling', an image of 'some woman in whom we could put as perfect faith and trust, as if we were children' (p. 20). Clara's moral purity and virtues hardly have a place in the modern world (the first, three-volume edition of the novel was subtitled 'A Story of Modern Life'); she represents a woman 'whom we could scarcely venture to look for, except in solitary places far away in the country; in little rural shrines, shut up from society, among woods and fields, and lonesome boundary-hills' (p. 20). In narrative terms she is shown to be ill at ease in London society, preferring the seclusion of the family's country house, and she is represented only in her familial relationships, particularly insofar as she provides moral guidance and emotional support. But she also has an important role to play in terms of the novel's symbolic economy which I shall be discussing later. Clara's resemblance to her father and her close affinity with him separates them from Basil and his attempt to enter into the modern world, and also from Ralph, the eldest son.

Introduced in terms of his apparent unsuitability for the responsibilities of heir to a large landed property, Basil's brother, Ralph, offers an alternative, more conventional image of boisterous masculinity. A good sportsman, he is 'gay, hearty, handsome' and carries 'a charm about him that subdued everybody' (pp. 11–12). Ralph absolutely refuses to be bound by the ambitions and constraints set by his father and leads a disreputable life in town until, after an 'awkward love adventure' with one of the tenants' daughters, he is persuaded to take up the post of an attaché in a foreign embassy. Returning home after a long absence, he astonishes the place with his continental habits: 'It was as if the fiery, effervescent atmosphere of the Boulevards of Paris had insolently penetrated into the old English mansion and ruffled and infected its quiet native air, to the remotest corners of the place' (p. 15). The suggestion of sexual activity is accompanied by anecdotes of Ralph's sexual adventures, and the use of the word 'infected' indicates the conventional fear of the 'French disease' associated with such adventures, but Ralph is eventually reformed during a second stay on the continent by a 'resolute female missionary', the 'morganatic' Mrs Ralph, and himself plays an important role in rescuing his younger brother from his social and ethical predicament. The contrast is thus drawn between the degenerative tendency of a life that eschews stimulation from outside the family and the regenerative possibilities of external influences.

Basil's experiences, however, point to a counter-tendency when the external influence is malign or inappropriate. His pursuit of a girl he has fallen in love with in such prosaic and public circumstance as riding on an omnibus is a significant bid for independence; not only is he taking the first step in forming a relationship outside his family of origin, but in his manner of doing so and in his choice of girl, he is contravening everything that his father stands for. Falling in love precipitates Basil into an alternative family and provides him with the option of an alternative father figure in Mr Sherwin, a representative of the brash commercial world of modernity. This option is not played out, however, since the relationship between them is, rather, a commercial one, in which Mr Sherwin uses his daughter in a bargain for social prestige, a bargain that is governed by the principles of the modern world where transactions can not be safely trusted to the honour of the participants. Basil has as it were entered into the world of work, but he is still economically dependent on his father, having, he says, only 'a very small independence left me by my mother' (p. 70), and finds himself domestically dependent now on his father-in-law, as he explicitly acknowledges at the start of Part II: 'Up to the time of my marriage, I have appeared as an active agent in the different events I have described. After that period ... my position changed with the change in my life, and became a passive one' (p. 101).

In this strange limbo, forbidden from consummating his marriage with Margaret, he meets Robert Mannion, Sherwin's enigmatic clerk. Mannion is important in Basil's route to manhood because he provides the competition that must be faced in a young man's assertion of independence. In this case, however, the competition is, at least to begin with, covert; Mannion, an older man, pretends to be a mentor, and the fact that Basil now has a legal right to Margaret does not stop Mannion from competing for her favours. This is how the situation between the two men looks as the narrative unfolds from Basil's perspective. However, we later have Mannion's perspective in a long letter that forms a narrative within a narrative, and it becomes apparent that there is not only a conflict between two men, but between two value systems, since Basil, naïve and self-deluded, operates according to a code of love and honour. On the other hand, Mannion, who has for a long time been interested in Margaret for himself, has learned through hard experience that the chivalric code is inappropriate in the modern world and is interested only in mastery: 'She shall grow up to maturity for *me*: I will imperceptibly gain such a hold on her affections ... that, when the time comes, and I speak the word ... she shall ... come to my side, and of her own free will put her hand in mine, and follow me wherever I go; my wife, my mistress, my servant, which I choose (p. 236). There is a startling similarity here with the lust for power and insistence on voluntary surrender that we shall find in *Dracula*. Mannion's father has been hanged, a victim of the over-zealous and inhumane sense of honour of Basil's father, and Mannion himself, warped by the desire for revenge, has turned into a sort of monster, and in competing for Margaret he now finds a potent way of avenging himself on the father through the son.

It is the discovery of Mannion's success with the woman that precipitates physical conflict and Basil's breakdown. Janet Oppenheim in, 'Shattered Nerves', gives evidence of the recognition in nineteenth-century psychology that nervous breakdown was not uncommon in men as a response to trauma; there is also evidence that breakdown was in fact not infrequently observed among young men on the verge of adulthood and, like Basil, often in conflict with their fathers.[17] What I am arguing is that Basil's mental breakdown, closely allied to madness, can be interpreted as his response to emotional trauma, and a consequence of his failure to achieve masculine independence from his father, and by looking more closely at the descriptions of alternative states of consciousness that Basil undergoes, it can be read in terms of his psychic development. But his psychological crisis is also important in terms of the novel's structure; it follows the revelation of Margaret's perfidy and Mannion's duplicity, and marks a peripeteia. This reversal is expressed in two ways, one having to do with Basil's relationship with his family, the other concerning his relationship with Mannion.

Collins's fiction is typically concerned with questions of identity, and the schematic nature of many of his novels is indicative of his awareness that identity is not simply a matter of socio-economic parameters, but of a sense of consciousness – its psychic dimension. One way of exploring this it to eschew the referential language characteristic of realism in favour of symbolism, metaphor, doubling and allegory. The literary critic of the *Times*, E.S. Dallas, was unusual in his time for recognising and appreciating the contribution that sensation fiction makes to our understanding of human nature. In *The Gay Science* he argues that 'our minds lead a double life – one life in consciousness, another and a vaster life beyond it', and that imaginative literature is important in exploring what he calls this 'Hidden Soul'.[18] Dallas writes about the unconscious in language that is vividly metaphorical:

> In the dark recesses of memory, in unbidden suggestions, in trains of thought unwittingly pursued, in multiplied waves and currents all at once flashing and rushing, in dreams that cannot be laid, in the nightly rising of the somnambulist, in the clairvoyance of passion, in the force of instinct, in the obscure, but certain, intuitions of the spiritual life, we have glimpses of a great tide of life ebbing and flowing, rippling and rolling and beating about where we cannot see it.[19]

The vigour of his language, and his choice of 'sea' imagery convey Dallas's sense of the reality of this unconscious life; like the sea, it is part of our physical existence, but like the sea it is uncontrollable and potentially overwhelming. Dallas's thesis relates closely to Collins's fictional practice. In *Basil* the language is similarly vigorous and the use of imagery unites Basil's unconscious with his conscious life. The symbolism of the novel, that is, is both a matter of aesthetics and a way of describing the life that lies beneath consciousness. Two strands of imagery are particularly prominent in the symbolic structure of the book: one of these is an emphasis on eyes and visual appearance; the other is the polarity of darkness and light.

In the course of the novel Basil suffers two mental and physical breakdowns, and describes several different states of consciousness. I shall trace the sequence focusing on the variations on the two imagistic strands, both of which contribute to the moral purpose which, as Collins declares in the dedication, is his aim in describing 'scenes of misery and crime' (p. xxxviii). Soon after meeting Margaret, he has a dream, which in effect elaborates on the contrast that has already been drawn between the fair Clara and Margaret, who is dark, 'darker than usual in English women' (p. 30). Standing on a plain, he sees a tall dark woman emerge from the 'dark secret depths' of the woods on one side, while another woman, dressed in white and 'illumined with a light', descends from the hills on the other side. The dark woman has 'the eyes of a serpent' (p. 45), her touch sends fire running through him and he follows her, his 'blood burning' and his breath failing him, into the 'secret recesses' of the woods: 'There, she encircled me in the folds of her dusky robe, and laid her cheek close to mine, and murmured a mysterious music in my ear' (pp. 46–47). The imagery and the echo of Keats's 'La Belle Dame sans Merci' imply a sexual awakening that is also a bewitching, and the woman in white, miming her protest and sorrow, is powerless to break his thraldom. The moral message is expressed not only in the dark/white contrast but through the landscape, with the woman in white retreating to the high ground, and the dark woman leading the way in the murky woods. Foreshadowing the direction his life will take, the dream expresses symbolically the significance of each woman in his life, and is powerfully evocative of the ambivalence of a young man's first experience of sexual passion.

The breakdown that follows the trauma of Basil's discovery of sexual betrayal falls into three stages. First, as he listens outside the room in the hotel where Mannion and Margaret are talking, there is a moment of apparent paralysis, when his anguish implodes in intense sensations of blood and heart: 'Whole years of the direst mental and bodily agony were concentrated in that one moment of helpless, motionless torment' (p. 160). All Basil's consciousness at this point is focused on internal sensations like those in the dream, only increased in intensity; he is momentarily oblivious of his surroundings. The second stage marks the return of physical strength as 'a quick vigour leapt hotly through my frame' (p. 161), and is the moment of overt physical contest between the two rivals, in which Basil nearly kills Mannion. There is no suggestion but that Basil is fully conscious at this point, however distraught he may be. Finally, having seen Margaret emerge from the hotel, having observed her face 'hideous' with guilt and terror, and having heard her 'abject inarticulate murmurings for mercy' (p. 165), he stumbles through the streets in vain and aimless pursuit of her. The incident not only refers back to the dark woman of his dream, whom he follows blindly into the unknown, but elaborates on one term of the light/dark polarity that runs through the novel: 'I had pressed onward, hitherto, because I saw a vision that led me after it – a beckoning shadow, ahead, darker even than the night darkness' (p. 166).

This third stage of delirious wandering comes at the end of Part II and is worth looking at in some detail. Basil does not lose all sense of what is going on around him, for he describes how he passes two men:

> One laughed at me, as a drunkard. The other ... told him to be silent; for I was not drunk, but mad – he had seen my face as I passed under a gas-lamp, and he knew that I was mad.
>   'MAD!' – that word, as I heard it, rang after me like a voice of judgment. 'MAD!' – a fear had come over me, which, in all its frightful complication, was expressed by that one word – a fear which, to the man who suffers it, is

worse even than the fear of death; which no human language ever has conveyed, or ever will convey, in all its horrible reality, to others. (p. 166)

Just as earlier the waiter at the hotel has been a witness of Basil's fainting fit at the hotel and has seen the 'horrid' look on his face, so here passing strangers act as external assessors of the extremity of his suffering. This is a text that emphasises appearances and seeing, even whilst recognising the difficulties of interpretation and acknowledging that seeing should not always lead to believing. Basil's awareness of the people he passes may be a device to allow the reader a momentary glimpse from a different perspective, to present himself from outside, as it were, but it also shows that he is not so self-absorbed as to have lost all contact with his surroundings. Basil's hyperbolic description of his mental state draws on two clichés: one that madness is more to be feared than death; the other that madness is a state of being which human language is powerless to fully represent. Nevertheless, Basil defies the second cliché by describing his state of mind and the actions it motivates. The physical violence of his attack on Mannion and of dragging Margaret away from the hotel is transformed into mental disturbance, and the directionless motion of his body expresses physically the confusion of his thoughts and emotions. His increasing disturbance is reflected in a series of questions that show his doubt of his own sense perceptions: 'Darkness? – *Was* it dark?'; 'Did I know what I saw?'; 'What was this thing under me?' (p. 167), before he attempts to bring his mind under control, employing another cliché, the attempt to repeat the words of the Lord's Prayer. The dark/light polarity dominates the end of the episode: 'lurid sunshine' flashes before his eyes in 'a hell-blaze of brightness', he is then plunged in darkness, 'the darkness of the blind', then he finds 'God's mercy ... the mercy of oblivion' (p. 167). The usual identification of dark with evil or the morally disreputable is countermanded by an alternative correspondence of darkness and oblivion, the merciful deliverance from seeing any more. The final paragraph, typographically separated from the rest of the chapter, so as to mark the elapse of time, describes the tableau of his recovering consciousness, surrounded by the authoritative male figures of father, doctor and policeman. They are all there, however, in a caring relationship; like a child, he is literally supported by his father, the doctor feels his pulse and the policeman is telling them how he found him and brought him home. It is a tableau representing a regression to childhood. It is written with complete coherence, a scene of relative normality after the nightmare synaesthesia of the preceding scene.

Just as Part II starts with Basil's consciousness of being in a new state of agency, so Part III starts with his description of being in a new state of consciousness: the delirium of what comes to be identified as brain fever. Brain fever is a common phenomenon in nineteenth-century fiction (Jonathan Harker in *Dracula*, for instance, is another sufferer), which, as Audrey Petersen has shown was not only recognised by contemporary medical practitioners, but was usefully vague, a serious illness which was nearly always fatal in reality, but from which fictional victims usually recovered, though in an altered state.[20] She shows that both physicians and non-medical people believed that brain fever could be brought on by emotional shock or excessive intellectual activity. In fiction, however, the great majority of instances are attributed to emotional shock, as indeed is the case for Basil. For him, total physical collapse is accompanied by intense internal activity. It is a way of exploring Basil's psychic development, the counterpart to the restructuring of family relationships.

Before describing his delirious visions, Basil takes up the idea of blindness from the end of Part II and uses an extended simile to compare the experience of an operation for the restoration of physical sight with his own mental vision, compounding his literal in-sight, the mental visions he experiences, with the insight he now has into the events of the past. Basil is able to reinterpret events from a new cognitive basis; he now knows that Margaret is perfidious, that Mannion is duplicitous, that Mrs Sherwin knows and disapproves of what is happening, and that Mr Sherwin is a dishonourable go-getter. Basil differentiates between the oblivion that fell on him initially, with the 'new darkness' (p. 168), which is not 'utter oblivion', but is filled, distressingly, with visions relating to his new awareness. He now 'sees' the events which have taken place in the past year from a new perspective, a position of enlightenment. No longer trusting, but suspicious from the start, Basil reruns the course of his relationship with Margaret, her mother and Mannion. The theme of blindness reappears in the conventional trope of the blindness of love: 'Now, no generous, trusting love blinded me to the real meaning of such events as these' (p. 171). It is the evidence of his eyes that has led Basil into trouble; he has been seduced by Margaret's beauty and failed to comprehend her trivial, shallow nature. Margaret has been represented in the earlier part of the novel as even more of a cipher than Clara is; she represented primarily in visual terms (it is, after all, her beauty of face and form, not her spiritual beauty that has captivated Basil); he tells us about his feelings for her and about his impressions of her, but the only times she is 'shown' in direct speech is when he overhears conversations that betray her baser nature, badgering her mother for a new dress and later threatening to kill the cat. Now, enlightened, Basil replays these particular scenes and this time, instead of making allowances for them as 'little weaknesses of beauty', he interprets them as warnings of her vileness.

As well as the symbolism of sight and blindness, Basil's delirium takes up the theme of darkness and light. Significantly his amended memories always stop at the point when he realises that the conspirators have not deceived Mrs Sherwin and determines that they shall not deceive him. Grammatically this point is interesting because instead of simply describing events that have already happened and reviewing them with new awareness, he expresses volition: the shift is from 'I saw' and 'I heard' to 'I was determined': 'I was determined', he says, 'they should not succeed in deceiving me' (p. 172). At this point he wants to alter the past, and it is at this point that he encounters darkness. It is as though, unable to follow the course of events through to the scene of discovery and of his fight with Mannion, he launches instead into a delirious replay of his 'mad' wanderings in the night streets of London, only this time it is his thoughts that are wandering 'over their own fever track' (p. 172). As at the end of the earlier wandering scene darkness gives way to a 'blaze of lurid sunshine', 'a hell-blaze of brightness', before he is consigned to the 'darkness of the blind', so now darkness gives way to 'a world whose daylight was all radiant flame' (p. 172). The language is less avernal, but he is still whisked away into a new, phantasmagoric phase of delirium by 'Giant phantoms', and the references to 'thunder-music', 'earthquake' and 'whirlwind' (p. 173) are scarcely comforting. The delirium represents here a symbolic scene, as in the dream of the two women, but instead of a generalised landscape of woods, plains and hills, we have an apocalyptic vision that has the architectural grandeur of a scene painted by John Martin and the hectic movement of the demonic finale of Berlioz's *Symphonie fantastique*. The light gives way to an impenetrable darkness out of which emerge two monstrous figures, Margaret and Mannion, their moral corruption made visible as physical corruption. It is at this point that Basil finds himself by 'a still, black lake of dead waters', and is shown the dead white bodies of his sister and father, spotlighted by a 'white light' (p. 174). Symbolically, he finds himself in 'cold contact' with them as they all eddy round in the waters, but is unable to grasp them, since they are continually separated by 'the demon pair' (p. 174). The imagery recalls the mythology of the Eleusinian mysteries and suggests, as has the tableau at the end of Part II, that Basil is symbolically starting his life again. When he recovers it is indeed to 'a new existence – to a life frail and helpless as the life of a new-born babe' (p. 175).

Delirium, one of the symptoms of brain fever, is not only (as Dallas recognised) a channel to the unconscious, but, as Jane Wood points out in *Passion and Pathology*, her study of mental disorders in literature and medicine, it is another useful device for the novelist.[21] It can range in form from 'a simple narrative device to the paralysing crisis of identity' (p. 113). It can mark a turning point in the plot, or it can create a liminal area where the 'laws and codes which fix consciousness in the material present' are temporarily suspended'.[22] 'Delirium', she continues, 'harbours the uncanny in its seeming power to facilitate insights and mental processes alien to the rationality of wakefulness whilst, at the same time and more disturbingly, revealing aspects of the human mind which operate outside the control of the will.'[23] Basil's delirium marks a turning point in the plot; it confirms a significant psychic transformation and allows him to replay events with his new-found insight, up to the point where he would actually act differently. Like Pip in Dickens's *Great Expectations*, another victim of disappointed love and of brain fever, Basil recovers to a new awareness of the significance of his relationships. But whereas Pip emerges from delirium to the comfort of his adoptive father, Joe Gargery, and an appreciation of Joe's true worth, Basil is 'reborn' into the same relationship with his father that he has tried to escape by 'marrying' Margaret. When he finally gets round to telling the story of his escapade, his father, outraged at the offence to the name of the family, disowns him: 'You are Mr. Sherwin's son – not mine. You are the husband of his daughter – not a relation of my family' (p. 204).

Basil has also to confront his 'demon', Mannion, and as the opening quotation makes clear, it is the thought of that confrontation that gives him back his sense of 'manhood'. Although the working out of Basil's relationships with his family and with the Sherwins is accomplished mainly in the mode of realism, so far as the other aspect of the reversal, Basil's relationship with Mannion, is concerned, the text moves towards fantasy, emphasising the extent to which the struggle has now become a psychic one. Having failed to effect a reconciliation with his father, Basil removes himself from his home and family and retires to a fishing hamlet not far from Land's End. It is made quite clear that this is a place removed from civilisation, and, since it is the childhood home of his nurse, there is the sense of returning to a place of beginnings. Furthermore, the description of the meeting with Mannion in Cornwall has some of the qualities of the delirious vision; there are no buildings here, but the menacing grandeur of the coastal scenery has the same apocalyptic significance. Mannion emerges (alone of course) out of the mist, and Basil's noting the removal of the shade that has covered his deformities recalls the 'net-work of twining worms' that has veiled his face in the delirium. The fight in the street has left Mannion facially severely deformed; it is as if Basil has created Mannion as a monster. He has literally caused his disfigurement by hurling him face down on a road which has been newly mended with granite, and, as he himself acknowledges, has been about to 'beat out of him ... not life only, but the semblance of humanity as well' (p. 164). Mannion's letter expresses his understanding of the situation in terms that recall the monster's reproaches to Frankenstein: 'Do you still exult in having deformed me in every feature, in having given me a face to revolt every human being who looks at me?' (p. 249). The letter itself, Mannion's personal narrative, operates within the text as does the monster's, and like Frankenstein, Basil, living in isolation from his family, is pursued by his 'monster' through wild, hostile territory. Basil's retrospective 'confessional' ends before he encounters Mannion again, and it is in journal form with its greater immediacy (and again a similarity with the letters which tell the final part of the story of Frankenstein) that Basil gives the narrative of the final instalment of his relationship with Mannion.

In the quotation with which this chapter started Basil expresses his sense of finding a manly purpose in life in tracking down his opponent, but in the end it is Mannion who tracks him down, and, whereas the earlier struggle was, I suggested, more like a contest between two different value systems, here the struggle between them seems less a stage in the attainment of masculinity than a wrestling match between two aspects of Basil's personality in a more fundamental definition of self-identity. I suggested above that Basil creates Mannion as a monster by dashing his face on the rough road, but this action could also be interpreted as Basil's grinding off Mannion's mask to reveal the expression of villainy beneath. Up to the moment of his exposure, Mannion has presented an appearance of enigmatic coldness. When Basil first meets him, it is his expressionless countenance that the young man finds uncannily disconcerting: 'No mask could have been made expressionless enough to resemble it; and yet it looked like a mask. It told you nothing of his thoughts, when he spoke: nothing of his disposition, when he was silent' (p. 110). Later, in a dramatic scene of thunder and lightening, as Basil leaves Mannion's house a lightning flash illuminates Mannion's face in such a way as to create the illusion of a fiend-like expression: 'It [the lightning] gave such a hideously livid hue, such a spectral look of ghastliness and distortion to his features, that he absolutely seemed to be glaring and grinning on me like a fiend' (p. 130). Then in the delirious vision the image of a mask is converted to the image of a veil, 'one hideous net-work of twining worms' (p. 174), that Mannion raises to reveal his corruption. These two instances support the idea that, rather than Basil creating Mannion as a monster, he is a monster already beneath a mask of impassivity. But agency here is ambiguous as indeed is the relationship between the two men. As Dorothy Goldman convincingly argues in the introduction to the World's Classics edition of the novel, if Mannion is Basil's dark double then his death, which also seems to be Basil's 'death', is a killing off of sexual aggression, of the desire to enter the market of sexual competition.

Basil's 'death' takes the form of a second breakdown, following this second close encounter with Mannion which brings to a climax the extraordinary relationship between the older and the younger man. As in the preceding episode, he enters a state of 'oblivion' from which he awakens to a transformation of the scene, which has been one of wildness, danger and violence, into one of paradisiacal beauty: 'When I rose and looked around me, the seaward sky was lovely in its clearness; the foam of the leaping waves flashed gloriously in the sunlight: and all that remained of the mist was one great cloud of purple shadow, hanging afar off over the whole inland view' (p. 326). But Basil has not entered paradise; he must drag himself back to his place in the real world, where this time there are no significant supportive figures, since he is living as an outcast. The relief that one would expect Mannion's death to bring is absent, and instead Basil is obsessed by visions of his opponent, of Margaret, Clara and Ralph. The visions pass like a dumb show, like ghosts, with scarcely even the fragmentary narrative of a dream. Nevertheless, through his journal, Basil continues the narrative of his own breakdown, retaining enough self-awareness to be able to question his mental state: 'I am afraid my mind is seriously affected ... My nerves must have suffered far more than I suspected at the time' (p. 328). His power of communication, however, gradually diminishes; he is unable to articulate the words that would enable him to tell the doctor what ails him and cannot write a letter to Ralph. Like Jonathan Harker in Castle Dracula, he is aware that writing his journal is keeping him sane. Unlike Harker, his journal disintegrates into brief entries, no longer marked by date, the syntax broken and the final sentence trailing off. An editorial note comments on the way the writing drifts into illegibility. The mental breakdown is thus mimicked in the graphical breakdown. At this point Basil disappears as the first-person narrator and the story is continued in the form of letters between a Cornish miner and his wife, who is on a visit to London, and a final letter from Basil, which acts as an epilogue, summing up the lessons to be learned and looking to the future.

This letter to his doctor friend ties up the ends in the traditional way by telling us about his recovery and about the death of his father, with whom he has been reconciled. The fact that his letter is written to a doctor makes it a sort of post-recovery check-up, a confirmation that healing has taken place. It tells us that he now lives in retirement with Clara, with Ralph fulfilling his appointed role as new head of the family. But it also reflects self-consciously on the difficulty of finding an ending:

> One difficulty, however, still remains: – How are the pages which I am about to send you to be concluded? In the novel-reading sense of the word, my story has no real conclusion. The repose that comes to all of us after trouble – to *me*, a repose in life: to others, how often a repose only in the grave! – is the end which must close this autobiography: an end, calm, natural, and uneventful; yet not, perhaps, devoid of all lesson and value. Is it fit that I should set myself, for the sake of effect, to *make* a conclusion, and terminate by fiction what has begun, and thus far, has proceeded in truth? In the interests of Art, as well as in the interests of Reality, surely not! (p. 339)

Basil simultaneously exposes the contrivance of the conventional closure of nineteenth-century fiction and adopts it, since Basil is being enclosed in the moral world of his sister. He retreats into a feminised space, away from the public sphere, intent on doing good works on a small scale: 'To serve the cause of the poor and the ignorant, in the little sphere that now surrounds me ... to live more and more worthy, with every day, of the sisterly love which ... watches over me in this last retreat ... these are the purposes, the only purposes left, which I may still cherish' (p. 342). The emphasis on 'repose' as an ending reinforces the impression already conveyed through the mental breakdown that Basil has in a sense 'died'. He has abandoned the attempt to enter the modern world, and to adopt the 'modern' definition of masculinity.

Maud, too, is a poem about conflict. The speaker sees conflict all about him, but is also himself in conflict with society, with his closest acquaintances, and – most importantly – with himself. Written in the present tense, drawing on the traditions of the monodrama, the mad song, and the dramatic monologue, the poem is constructed from vividly contrasted sections, narrative and lyric, representing the different emotional states of the speaker. Like *Basil*, the poem also tells the story of a failed romance, of fighting and death, leading to a breakdown in which the speaker is confined away from society. Like *Basil*, *Maud* is in three parts: there is an abrupt switch from the end of Part I and the famous love song to Maud in the garden, to Part II, when the speaker describes the fight and killing retrospectively amidst the more detailed description of his own disturbed state of mind and being. Part III describes what appears to be his recovery from madness. Although in both texts the madness can be seen to be triggered by trauma and by the disastrous end to a love affair, in *Maud* the speaker's psychological problems are even more complex; his sense of self and of manhood is pathologically insecure. This young man is particularly deracinated; he appears to have no occupation, no remaining family and no home to go to. In fact, he does have a *house*, which he represents as an environment of nightmarish decay and desolation, a shelter only rather than a home, and in his madness, unlike Basil, who is confined at home, tended lovingly by his sister and supported by his brother during his brain fever, the speaker of *Maud* is confined in a madhouse, a place of anonymity. Bereft of the normal domestic and social contacts, he provides himself with a psychic framework by dwelling on the death of his father, indulging in hatred of the old man up at the hall, bewailing the corruption of society, and developing an obsessive love for Maud.

In his ' "Morbid Introspection", Unsoundness of Mind, and British Psychological Medicine, c.1830–c.1900', Michael J. Clark discusses Victorian thinking about the dangers of intense introspection: '…"introspection", almost invariably in conjunction with habitual self-absorption and unnatural egoism, forms one of the principal constitutive elements of their [later nineteenth-century psychological authorities] conception of "unsound Mind".'[24] Such total absorption in subjective states of consciousness disabled, it was thought, the capacity to receive and react to external impressions; crucially there was a loss of self-control and reason was displaced by emotion: 'This dethronement of reason and will in turn favoured the development of "dominant", "imperative", or obsessional ideas or trains of thought, of morbid emotional states, and of mental automatism, and thus by degrees passed over into actual mental disorder.'[25] Linked with these dangers was the problem of imagination exercised without the control of reason and judgement. Imagination was not in itself intrinsically unhealthy or immoral, but its excessive, unregulated cultivation could lead to mistaking imaginary phenomena for reality. The speaker in *Maud* could be taken as a case study of the dangers of morbid introspection; obsessed by his father's death and then by thoughts of Maud, the form of the poem both reflects and determines the speaker as the centre of thought and feeling from the very first line.

The melodramatic opening of *Maud*, vibrating with hatred, sets a very different tone from the considered and contemplative start of *Basil*. Instead of a retrospective narrative, starting in conventional (auto)biographical form with an account of family background we have a poetic stream of consciousness, in which the reader must make out the narrative as best she or he may. Whereas Basil starts from a position of security, the speaker of *Maud* starts from a position of instability, mental and circumstantial. That opening plunges into a nightmare of hectic emotion:

> I hate the dreadful hollow behind the little wood,
> Its lips in the field above are dabbled with blood-red heath,
> The red-ribbed ledges drip with a silent horror of blood,
> And Echo there, whatever is asked her, answers 'Death.' (I.I.i)

Hovering between metaphoric and literal status, the repeated word 'blood' hints that something has happened to taint the place, but also warns us that we are entering the speaker's mind, even as we view the scene. The emotion is so immediate it comes as a shock in the second stanza to find that the body was found in the pit 'long since'. Whereas Basil's problem is to escape the control of a father who is very much alive, for the speaker here the problem is to escape the emotional legacy of a father who is dead. However, the speaker is less inclined to escape a liaison with Maud, which is in fact another legacy from his father – or at least is seen as such by the speaker in one of the vignettes of memory.

She is the only character who is named, but that does not make her any more concrete a presence, for she is singularly elusive. On a narrative level she functions, like Margaret Sherwin, as the cause of the fight between the rival lovers and as part of a contextual plot concerning property. But she is a shadowy figure, more like a figment of the speaker's imagination than a creature of flesh and blood. She is consistently accompanied by the imagery of jewels: her face is 'cold and clean-cut', 'icily regular' (I.II), she is 'a pearl' (I.XVII.v), and she is set, still and enclosed, in vignettes: the village church, where she seems as lifeless as the stone angel (I.VIII), or her 'own little oak-room' which she lights 'like a precious stone' (I.XIV.ii). Such imagery emphasises her value, but it tends to commodify her; it emphasises the degree to which her would-be lover sees her as artificial and as displaying her wealth. In his eyes she may reflect light but there is no warmth. As the poem progresses, however, and the relationship between them starts to blossom, the jewel imagery associated with her melds into that of flowers, and she herself becomes a 'Bright English lily' (I.XIX.v) before being absorbed in the crescendo of sensual outpouring in the lyric, 'Come into the garden, Maud'. Unlike Clara in *Basil,* she does not represent Christian womanly virtues; like Clara, though, she does seem to represent an ideal, an ideal of the past regained. The lover supports his love with his insistence on his right to Maud as a legacy left by his father, who with her father had pledged them to each other at her birth. Now, estranged from Maud's father, he sees her sweetness as she mellows towards him as inherited solely from her mother. Whereas before she is seen as implicated in the cold commercial relationship that has led to the breakdown of affective relations between the two families – she has been a pawn in their bargaining – now she is seen as a having restorative powers, and a union with her holds out the promise of healing the rift, not between the two families but within himself.

Whereas in *Basil* conflict is externalised but given psychological significance through the device of doubling, in *Maud* the conflict in the speaker's mind is represented more literally in the expressions of a divided self which enter early in the poem and become increasingly inharmonious. From seeing himself as his own refuge ('I will bury myself in myself', I.I.xix) he moves to wariness ('myself from myself I guard', I.VI.vii), before finding himself 'At war with myself' (I.X.ii). The idea of warfare carries through the next stanza of canto X which expresses his outrage at the preacher who is condemning war in the town, and carries enmity into the most domestic of contexts, 'at your own fireside', for conflict is endemic to society and 'each is at war with mankind' (I.X.iii). This raging is juxtaposed in the next stanza with the memory of Maud singing her 'chivalrous battle-song'; it is a memory he holds on to, not so much to comfort himself in his anger with societal wrongs, but to save himself from jealousy of the 'wanton dissolute boy' he fears is his rival (I.X.iv). As he gathers courage to make a declaration of his love, he emphasises her significance for his psychic well-being: 'if *I* be dear to some one else, / Then I should be to myself more dear' (I.XV). And in the next canto this becomes still more extreme: he knows her beauty to be

> the one bright thing to save
> My yet young life in the wilds of Time.
> Perhaps from madness, perhaps from crime,
> Perhaps from a selfish grave. (I.XVI)

Once assured of Maud's love, he resolves to 'bury / All this dead body of hate' (I.XIX.x), as though the emotion is an entity physically separate from himself.

His resolution, however, is thwarted by the return of Maud's brother and the fight in the garden and the sense of a divided self increases in Part II. Here the split in the speaker's psyche is envisaged as one between himself and his 'passionate love', his 'harmful love' (II.II.ix) and his psychic estrangement is given still more graphic expression as he addresses his 'heart of stone' in the second person (II.III). In his new predicament, Maud is still a presence, though, even before the strangely muted announcement of her death, it is a ghostly presence: 'a hard mechanic ghost' , 'flitting to and fro' (II.II.v). This is not a comforting ghost, but a 'disease' that plagues him, and the speaker reveals his awareness that it is neither a heavenly nor a hellish emanation, but 'a juggle born of the brain' (II.II.v). As his distraction increases there is, in a stanza resonant of Macbeth's guilt-crazed hallucinations, a confusion between the phantom of Maud and the haunting of his own guilt, and two stanzas later his living presence is further confused with her ghostly presence as he describes himself stealing through the market, 'a wasted frame'. Like Basil he plays over in his hallucination the significant scenes of the past, but here they are not caricatured. The speaker of *Maud* is still obsessed with the image of the woman he loves; the figure of his rival plays no part in his replaying of the past.

In fact the rival plays a far less important role in the psychological torment faced by Maud's lover than he does in Basil's problems. So far as conflict over rival claims for Maud's hand is concerned, it is her brother who is the significant other. In terms of social convention, it was not unusual for a brother to assume responsibility for a sister's disposal in marriage, and to defend her honour against the advances of an unsuitable lover. In such circumstances, it is not the woman herself who is the focus of consideration, but the family, and it is difficult to ignore the further significance the brother takes on as an incestuous rival. In Maud, unlike *Basil*, it is the brother who dominates the speaker's consciousness of Maud's alternative loyalties, he who fights and is killed, whilst the 'babe-faced' lord stands 'gaping and grinning by' (II.I.i). The ostensible rival lover is depicted in derogatory terms as a passive figure, an adjunct of the brother. He is introduced in canto X as a 'new-made lord', his wealth the legacy of his grandfather, a tainted legacy since it derives from the grime and poison of the pits. The 'splendour' that derives from the alchemy of 'coal all turned into gold' and the newly conferred title is not the splendour of manliness

(I.X.i). He is characterised as being 'Rich in the grace all women desire', an ambiguous phrase that could mean that insofar as he possesses grace he is desirable to women, or that he is womanish in that he possesses grace that women would like to imagine they hold in themselves (I.X.i). The second way in which he is characterised is less ambiguous: he is 'Strong in the power that all men adore' (I.X.i). Although this phrase contains within it the suggestion that men want power for themselves, the stronger meaning is that they adore power more abstractly, for they 'simper and set their voices lower, / And soften as if to a girl' (I.X.i). The ownership and exercising of power may in the popular stereotype be characteristic of masculinity, but here it appears, on the contrary, to emasculate. He is 'a padded shape, / A bought commission, a waxen face, / A rabbit mouth that is ever agape' (I.X.ii). Maud would never, the speaker hopes, take this 'wanton dissolute boy / For a man and a leader of men' (I.X.iv).

The brother, who stands *in loco parentis*, is represented initially and synecdochally through his head: 'That jewell'd mass of millinery' (I.VI.vi), the language redolent of decadence. A second vision of him extends the picture to encompass his whole, six-foot-two body, but the idea of decadence remains in the description of 'his essences' which 'turn the air sick' and the 'barbarous opulence jewel-thick' of his breast and hands (I.XIII.i). Such excessive attention to appearance is not consistent with an approved model of masculinity, and the brother's pleasure-seeking habits conflict with the ideal of industriousness. Like the rival lover, he is able to pursue an idle life because of his inheritance; the legacy of an older generation of men is important in one way or another for all three young men. The two fathers and the lord's grandfather have involved themselves in the world of commerce and industry, and the younger men cannot escape its consequences, even if they do not buy into it.

From the emotional mêlée one positive image of masculinity emerges, that of a 'still strong man', who, whether 'Aristocrat, democrat, autocrat' is one who 'can rule and dare not lie' (I.X.v). Strength and honesty are here the two prized virtues and they are coordinated in the ending of the poem with its depiction of war in a just cause. It might seem that this provides an escape from insanity and a solution to the speaker's desire: 'And ah for a man to arise in me, / That the man I am may cease to be!' (I.X.vi). Whereas Basil finds mental and physical security by retreating into a feminised space, the speaker of *Maud* seeks his salvation in the typically masculine pursuit of war. He thus becomes a man of action, fighting in support of righteous principles and drowning his egotistical obsessions in the general cause. But there are problems with this ending, since not only was Tennyson a known opponent of the war, but it not clear how fighting abroad can in any way remedy the social ills he rails at in the beginning; nor is it clear how the war can be condoned as 'the purpose of God'. But, as always, with a dramatic monologue the problem is one of knowing how to judge the speaker's values without external referents.

Carol Christ, in 'Victorian Masculinity and the Angel in the House', argues that in idealising women's passivity and asexuality, male writers in fact are depicting the qualities they would prefer to find in men, rather than the aggressive sexuality they find difficulty in accepting. As she says: 'The fear of sexual energy seems to permit two alternatives of characterization and sexual identity: the man who gives way to his energy is a beast; the good man wishes to retreat from the world of male energy and action.'[26] In *Basil* it is Mannion who indulges his sexual energy, and through Basil's actions he is turned into, or revealed as, a beast. Basil himself, the eavesdropper, is denied the consummation of his marriage and chooses to spend the rest of his days removed from both sexual and commercial competition, living a life of Christian virtue in an asexual relationship with his sister, the angel in the house. The situation for the speaker of *Maud* is different. The fight with the brother follows what appears to be a coitus interruptus and the speaker, denied sexual fulfilment, seeks personal salvation by fighting in the Crimean War. Christ maintains that 'the conclusion of the poem is bombastic and unconvincing' and suggests that this is because Tennyson is ambiguous about the conventional association of masculinity with a world of action.[27] Ann C. Colley, on the other hand, argues in *Tennyson and Madness* that the lover has not really recovered full sanity at the end of the poem and the last part represents his unstable imaginings of a war that suits his needs and of a new world purged of the greed he so detests, capable of liberating him from his rage.[28] However, unlike 'Ulysses', where the ending expresses determination rather than action, there is evidence of the speaker actually going to fight, since he describes himself on the 'giant deck' with 'loyal people shouting a battle cry' (III.VI.iii). Colley is right though, I think, to concentrate on the degree to which the final part maintains the internal focus of the rest of the poem. The speaker may be describing his move away from the madhouse and out to the Crimea, but it is what is going on in his mind that is important. Furthermore, the obsessions of the poem, which have formed unifying *leitmotiven*, continue to provide, in this third part, an aesthetic coherence that confines the poem to its own form.

Most particularly, the ending is associated with Maud. The speaker's sudden resolve is prompted by a dream-vision in which she divides from 'a band of the blest' in their celestial environment and points to Mars 'As he glowed like a ruddy shield on the Lion's breast' (III.VI.i). And the martial imagery of the concluding part is a reminder of the 'chivalrous battle-song' she has sung earlier. So his going off to war seems like a response to her image of fighting men; it is the fulfilment of her ideal. Listening to her song, he has felt himself to be 'languid and base' (I.V.ii); determined actually to go and fight, he feels that he has 'awaked, as it seems to the better mind' (III.VI.v). Once he has taken the decision, shown a masculine resolution, he sees the 'dreary phantom arise and fly'; it seems that her insidious ghostly presence has been part of his madness, as much as her real, if elusive, presence has been part of his pre-madhouse life. By stanza iv, as the poem comes to a conclusion, the use of hyperbole, the prominent alliteration and the piling up of clauses introduced by 'And' echo the hectic quality of the opening; the 'deathful-grinning mouths of the fortress' and the 'blood-red blossom of war' recall the death and blood associated with the hateful 'hollow'. Furthermore, in the ideas of coming to life after having been buried and of the 'blood-red blossom' there are echoes of the last stanza of 'Come into the garden', where the speaker in an ecstasy of anticipation imagines how, even though he had been dead for a century, his 'dust' would respond to her walking over his grave and would 'blossom in purple and red' (I.XXII.xi). Rather than reading the ending as evidence of his recovery and of his determination to enter into the world of masculine activity, I am more inclined to read it as expressing his desire for death, which is the only way he might now be reunited with Maud. In the mad cell he has bemoaned 'their' failure to bury him 'deep enough'; now the literal death that beckons could lead, unlike the metaphorical death of madness, to his being buried 'Deeper, ever so little deeper' (II.V.xi).

In *Basil* there is a clear distinction between different states of con-sciousness, however closely they are linked to each other and to Basil's con-scious life by imagery, and the text distinguishes the periods of mental instability. His development is explored on both the social and psychic level, masculinity being represented as both a cultural construct and a matter of psychic identity. However, it is more difficult to authenticate the experience of the speaker of *Maud* by reference to his social and domes-tic context because his view is so inward-looking. The relative lack of reference to his environment contributes to the sense that he is merely a consciousness, a voice, a voyeur. Unlike the moments in *Basil* when the narrator adopts devices which will allow for external representation, the speaker of the poem has a single perspective, with the direct speech of others included only rarely. This solipsism is intrinsic to the genre of the piece, but also it is expressive of the speaker's egoism. I have argued that the speaker's introspection holds right to the end; his internal conflict appears to be resolved ('I am one'), but the resolution is ambiguous, for, the quotation continues, 'I am one with my kind', and the unity in which he now places his faith seems inextricably linked to death:

> I have felt with my native land, I am one with my kind,
> I embrace the purpose of God, and the doom assigned. (III.VI.v)

Whereas in the previous chapter madness was seen predominantly in terms of external appearance and behaviour, in the two texts discussed here the representation is focused on the unique internal experience of madness. Although there are traces of conventional iconography in, for instance, Basil's restless wandering, or the other delusional patients in the asylum in *Maud*, and the representations draw on contemporary ideas about brain fever and monomania, these texts develop their own patterns of imagery generated by the imaginative activities of the unconscious or poetic sensibility. The father–son relationship, which in *Barnaby Rudge* is seen in both personal and societal terms, is here central to the domestic aspect of a man's life. Madness is the result of thwarted love; it is both expressed in terms of conflict and seen as the result of the conflict that is an intrinsic part of the move towards independence. Both texts question any easy separation of masculine and feminine qualities, but the feminine in *Maud*, as seen in the representation of the brother, is derided as effeminate vanity, whereas in *Basil* feminine qualities are valorised. Interestingly, whereas the mad woman is seen by Helen Small as being liberated by madness to take on significance in the political sphere, the man driven mad by thwarted love in *Basil* seeks sanctuary after recovery in the female space of home, sequestered, like Barnaby, from engagement in the world of men's affairs. In *Maud*, on the other hand, the particular features of the dramatic monologue make for a complex interplay of social and political issues within the intense interiority of the speaking voice, so that the movement outward is always accompanied by a contrary motion inward. As I have argued, the ending of the poem, for all the rhetoric of going to fight abroad, seems scarcely to move; the speaker remains rooted in his obsessions. The loss of self-control, which for both this character and

Basil has led to violent action, is figured as morbid introspection, where the solipsism of the poetic form represents the egoistic introspection of the neurotic, if no longer actually mad man. His involvement in the Crimean War, then, can be seen less as serving the interests of his country than as personal therapy. If in these two texts the emphasis has been on representing madness from within, and on the masculine negotiation of a place in society, in the following chapter attention is focused on an external view of madness, and on the responsibilities of society for the treatment of madness.

Notes

1 Collins, *Basil* [1852], ed. Dorothy Goldman (Oxford: Oxford University Press, 1990); Alfred Tennyson, *Maud* [1855], in *The Poems of Tennyson*, ed. Christopher Ricks (London: Longman, 1969). All subsequent references are to these editions and are incorporated in the text.

2 Basil explains that he is starting his retrospective narrative on his twenty-fourth birthday. The speaker of *Maud* says that he is twenty-five years old.

3 Small, *Love's Madness*.

4 Taylor, *Secret Theatre*.

5 Tosh, 'What Should Historians Do?', pp. 179–202.

6 Tosh, *Man's Place*, p. 2.

7 Tosh, *Man's Place*, pp. 6–7.

8 Tosh, *A Man's Place*, p. 4.

9 Wilkie Collins, *The Law and the Lady* [1875], ed. David Skilton (Harmondsworth: Penguin, 1998).

10 Collins, *Law and the Lady*, p. 163.

11 Collins, *Law and the Lady*, pp. 215–6.

12 Collins, *Law and the Lady*, p. 216.

13 Collins, *Law and the Lady*, p. 219.

14 Wilkie Collins, *The Woman in White* [1860], ed. John Sutherland (Oxford: Oxford University Press, 1996).

15 Collins, *Woman in White*, p. 32.

16 Collins, *Woman in White*, p. 41–42.

17 Oppenheim, *'Shattered Nerves'*.

18 Dallas, *Gay Science*, vol. I, p. 251.

19 Dallas, *Gay Science*, vol. I, p. 250.

20 Audrey Petersen, 'Brain Fever in Nineteenth-Century Literature: Fact and Fiction', *Victorian Studies*, 19 (1976), pp. 445–64.

21 Wood, *Victorian Fiction*.

22 Wood, *Victorian Fiction*, p. 113.

23 Wood, *Victorian Fiction*, p. 116.

24 Michael J. Clark, ' "Morbid Introspection", Unsoundness of Mind, and British

Psychological Medicine, c.1830–c.1900', in W.F. Bynum, Roy Porter and Michael Shepherd (eds), *The Anatomy of Madness: Essays in the History of Psychiatry*, vol. III, *The Asylum and Its Psychiatry* (London: Tavistock, 1985), pp. 71–101 (72).

25 Clark, 'Morbid Introspection', p. 72.
26 Carol Christ, 'Victorian Masculinity and the Angel in the House', in Martha Vicinus (ed.), *A Widening Sphere: Changing Roles of Victorian Women* (Bloomington, IN: Indiana University Press, 1977), pp. 146–62 (161).
27 Christ, 'Victorian Masculinity', p. 158.
28 Ann C. Colley, *Tennyson and Madness* (Atlanta, GA: University of Georgia Press, 1983).

3

Wrongful Confinement, Sensationalism and *Hard Cash*

Even before the large-scale building of county asylums promoted by the 1845 Lunatics Act, the fear of wrongful confinement was apparent. In 1728 Daniel Defoe castigated the 'vile Practice now so much in vogue among the better Sort, as they are called, but the worst sort in fact, namely, the sending their Wives to Mad-Houses at every Whim or Dislike, that they may be more secure and undisturb'd in their Debaucheries'.[1] John Conolly voiced a similar anxiety over the possible abuse of the system in 1830:

> The facts which have been alluded to in the foregoing Inquiry, show, that the present regulations regarding the insane are at once inefficient for the protection of the insane themselves, and dangerous to the public; – that it results from them that some are improperly confined, and others improperly at large; – that whilst the eccentric are endangered, those actually mad are often allowed a dangerous liberty; – that the public are dissatisfied, and medical men harassed and perplexed.[2]

One of the first novels to exploit the possibility of a man being wrongfully confined, is Henry Cockton's *The Life and Adventures of Valentine Vox, the Ventriloquist*, which was first published in monthly serial form and reissued as a book in 1840. Following in the tradition of the picaresque, it exploits the double shortcoming of the early Victorian asylum system, where someone could be wrongfully confined to suit greedy relatives, whereas a real lunatic could be left at large. Having witnessed a magician's display of ventriloquism, Valentine resolves to try it himself and discovers that he possesses an amazing 'power of speaking with an abdominal intonation'.[3] He first tries out his powers on a grand scale at a local political meeting, where he causes great confusion to others and great amusement to himself. Eventually he goes up to London and for the remainder of the book entertains himself by similar displays, with similar results, in a variety of different locations. Interwoven with the vocal mischief is another more continuous and more serious narrative. Valentine goes to stay during his London visit with an old friend of his Uncle John, Mr Grimwood Goodman. Goodman, unmarried himself, has, as his only relatives, a brother, a nephew and their wives. He also has a considerable fortune. Fearing lest Valentine should dispossess them of what they conceive to be their inheritance, the relatives arrange for Goodman to be abducted to a private lunatic asylum. There he remains for much of the novel – nearly 300 pages. Despite periodical concern for his host, Valentine exerts little effort on his behalf, until his Uncle John, alarmed at his friend's prolonged disappearance, comes up to town to pursue investigations. Uncle John, distracted by the delights of town, delays his investigations for more than a month, but eventually secures the release of his friend. Goodman dies soon after his release, leaving his money, despite the wrongs done to him, to his predatory brother, Walter, who is so overcome by remorse that he goes mad in earnest: '… his eyes seemed to be starting from their sockets, while he groaned and ground his teeth and with his clenched fists struck his head with violence.'[4] Drawing on the conventional iconography of madness, Cockton never goes beyond the superficial. Walter's madness is represented in Macbeth-like hallucinations, which have a generic similarity with the illusions of ventriloquism, and, like them, provide an opportunity for humour rather than pathos. Walter, left unconfined, is unexpectedly encountered by Valentine towards the end of the book, 'an emaciated form' who rushes off to commit suicide by throwing himself off a bridge into the river.[5]

In the extended preface to the later editions of *Valentine Vox*, Cockton draws attention to the deficiencies of the 1828 Madhouse Act, which, he maintains, would not prevent wrongful confinement for reasons of adultery, re-appropriation of property, revenge, or the prevention of unapproved marriages. Despite what would appear to be a claim for the novel as part of the campaign against the asylum system ('if, in these hastily written pages, the dreadful system shall have been sufficiently illustrated to induce the legislature to take it into serious consideration, it must of necessity be the means of effecting a revision'), it is difficult to read it as having more serious intent than entertainment. Cockton inveighs against a system under which men

> can at any time be seized, gagged, manacled, and placed beyond the pale of the constitution, within the walls of an asylum, there to be incarcerated for life, with no society save that of poor idiots and raving maniacs, shut out for ever from the world as completely as if they were not in existence, without the power of communicating with a single friend, or of receiving from a single friend the slightest communication.[6]

But he undermines his case by the hyperbole of his own rhetoric. Goodman is neither gagged nor manacled, and the reason that he has little communication with his friends is that they do not readily communicate with him.

Defoe's recommendations (licensed houses subject to 'proper Visitation and Inspection', no confinement without 'due Reason, Inquiry and Authority')[7] were finally embodied in legislation in 1845, but legal safeguards did not calm the fears, and in the same year John Perceval's Alleged Lunatics' Friends Society was founded, achieving sufficient credibility to present evidence of abuse of the system to the 1858 Select Committee. At the same time, and for some years to come, stories of fictional and documentary cases continued to publicise the issue of wrongful or unjustified confinement. One of these was of Herman Charles Merivale's narrative of his experiences in a lunatic asylum. Like Charles Reade, Merivale was trained for the law but earned his living as a writer. But whereas Reade is known now primarily as a novelist, despite his close involvement in the London stage, Merivale is known, if he is known at all, for his plays, though he did write a small amount of fiction. In 1879, however, he brought out a volume that was neither play nor prose fiction.[8] In it he recounts, anonymously, his experiences of twice being confined in a private madhouse. The narrative is not always easy to follow, since no names are given, so that identities become confused and, moreover, the story is constantly interrupted by polemic; Merivale is vituperative about the ease with which the commercial world of private enterprise in the mad business can be exploited by relatives for their own selfish concerns.

Merivale's story is that he was indeed in a weakened state following the death of a 'near and dear relative under circumstances of exceptional pain',[9] compounded by taking the waters at Carlsbad, which he found anything but beneficial, and by taking also hydrate of chloral, which was commonly used as an anaesthetic and hypnotic in the nineteenth century. But he calls his condition 'hypochondria': 'In these coddlesome and unmanly days of ours it is becoming almost rare to meet, in London life at all events, with a man who is not more or less of a hypochondriac about that unlucky scapegoat of modern times, his liver.'[10] Hypochondria was a term widely used in the later part of the nineteenth century (replacing the earlier 'hypochondriasis') to describe a condition which was assumed to have a physiological foundation, but was accompanied by emotional symptoms and changes in behaviour. It was frequently confused with 'nervous collapse' or 'nervous exhaustion', all three terms being preferred to that of insanity in borderline cases, since they lacked social stigma and were unlikely to lead to confinement in an asylum.[11] There are frequent protests throughout the text that he was not insane and that various doctors had vouched for his sanity. Nevertheless, a relative organises for him to be sent to a private asylum. It is not clear how long he spends there, but he is eventually sent to a seaside 'annexe', where a sympathetic matron sends for an 'impartial' relative who secures Merivale's release. He spends the next ten months in aimlessly and unhappily wandering about Paris and London, tormented by dreams of the asylum and fears of being recaptured. This, he maintains, was the time when he might really have been considered mad. He is tracked down by a detective and sent to a doctor who prescribes treatment, as was common for hypochondria, at a hydropathic establishment. Here Merivale continues to be beset by dreams and fears, until:

> At last came the realization of my constant fear; and I fell into a fit of light-headed wandering, and began calling out at intervals various silly things. What should have been done was to nurse me and pour wine down my throat, and apply the common means of homely restoration. What was done was this: the stout bathmen and servants of the place were sent to hold me down; and I was gagged, and left gagged, till the blood ran down from my mouth.[12]

Once again he is certified and sent back to the asylum of his first confinement. He spends another eight months there, before being examined and released by two doctors for the commission in lunacy. Thereafter Merivale effects his own recovery by fighting the dreams and fears, travelling and making a determined effort to interest himself in new scenes and people, before marrying, despite the criticism of relatives.

In terms reminiscent of madhouse brochures, Merivale describes the asylum to which he is sent as a pleasant enough place in itself, 'a castellated mansion in one of the prettiest parts of England', which offered carriages to take him out, cricket, bowls, archery, harriers, as well as evening parties and entertainers from the town.[13] When he first arrives, he believes, like Maud Vernon in Sheridan Le Fanu's *The Rose and the Key* (1871), that he has come to an hotel.[14] Again, like Maud, this impression is only corrected after an encounter with one of the other more eccentric inmates:

> Left alone in a big room on the first evening, I was puzzled by the entrance of a wild-looking man, who described figures in the air with his hand, to an accompaniment of gibber, ate a pudding with his fingers at the other end of a long table, and retired. My nerve was shaken to its weakest, remember; and I was alone with him! It was not an hotel. It was a lunatic asylum.[15]

Another similarity with the earlier fictional text is in the reference to servants who function as custodians. But, whereas Maud's mother has arranged her confinement in a private madhouse to punish her for defying her wishes, the reasons for Merivale's confinement are less clear. What is clear, however, is that he feels himself to be at the mercy of his relatives, who are not acting in his best interests, and in a position that is more usually associated with a gothic heroine. Writing of his second 'apprehension' he makes it obvious that he sees himself as a (female) victim, complaining that he was 'drugged by authority, as effectually and deliberately as ever was heroine of a novel'.[16] At the same time he distinguishes himself from the female sex: 'The nervous maladies which attack us, attack tenfold their more delicate organisation; and they are no safer from wrong or selfishness than we.'[17] To the explicit comparison with the female situation is added a sense of powerlessness induced by the references to things being done to him and actions taken against (and occasionally for) him by unnamed individuals. No doubt, as a trained lawyer, Merivale was aware of the danger of libel, but the effect of this anonymity is to increase the sense of Merivale's powerlessness; the object of their machinations or ministrations, he is unable even to name either his adversaries or his rescuers. In fact the only individual named in the text is his fellow author, Charles Reade.

Merivale writes about his experiences with overt reference to Reade's novel, *Hard Cash* (1863). After recounting the problem that patients have with ensuring that letters they send arrive in the right hands and are not appropriated by the doctors at the asylum or redirected to the relatives responsible for their confinement, Merivale asks a series of rhetorical questions: 'Does this read like "England in the Nineteenth Century", I wonder? Or need we go to the Alfred Hardy's and Mrs Archbolds of Charles Reade to tell us again that fiction is not so strange as truth? He imagines; I describe. Which is the stronger?'[18] Merivale's account in fact contains many of the elements of Reade's fiction. He protests that the doctors find someone mad because they have been told that person is mad; he draws attention to the importance for the patient of keeping calm lest anger be considered yet another symptom of insanity; he describes oppressive treatment and the use of drugs to procure docility; he comments on the attitudes of doctors who seem to be as mad as their patients. And he faces up to the charge of 'sensationalism': 'This story has been called "sensational", when it is simply true. When a direct description of things as they are is sensational, things as they are not things as they should be.'[19] At the time that Merivale was writing, 'sensational' denoted a particular literary genre, so he can be seen as objecting to the way in which his life is being turned into a fiction. He has lost control of the living of it and can only regain control by writing and exposing the false premises.

In his article 'Liberty and Lunacy: The Victorians and Wrongful Confinement', Peter McCandless investigates the extent to which such fictional anxieties were warranted by the actual incidence of wrongful confinement.[20] Like many other twentieth-century medical historians, he cites Reade's *Hard Cash* for its sensational account of wrongful confinement, which by its very popularity helped to publicise the issue and to fan public fears. Recognising the emotional heat generated by this issue, he tries to discover to what extent the fears of conspiracies to confine people who were not really insane were founded on fact, and concludes that, although there were undoubted dangers to individual liberty, deriving from widespread ignorance within the medical profession as to what constituted insanity, occasional malpractice, subjective indices of madness and the tendency to confuse insanity with immorality, nevertheless there is no firm evidence of conspiracy or corruption. There was indeed the suspicion of conspiracy in a few cases, but on the whole 'the men who certified and confined lunatics did so because they believed that it was in the best interests of society and the individuals concerned'.[21] This may well have been true in the case of Merivale, since there is clearly no shared understanding about what constitutes insanity, and there is no claim on his part that the relatives who arranged for his confinement profited from it in any way. Whatever the actual incidence of wrongful confinement, it continued to appear in fiction well after the heyday of sensation writing in the 1860s. In 1874 Mary Braddon published *Taken at the Flood*, for instance, in which Lady Perriam, the beautiful and unscrupulous heroine for which sensation fiction was notorious, has Sir Aubrey, her ageing and ailing husband, confined in an asylum.[22] As so often, it is money that is at stake and the plot, possibly indebted to *The Woman in White*, also involves confusion of identities. The character of the impecunious and unprofessional mad doctor to whose care she consigns Sir Aubrey further emphasises the degree to which madness and confinement are matters where finance is paramount.

Recognising the sensationalism inherent in stories of enforced and illegitimate confinement, Collins appended an authorial note to his short story 'A Mad Marriage' (1875), which he claims is 'founded, in all essential particulars, on a case which actually occurred in England, eight years since'. It tells of a young man, Roland Cameron, who finds himself confined in the first place because his father wants to prevent his marrying a young French woman (a 'nursery governess') he has met on holiday.[23] He endures five years 'arbitrary imprisonment'[24] until the death of his father, when he is freed, after a year in what we might call sheltered accommodation. Three years later an uncle dies and leaves him a large fortune, sufficient inducement for self-interested relatives to drag up a story of an 'act of violence' as an excuse to bring him before a commissioner in lunacy who declares him to be of 'unsound mind'. The proprietor of this asylum allows him to take a holiday in a seaside annexe, where he has complete freedom, provided he returns before nine-thirty each evening. During his hours of liberty he meets a young woman, the narrator of the tale, falls in love with her and marries her. In the circumstances it is not surprising that this causes objections all round, and it is only after a failed petition to the Lunacy Commission and prolonged scheming that he escapes from the asylum and runs away to America with his wife – but without his fortune. The reasons for the first confinement, parental disapproval of marriage plans, puts Cameron into a female stereotype; like Maud Vernon, he is powerless to resist punishment for disobedience. No details are given of the process by which the two medical men necessary for certification arrive at their diagnosis of insanity, and no suggestions are made about eccentricity of behaviour, other than the unsuitability of his desired partner in marriage. On the other hand, the 'act of violence' that is used to justify the second confinement might be described as behaviour more typical of the male than the female: 'He had lost his temper and had knocked a man down who had offended him.'[25] And when finally he makes his escape from the asylum it is by 'committing another "act of violence"';[26] he springs on the keeper who is bringing food to his room, binds and gags him, and lays the man on his bed, covered, as his substitute. He then gets out of the room from the window using sheets tied together, runs through the grounds, climbs the garden wall and walks to Manchester, over thirty miles away. Although it is not unknown for fictional females to behave with physical bravado (Collins's own Marion Halcombe is a case in point), when they do, it is represented as exceptional, daring and unfeminine. Cameron here is seen as acting with proper resolution and courage. Interestingly, though, the description of his appearance and demeanour given by the narrator before she knows anything of his history emphasises what may be thought to be feminine qualities: he is a 'modest, gentle, and unassuming person', he has 'a winning charm of look and voice', his complexion is pale, his hands and feet small, and he tends the narrator's brother 'tenderly'.[27] The only clues to an unusual state of mind are his occasional periods of blankness (as if he had 'suffered some terrible shock … and his mind never quite recovered it') and 'violent outbreaks of temper, excited by the merest trifles'.[28] It is as though the evidence of his fundamental sanity rests on his femininity: the suspicion of insanity is associated with masculine aggression. Like Merivale's narrative, this story attests to the ease with which aspects of behaviour that others find disturbing for one reason or another can be twisted into evidence of insanity with the connivance of incompetent or corrupt doctors. Despite differences in emphasis in these two accounts, there is a shared insistence on the blighting that results from being labelled insane and of the effectual silencing that label entails.

Charles Reade, ill at ease with his reputation as a writer of sensation fiction, was also anxious to assert that there was a factual foundation for his novel, *Hard Cash*. Published in serial form in Dickens's periodical *All the Year Round* from March to December 1863, before coming out in three-volume form a week or so before the conclusion of the serial, it forms part of a campaign that Reade was conducting to publicise and reform the abuses of private lunatic asylums.[29] It was preceded by letters to the press, which Reade later published under the title 'Our Dark Places' in *Readiana*, and the text of the novel was accompanied in its later editions by 'Correspondence elicited by the first edition of "Hard Cash" '.[30] He called his novel a 'Matter-of-Fact Romance', a favourite designation that he applied to five of his fictional works, and prided himself on his meticulous research: '… these truths have been gathered by long, severe, systematic labour, from a multitude of volumes, pamphlets, journals, reports, blue-books, manuscript narratives, letters, and living people, whom I have sought out, examined, and cross-examined, to get at the truth on each main topic I have striven to handle.'[31] But he also worried over the relationship between fact and fiction: 'Sometimes, I say, it must be dangerous to overload fiction with facts. At others, I think fiction has succeeded in proportion to the amount of fact in it.'[32] Reade considered himself to be a reformer who could transmit his message to a wider audience by working through fiction:

> I have taken a few undeniable truths out of many, and have laboured to make my readers realize those appalling facts of the day which most men know, but not one in a thousand comprehends, and not one in a hundred thousand real-izes, until fiction – which, whatever you have been told to the contrary, is the highest, widest, noblest, and greatest of all the arts – comes to his aid, studies, penetrates, digests the hard facts of chronicles and blue-books, and makes their dry bones live.[33]

Reade's statements about fiction are not always as positive as this. In *A Terrible Temptation* (1871), another novel concerned with madness and questionable confinement, he draws what, according to his biographer Wayne Burns, is an 'acknowledged self-portrait, in the character of Mr. Rolfe, a novelist and dramatist who is also a lawyer, and whose fictions are 'works of laborious research'.[34] Rolfe's books, says the rector, Mr Angelo, 'bring about the changes he demands ... he has taken a good many alleged lunatics out of confinement'.[35] But it is not as a writer of fiction that Rolfe helps to release Charles Bassett from the asylum; he is effective insofar as he is an active campaigner rather than a novelist, and the text indicates the queasiness about the status of fiction that is reflected also in Reade's protestations about the factual basis of his novels. Rolfe articulates a cynical point of view:

> 'Well, you are a writer [says Dr. Suaby, the 'mad-doctor']; publish a book, call it "Medicina Laici", and send me a copy.'
> 'To slash in the *Lancet*? [replies Rolfe] Well, I will: when novels cease to pay, and truth begins to.'[36]

Rolfe confirms his position a little later: 'Oh ... all work and no play makes Jack a dull boy. My business is Lying, and I drudge at it; so to escape is a great amusement and recreation to poor me. Besides, it gives me fresh vigour to replunge into Mendacity; and that's the thing that pays.'[37] These comments might be taken as dinner party repartee in the first case and a self-deflating escape from gratitude in the other, were it not that lying, especially insofar as it leads to abuse in the private asylum system, comes in for strong condemnation.

The ambiguous status of books is also evident in *Hard Cash*. Having been lured to Silverton Grove House, Alfred, still officially a free man, is left in an unkempt room, one side of which appears to be all books, including the door by which he has entered. Having 'learned to pick up the fragments of time', he goes to take a book from the shelves, only to find that it and all the others are 'iron and chilly' (p. 261). There seems to be no reason for the deception: 'What a fool the man must be!' thinks Alfred, 'Why he could have bought books with ideas in them for the price of these imposters' (p. 261). Further exploration reveals that he is in a topsy-turvy world where the door has no door-knob and the door-knob no door. He also realises that he is a prisoner within these illusions. The room is never referred to or visited again, and its function here seems to be to emphasise symbolically the degree to which the hero has been trapped in a world of delusion and hallucination. Not only has he entered the domain of the mad, where the madness is not confined to the kept, but he has himself arrived under the illusion that he is to meet Peggy Black, and there is to be a further conspiracy of pretence and misconception that he is mad. But if we take the symbolism to be of psychological rather than structural significance, the inclusion of books as an element of deception can be seen to indicate Reade's own mixed feelings regarding the craft of fiction. It is the fact that the 'books' are revealed to be made of iron that makes the room so curious; doors pretending to be book-shelves are not unknown in the English country house and a wall painted *trompe l'oeil* fashion is conceivable. Iron, on the other hand, is associated throughout the novel with constraints on individual freedom – iron gates, iron manacles, iron handcuffs, iron bars – and Alfred is shortly to be strapped to an iron bedstead. It is possible, then, to read this scene as having a significance beyond that of mere plot and as expressing anxieties similar to those that are aired more explicitly in *A Terrible Temptation*. Books here are not simply empty of ideas, but are implicated in the idea of imprisonment and constraint.

Reade did in fact communicate his feelings of being overwhelmed by the material he had accumulated as source material for his fiction. In his biography of Reade, Malcolm Elwin refers several times to the difficulty Reade expresses about keeping his narrative alive through the masses of documentary material he considered necessary for *The Cloister in the Hearth* and later for *Hard Cash*, and quotes from a letter to Mrs Seymour, his long-term housekeeper and confidante, where he reflects on the pull between research and creative writing: 'Sometimes I say, it must be dangerous to overload fiction with facts. At others, I think fiction has succeeded in proportion to the amount of fact in it'[38] Wayne Burns explains what seems like a neurotic dependence on facts as a camouflage for the emotional scars left by the deficiencies of his childhood relationships. He advances, furthermore, the theory that Reade exerted an unusual degree of control over his material and prized self-control so highly because he feared the encroachment of insanity that would be the all too swift consequence of loss of control. Whatever the truth of this claim it is certainly true that, as we shall see, control, whether of self or of written material, is highly valued in the text under consideration.

For *Hard Cash*, a novel which wavers uneasily between lurid sensationalism and polemic, Reade drew on his own experiences. Like Rolfe in *A Terrible Temptation*, he was actively involved in a case of wrongful committal of a young man called Fletcher, which is documented in the series of letters that was eventually published as 'Our Dark Places', and in writing

Hard Cash he added to the material he had already accumulated by con-
sulting Dickson, the Scots doctor he had had dealings with over the
Fletcher case and who served as a model for Dr Sampson.[39] A number of
critics have discussed the relationship between fact and fiction in Reade's
work, frequently finding it problematic. The deleterious effect of over-
researching his fiction is, for instance, commented on by Winifred Hughes
in her study of sensation novelists.[40] She notes that a 'crazy-quilt effect'
results from the cramming in of as many sensational occurrences as possible in *Hard Cash*, without allowing for the inclusion of intermediate
matters to give a sense of perspective. I would add that the concomitant
absence of psychological exploration not only weakens the characterisation
but reduces the polemical drive of the text. Reade's earlier 'Matter-of-Fact
Romance', *It Is Never Too Late to Mend* (1856), which also aims at social
reform, lacks neither sensationalism nor polemic, but it also makes a
greater emotional appeal than *Hard Cash*. In the earlier work it is the 'separate and silent' system that Dickens had so condemned in *American Notes*
that Reade attacks. Concentrating on a single prison, its governor, a
handful of warders and prisoners, he powerfully conveys the deleterious
effects of the system itself and of the additional punishments that are the
whim of a sadistic governor who is ill-controlled by the feeble inspectorate.
Hard Cash tells a similarly harrowing story, but its impact, for all the doc-
umentation, is weaker in terms of psychological verisimilitude.

The embarrassment its close modelling on the people and events of 'real
life' caused the editor of the journal is discussed in an article by Hunter
and MacAlpine which I shall return to later, but the novel's reception seems
also to have caused Reade himself some embarrassment. The preface,
which was not written until 1868, says that the madhouse scenes have not
only led to 'bold denials of public facts', but to 'a little easy cant about
Sensation Novelists'. Although Reade shuns the label ('This slang term is
not quite accurate as applied to me'), it has regularly been attached to him
by critics of the twentieth century as well as those of his own period, and
it is Dickens himself, in an article published in *All the Year Round* two
months after the three-volume publication of *Hard Cash*, who gives a justification of sensationalism that Reade himself must surely have endorsed.
He writes: 'Now, there can be no doubt that very beautiful and interesting
fictions may be made, and have been made, out of the simplest elements
of every-day life ... But why is all art to be restricted to the uniform level
of quiet domesticity?'[41] He wants to include also 'adventures, crimes,
agonies', 'the awful visitations of wrath and evil and punishment' and

'wonderful and unwonted accidents of fortune'. 'Let it be granted', he goes on, 'that such things *are* sensational; but then life itself is similarly sensational in many of its aspects.'[42] Reade, reversing the assumptions, says something similar towards the end of *Hard Cash*: 'No life was ever yet a play: I mean, an unbroken sequence of dramatic incidents. Calms will come ...' (p. 415). He then compares the detailed record he has given of the events of one year with the abridged account of the succeeding year that he is to trace next, where chronology is to be subservient to topic. His justification for this proceeding is that all narratives do the same thing, because no-one wants to read about the normal and the mundane. Thus does he echo the sentiment of his prefatory footnote: 'Without sensation there can be no interest.'

In *The Maniac in the Cellar* Winifred Hughes contrasts Reade's sensationalism with that of Wilkie Collins. Collins, she points out, preferred to interest himself in mystery and suspense, the narrative frequently concerned with the past as much as the present, whilst Reade offers a series of climaxes in a predominantly forward-moving narrative. Although sensation fiction has been particularly associated with the use of formidable and frequently morally dubious female protagonists, the plot of *Hard Cash* focuses on the plight of male characters, with the females playing supporting roles. The early chapters deal with pretty mundane affairs concerning undergraduate life and the burgeoning love between Julia and Alfred; the sensational element is only introduced later with the financial wheeler-dealings of Hardie senior and thereafter is to be found in just those elements of life that Dickens recognises as co-existing with the cosily domestic: 'adventures, crimes, agonies', and the 'wonderful and unwonted accidents of fortune'.[43] The sensationalism of the text lies in the adventures at sea in the first part and the various madnesses that are triggered off by the collapse of Hardie's bank in the second half. In the interest, presumably, of a wide coverage of the different aspects of lunacy and its treatment, cases are crammed in past the bounds of credibility. Two victims of the fraudulent banker, Richard Hardie, are Captain Dodd, who, tricked out of his savings, falls into a fit and loses his senses as well as his money and the labourer Maxley, who becomes subject to hallucinations and fits of violence, having lost his savings in the bank's fall. The third victim, and the hero of the novel, is Hardie's son, Alfred.

Alfred remains obstinately sane, but is accused of lunacy and tricked into confinement at Silverton Asylum in order that his money should become available to alleviate his father's financial embarrassment. His conviction that his father has appropriated David Dodd's fourteen thousand pounds is taken as further evidence of susceptibility to delusions. Later he is moved to Wycherley's establishment, which is run on the most enlightened principles, though Dr Wycherley is represented as being himself monomaniacal on the subject of Hamlet's madness, and then to Dr Wolf's asylum at Drayton House, which is 'conducted on the old system' (p. 341). At Drayton House he meets Dodd as a fellow inmate and together they escape under cover of a fire that has conveniently broken out and that Dodd's son, Edward, is helping to extinguish. The final part of the book concerns Alfred's attempts to prove that he has been wrongfully confined. It is at this stage that Alfred's uncle, whose signature has confined him to the asylum, is revealed to be feeble-minded, and his father's criminal obsession with money is finally classified by the author as a monomania, such as Alfred himself has been unjustly accused of. Cash is the pivot of the plot and, as the above shows, it is directly linked with lunacy. The world of Reade's fiction is grounded in the struggle between money and morality, and in this novel it is explored by exposing the commercial nature of the private asylum business, where therapy comes second (if indeed it comes anywhere at all) to profit. Reade's aim in writing was explicitly to campaign for a reform of the asylum system. In what follows I shall explore the concepts of madness that underlie his reformist pleas, and discuss the ways in which he represents his male victims as victims of institutions as much as of individuals.

In the year that 'Very Hard Cash' was being serialised in *All the Year Round*, Dr Thomas Laycock published an article in *The Journal of Mental Science*, 'On the Naming and Classification of Mental Diseases and Defects'. This was a prestigious journal in the profession and Laycock, a writer of some eminence, repeats there ideas that are also to be found in other clinical writings, so what he says here can, I think, be taken as reasonably representative of mid-century psychiatric thinking. Naming is important, Laycock says, because it indicates both the appearance and the causality of a mental disease. Having distinguished idiocy, or 'primary' mental defect, from the various 'secondary' mental defects 'consecutive to certain other morbid states occurring in a previously healthy brain', he defines mania or insanity as 'a disease characterized by disorder of the intellect, but without coma or fever'.[44] Given the impossibility of entering into the consciousness of another person, idiocy or insanity can only be established by an examination of external phenomena, action, conduct, speech and, in the case of idiots, formation of body generally, and head and face in particular. In all cases, though, the assessment of mental defect involves a comparative process, requiring, in the first place, a standard of 'mental soundness and completeness', and, in the second place, knowledge of the individual's customary state of mind. The article expresses both uncertainty in its recognition, for instance, of the difficulty of inferring a state of mind from external characteristics, as well as confidence in the possibility of defining ideal types. A similar confidence is imparted to *Hard Cash* through the narrator, who maintains an authoritative stance on the subject of madness; yet a lack of confidence is also evident in the exposure of the disastrous results of incompetence and of undue faith in the shaky procedures of diagnosis.

Malcolm Elwin, in an unattributed quotation, says that Fletcher, Reade's protegé, 'drank, had fits, wasted money' before claiming the money he believed to be his inheritance and being certified by his father's firm.[45] Alfred Hardie, on the other hand, is set up as an ideal type, a 'young Apollo', whose brilliant intellect is matched by outstanding achievements as a boatman and cricketer. There is no suspicion of wild living as far as he is concerned: '... young Hardie was a Doge of a studious clique; and careful to make it understood that he was a reading man who boated or cricketed, to avoid the fatigue of lounging; not a boatman or cricketer who strayed into Aristotle in the intervals of Perspiration' (p. 5). In the 1860s, the games-playing cult was sweeping through Britain, promoted in public schools and the universities as a way of maintaining health through exercise, and of developing character through leadership and team spirit.[46] Alfred, a product of Harrow, is now at Oxford showing his mettle in the boat races. He is not without weakness; 'the bloke really has awful headaches, like a girl' (p. 15), as one of his colleagues puts it. It is weakness that leads to his introduction to Julia Dodd (who is to become his intended) and her mother: '... they had heard of him as a victorious young Apollo trampling on all difficulties of mind and body; and they saw him wan, and worn, with feminine suffering: the contrast made him doubly interesting' (p. 17). In the adventures that follow, Alfred is to endure sufferings that are more characteristic of the female than the male situation as he loses autonomy and becomes subject to arbitrary authority, but he reacts with the vigour of his sporting exploits, showing not only the physical fitness he has acquired, but the value of the lessons in self-control and planned strategy he has learned.

Alfred is contrasted with the 'real' lunatic, Maxley, and a subsidiary plot concerning Captain Dodd's adventures and insanity elaborates on Reade's ideas about the causes of madness. James Maxley, a labourer, is described as 'a bit of a character'; he is 'scrupulously honest, but 'much too fond of money' (p. 47). David Dodd, similarly, has a weakness concerning money, though it is represented as deriving from the virtue of wanting to provide for his children. He has saved and invested fourteen thousand pounds in a bank in Calcutta. When he hears that the bank's security is threatened, he withdraws the money only to find it weighing heavily on his mind, as well as his body (it is in a pocket-book sewn into his waistcoat): 'The material treasure, the hard cash, which had lately set him in a glow, seemed now to load his chest and hang heavy round the neck of his heart' (p. 92). It is as though Reade is endowing his characters with a Bradleyan 'fatal flaw', which is what leads to their downfall. Having preserved his packet of money in the midst of life-threatening adventures, the first thing Dodd does when he reaches his home town, before even going to his own house, is to place the savings in Hardie's bank. However, he has no sooner done so than he discovers (from Maxley) that the bank is on the point of collapse. This discovery leads to Dodd's own collapse as rage leads to apoplexy, which, incorrectly treated, leads to insanity:

> there was David with his arms struggling wildly and his fists clenched, his face purple, and his eyes distorted so that little was seen but the whites; the next moment his teeth gnashed loudly together, and he fell headlong on the floor with a concussion so momentous that the windows rattled and the room shook violently; the dust rose in a cloud. (p. 176)

On the one hand, this hyperbolic moment is the culmination of a series of threats – from pirates, hurricane, shipwreck, land sharks; on the other hand, as the moment of Dodd's final breakdown, it signifies the lack of security at home (in the wider sense) and, since the Dodd family will as a result live in precarious circumstances, the threat to life at home (in the narrower sense) when society's institutions fail.

Maxley's insanity is explained as the result of the loss of his money compounded by the loss of his wife, who has died of 'Breast-pang', and it takes the form of hallucinations which he is able to explain in his lucid moments: 'I do see such curious things, enough to make a body's skin creep at times' (p. 209). These hallucinations, he fears, makes him a danger to the community and for that reason he requests confinement in the public asylum:

> Now suppose I was to go and take some poor Christian for one of these great bloody dragons I do see at odd times, I might do him a mischief you know,

and not mean him no harm neither. Oh dooee take and have me locked up, gentlemen, dooee now: tellee I ain't fit to be about, my poor head is so mazed. (p. 210)

Here Reade, like an examining doctor, relies on the external evidence of insanity that is provided by words, actions and appearance. The representation of the labourer's dialect adds to the effect of authentic testimony, and Maxley gives clear physical signs of the derangement his words assert:

His beard was unshaven, his face haggard, and everything about him showed a man broken in spirit as well as fortune: even his voice had lost half its vigour, and whenever he had uttered a consecutive sentence or two, his head dropped on his breast, pitiably: indeed, this sometimes occurred in the middle of a sentence, and then the rest of it died on his lips. (p. 209)

And his actions provide further corroboration in that he has, by his own account, already killed his 'missus's favourite hen' in an attack on an illusory 'fiery sarpint'. His subsequent fatal attack on Jane, Hardie's beloved daughter, vindicates his own fears and makes an ironic criticism of Hardie, who, as a magistrate, has been prepared only to follow the rules and give Maxley an order for the workhouse. Expressive of the Victorian belief that the insane *should* be confined, this case also allows for adverse comment on a system which refuses help to a man who is and knows himself to be dangerous, and furthermore it shows up the irresponsibility of medical men who are so obsessed with their own ideas of insanity that they fail to see the madness which is obvious. Subsequently Maxley is represented in terms of the pre-industrial conventions of madness, as he roams round the village with his madman's staff, taunted by the local boys (pp. 235, 306).

Again and again, the importance of external appearance is emphasised. The point is made in the case of David Dodd, who goes unrecognised by his old friend and cousin by marriage, Captain Bazalgette, because, amongst other reasons, 'insanity alters the expression of the face wonderfully' (p. 428). Dodd only resumes his former appearance after his almost-death by drowning and restoration to sanity. Appearance is also a give-away, in the case of Alfred's protegé, Frank Beverley, who is 'not the least mad nor bad, but merely of feeble intellect all round' (p. 349), and who, despite the poverty of his clothes, shows the ineradicable characteristics of his class: 'his hands, his features, his carriage, his address, had all an indefinable stamp of race' (p. 349). Alfred also follows the narrator's lead in realising the importance of external appearance as an indication of state of mind: 'Now Alfred had already observed that many of the patients looked madder than they were … So he made his toilet with care, and put his best hat on to hide his shaven crown' (p. 276). Thus arrayed, his 'dress, address, and countenance left no suspicion of insanity possible in an unprejudiced mind' (p. 276).

Given the importance of appearance as an indication of a person's mental state and social position, it is perhaps rather surprising that it receives little attention in the presentation of Alfred, whereas the question of intellect is what is emphasised. It is almost as though Reade had in mind a definition such as Laycock's where insanity is regarded as 'disorder of the intellect', and was determined to exonerate his hero from any suspicion of madness. Alfred is consistently and frequently referred to as 'brilliant' and evidence given of his ability to outwit anyone in argument or learning. At the second asylum he engages in studies for his degree and enjoys academic debates with Dr Wycherley, who warns the examining Commissioners that they 'might examine my young friend for hours and not detect the one crevice in the brilliancy of his intellectual armour' (p. 334). Alfred's status is made still more positive in that he frequently seems to speak for the author (he acts in fact as a surrogate), so that 'to give his [Alfred's] evidence would be to write "Hard Cash" over again' (p. 444). In the scene where Maxley begs to be put away, for instance, Alfred's comment on the labourer's predicament is representative of the narrator's indictment of the system:

'Look here, Maxley, old fellow,' said Alfred, sarcastically, 'you must go to the workhouse, and stay there till you hoe a pauper; take him for a crocodile, and kill him; then you will get into an asylum whether the Barkington magistrates like it or not; that is the *routine*, I believe; and as reasonable as most routine.' (p. 210)

But it is clear from the text that madness is not *just* 'disorder of the intellect', but loss of self-control. It is his ability to preserve his self-control that ensures Alfred's sanity, and in tracing the role he fulfils as authorial surrogate, it is worth noting the way that control is reflected in his writings. Time and again he is commended for his ability to present a 'well-governed narrative' (pp. 279, 295, 390, 407–08), and Dr Sampson, whose probity and authority is well established, comments on Alfred's SOS from Drayton House: 'There … didn't I tell you? This man is sane. There's sanity in every line' (p. 368). Reading a text here is analogous to reading a face; in both cases sanity will be obvious to unprejudiced scrutiny. It is the difficulty of finding readers, whether of texts or faces, who are free from prejudice that constitutes a leading theme of the novel. Reade returns continually to the problems of erasing labels and of evading the facile presumptions that labelling incurs. Because he has been labelled insane, for instance, Alfred's story of his father's misappropriation of the £40,000 is taken to be an hallucination and no attempt is made to check the truth of his statement. Also any outburst is automatically assumed to be a further indication of insanity.

Paradoxically, though, for all the reiteration of the ease with which madness can be known, what the novel actually shows is how difficult it is to diagnose insanity. During the legal proceedings Alfred is asked by the judge to define insanity and he does so by example, contrasting the madmen he has met with the sane who were to be found in the asylums:

> This was the most remarkable part of the trial, to see this shrewd old judge extracting from a real observer and logical thinker those positive indicia of sanity and insanity, which exist, but which no lawyer has ever yet been able to extract from any psychological physician in the witness-box. (p. 445)

It is noticeable that these 'indicia' are not spelt out at this point, so it is worth investigating what evidence is presented in the text to substantiate the claim that there are infallible ways of distinguishing between the mad and the sane.

In the third asylum of his confinement, Dr Wolf's Drayton House, Alfred is tricked into violent behaviour so that he can be punished by being sent to the 'noisy' ward, where

> His ears assailed with horrors, of which you have literally no conception, or shadow of conception, his nose poisoned with ammoniacal vapours, and the peculiar wild-beast smell that marks the true maniac, Alfred ran wildly about his cell trying to stop his ears, and trembling for his own reason. (p. 373)

The use of the second-person pronoun is a characteristic device to draw the reader into imaginative involvement with the text and shock her or him into sympathy with the plight of the wronged Alfred. Here, he is confronted with the 'true' maniac, who, in terms familiar to the eighteenth century, is represented as bestial, distinguishable by the senses of smell and hearing. The bestiality of these madmen, comprising both the wildness that has always been found so threatening in insanity and the lack of the supremely human power of reason, is insisted on in this episode. As Alfred approaches the ward he hears strange noises that gradually grow louder until they are discerned as 'Singing, roaring, howling like wolves' (p. 372). With a slight variation, the sounds that he hears throughout the night are described as 'Singing, swearing, howling like wild beasts!', whilst his left-hand neighbour 'alternately sang, and shouted ... and howled like a wolf, making night hideous' (p. 373). Alfred himself comes close to the level of these unfortunate creatures as he runs wildly about his cell, but, although to the naked eye his behaviour is that of a wild animal, Alfred makes no inhuman noises and, of course, emits no ammoniacal smell.

Smell was indeed one of the indices of madness in the eyes of Dr George Burrows, but his bulky treatise dates from 1828 and aroused ironical comment in the *Lancet* even then, so it is difficult to understand why a 'reformist' writer like Reade should adopt such a retrograde attitude, which seems here to be employed without irony.[47] It is not, however, a contention of the book as a whole that such 'symptoms' are the only ways of telling 'true' madness. Rather, the animalistic hyperbole is an aspect of sensationalist rhetoric that not only helped to give sensation fiction a bad name, but in this novel confuses the issue of diagnosis. Maxley, for instance, is established as truly insane and truly dangerous. In the scene when he attacks Jane Hardie he is given the usual animal characteristics: he appears 'all grizzly and bloodshot' and, like a bear, is 'baited' by the boys (p. 309); he cowers 'like a cur'; he finds out Julia's flagging courage 'by some half animal instinct'; he attacks Edward 'like a Spanish bull' (p. 310); and the place where he has fallen is so covered with blood that 'a bullock seemed to have been slaughtered at the least' (p. 311). But there is no mention of the sounds he makes nor of 'ammoniacal' smell; his maniacal behaviour is apparent to the eye alone.

As I have already commented, the novel emphasises the importance of appearance and a faith in the possibility of detecting insanity through the power of the eye, which echoes Reade's account of Dr Ruttledge's diagnostic process in one of the letters in 'Our Dark Places':

> Dr. Ruttledge ... sat down by me first, with an eye like a diamond: it went slap into my marrow-bone. Asked me catching questions, touched my wrist, saw my tongue, and said quietly, 'This one is sane.' Then he went and sat down by — drove an eye into him, asked him catching questions, made him tell him in order all he had done since seven o'clock, felt pulse, saw tongue: 'This one is sane too.'[48]

Although other tests are applied, the language highlights the acumen of the boring eye as paramount, if inexplicable. But if it is the most reliable means of ascertaining insanity, the eye is not infallible. Previous to the scene in the 'noisy ward' referred to above, Alfred has been depicted as being at the deepest pitch of despair: 'Pale, thin, and woe-begone ... Even an inspector with a naked eye would no longer have distinguished him at first sight from a lunatic of the unhappiest class, the melancholic' (p. 370). The implication is that although Alfred might *appear* mad, he is not really so, but what it is that distinguishes his state of mind here from that of the melancholic is not spelt out. Believing perhaps with Laycock that the individual consciousness is inaccessible to others, Reade makes little attempt to enter into it either here or at those other moments that focus on Alfred's tormenting predicament. This leaves the question of Alfred's sanity at the level of authorial assertion and implies, without accepting the consequences of the implication, that there is a liminal area between sanity and insanity that may be inhabited temporarily by people who would otherwise be declared 'normal'. One of the consequences of this position is surely the difficulty of diagnosis and the impossibility of relying purely on external appearances.

There are other occasions, too, when the young man behaves in a way that is to the naked eye indistinguishable from that of a maniac which are not acknowledged by the narrator. In the fight that precedes his relegation to the 'noisy' ward, the young hero is seen taking physical revenge on the keeper, Rooke, who has been victimising the feeble-minded Frank. On this occasion, however, not only is the motivation clearly different from Maxley's, since Alfred is defending, whilst Maxley is attacking, unaware in his insanity that Jane is coming to his rescue, but the fight itself is described in the manner of a boxing or wrestling commentary. Rooke is accredited with skill 'in the art of self-defence' (p. 371), and there is a suggestion, therefore, that this fight is governed by certain rules and that Alfred is behaving like the sportsman he was portrayed as at the start of the novel. All the rules are broken, on the other hand, in an earlier fight. At the first asylum, Silverton Grove House, Alfred arouses the enmity of the head keeper, Cooper, by revealing to the visiting justices the hidden instruments of restraint. In revenge, the keeper determines to administer a powerful dose of croton-oil, a drastic purgative; Alfred is equally determined not to be dosed. In the three-volume version the incident is taken as an opportunity to expose, fictionally, the brutality of keepers which Reade has already brought to the attention of the public in his letter to the *Pall Mall Gazette* that is reproduced in the prefatory 'Correspondence'. Alfred punches Cooper twice before he is handcuffed, put in a strait-jacket and given the 'kneeling' treatment, which is only halted by the interference of another keeper, Brown, and the handcuffing of Cooper (pp. 284–85).

The serial version is somewhat different, extending the struggle between Cooper and Alfred in a way that requires lengthy quotation. I give below the passage that appeared in *All the Year Round* after the sentence that describes Cooper kneeling on Alfred's chest, ending 'and he could scarcely breathe' (p. 285):

> Cooper warmed to his work and kneeled on Alfred's face. Then Cooper jumped knees downwards on his face. Then Cooper drew back and jumped savagely on his chest. Then Alfred felt his last hour was come: he writhed aside, and Cooper missed him this time and overbalanced himself; the two faces came together for a moment, and Alfred, fighting for his life, caught Cooper with his teeth by the middle of the nose, and bit clean through the cartilage with a shrill snarl. Then Cooper shrieked, and writhed, and whirled his great arms like a windmill, punching at Alfred's head. Now man is an animal at bottom, and a wild animal at the very bottom. Alfred ground his teeth together in bull-dog silence till they quite met, and with his young strong neck and his despair shook that great hulking fellow as a terrier shakes a cat, still grinding his teeth together in bull-dog silence. The men struck him, shook him, in vain. At last they got hold of his throat and choked him, and so parted the furious creatures: but not before Mrs. Archbold and nurses Jane and Hannah had rushed into the room, drawn by Cooper's cries. The first thing the new comers did was to scream in unison at the sight that met them. On the bed lay Alfred all but insensible, his linen and his pale face spotted with his persecutor's blood. Upon him kneeled the gory ruffian swearing oaths to set the hair on end.
>
> 'I'll stop your biting for ever,' said he, and raised a ponderous fist: and in one moment more Alfred would have been disfigured for life, but Brown caught Cooper's arm ...[49]

At this point the serial version coincides with the book version, which reads: 'But Brown drew Cooper back by the collar, saying, "D'ye want to kill him?"' (p. 285) and there are no further differences between the two versions in the succeeding description of Alfred being handcuffed by the nurses. Whatever the reason for the alteration, it is interesting to see the effect of the longer and more violent passage that was published in the periodical. The viciousness of Cooper's attacks on Alfred does indeed turn him into a savage, but the full weight of animal imagery falls on Alfred, who behaves with a scarcely credible ferocity. Furthermore, the general statement, 'Now man is an animal at bottom, and a wild animal at the very bottom,' suggests a continuum rather than a dichotomy between sanity and madness, and if that is so then, as I remark above, it becomes far more difficult than the text makes out elsewhere to tell the 'true maniac'. In fact the novel is torn in two directions. On the one hand, it is asserted confidently that an unprejudiced naked eye can detect insanity; on the other hand, Alfred, who is said to be unquestionably sane, is represented as behaving in a way that is indistinguishable from the behaviour of a madman. There is a firm belief that true madness is discoverable, but uncertainty as to how it is to be discovered.

This is not, however, exactly the quandary that *Hard Cash* is explicitly concerned with. According to this novel what causes so many problems and leads to travesties of justice is the difficulty of finding a diagnostician who is free from prejudice. Reade's novel makes a scathing indictment of the medical profession just at the time when it was establishing its scientific credentials and laying claim to the field of madness. He makes his attack in several ways. The tone of heavy irony with which he recounts the approaches taken by various doctors to Julia's 'illness' leaves no doubt as to his adversarial attitude, and their incompetence in the field of physical illness is stressed by having Captain Dodd's madness incurred through the administering of inappropriate treatment for apoplexy. As owners of, or attendants at asylums they are seen as negligent, insufficiently scrupulous, or downright corrupt. Dr Wolf is an extreme case, running an institution purely for money and prepared to countenance the admission of a man he suspects is sane. His name indicates a greedy bestiality which spreads throughout the asylum and is reflected in the brutality of the keepers, male and female. Then Dr Sampson, excitable and voluble, himself a proponent of a naturalistic approach he calls 'Chronothairmalism', is given a lengthy diatribe criticising the rogues' gallery of doctors who have been 'treating' Julia for being far more interested in cash and jargon than the patient. He denounces them as 'monomaniacs', interested to the point of obsession in their separate specialities, unable therefore to see the patient as a whole. It is the 'monomania' of the medical profession that is its most serious prejudice, and this is illustrated in the figure of Dr Wycherley.

In an article in the *Times Literary Supplement*, Richard Hunter and Ida MacAlpine shed new light on *Hard Cash* through their discovery of correspondence that not only pointed to a friendship between Dickens and John Conolly but revealed that Reade was lampooning Conolly in the character of Wycherley.[50] Conolly had won great acclaim for his abandonment of restraint in a large county asylum, but he was not without his critics. Dickens, however, was certainly not one of them. In 'Idiots' he and W.H. Wills describe their visit to Park House, Highgate, one of two establishments that Conolly and Dr Andrew Reed had opened for the care and education of idiots.[51] The institution is described in glowing terms, and commended for the quiet and orderliness that govern the activities there. A few years later *Household Words* paid Conolly the tribute of recording his career and achievements in the care of the insane in an article entitled 'Things within Dr. Conolly's Remembrance'. The article opens as follows:

> Most of our readers know that one of the best achievements of the present century is a complete reversal, in the treatment of madness, of opinions and practice which had previously been in force for five-and-twenty centuries at least ... The blessing of [the change] has been secured to England – and, by the example of England, more widely and certainly diffused among civilised nations – mainly by help of the wise energy of DR. JOHN CONOLLY.[52]

Conolly is placed in the reforming tradition of Pinel and Tuke and his first volume, *An Inquiry into the Indications of Insanity* (1830), approved for its recommendation that asylums be removed from the hands of private speculators, and its suggestion that many harmless lunatics are better cared for within the love and relative freedom of their families. Whilst acknowledging the pioneering work of Dr Charlesworth and Mr Gardiner Hill at Lincoln and Dr T.O. Prichard at Northampton, the writer sees Conolly as the man who brought non-restraint to public attention because of the size of the asylum that he ran and because of its proximity to London, then, as now, the seat of power and influence. He is further commended for his modesty, his prioritising of actions over words and the 'abundant store of anecdote and illustration, chiefly drawn from experience, partly from reading, with which he defines every point of his argument'.[53]

It is difficult to recognise this portrait in the character of Dr Wycherley in *Hard Cash*. Wycherley is represented as a verbose, canting 'monomaniac'; blinded to truth by his obsession with his pet theories, he is accused by Alfred of founding 'facts on theories instead of theories on facts' (p. 335). As proof of his moral superiority, it is Alfred, too, victim though he is, who delivers the only sustained praise of Wycherley:

> Dr. Wycherley is the very soul of humanity. Here are no tortures, no handcuffs nor leg-locks, no brutality ... And, gentlemen, I must tell you a noble trait in my enemy there: nothing can make him angry with madmen; their lies, their groundless and narrow suspicions of him, their deplorable ingratitude to him ... all these things seem to glide off him, baffled by the infinite kindness of his heart, and the incomparable sweetness of his temper; and he returns the duffers good for evil with scarcely an effort. (p. 335)

The narratorial comments are savage; Dr Wycherley is

bland and bald, with a fine head, and a face naturally intelligent, but crossed every now and then by gleams of vacancy; a man of large reading, and of tact to make it subserve his interests. A voluminous writer on certain medical subjects, he had so saturated himself with circumlocution, that it distilled from his very tongue: he talked like an Article; a quarterly one; and so gained two advantages: 1st, he rarely irritated a fellow-creature; for, if he began a sentence hot, what with its length, and what with its windiness, he ended it cool: item, stabs by polysyllables are pricks by sponges. 2ndly, this foible earned him the admiration of fools; and that is as invaluable as they are innumerable. (pp. 203–04)

The doctor's polysyllabic windiness is then demonstrated at length. Still more damaging, though, is the suggestion that Wycherley is himself insane. The 'gleams of vacancy' with their suggestion of idiocy, are replaced, later in the book, by the more sinister insinuation of monomania. Raging at Alfred's contention that Hamlet was not really mad, Wycherley falls down 'in a fit of an epileptic character, grinding his teeth and foaming at the mouth' (p. 340). Alfred's reaction again shows his superiority: 'Alfred had studied true insanity all this time, and knew how inhumane it is to oppose a monomaniac's foible; it only infuriates and worries him' (p. 340). Wycherley, convinced that 'consciousness of insanity is the one diagnostic of sanity' and, conversely, that 'an obstinate persistence in the hypothesis of perfect rationality demonstrates the fact that insanity yet lingers in the convolutions and recesses of the brain' (p. 332), becomes the lord of misrule of what, if left to him, would be a topsy-turvy world, where the sane are confined for asserting their sanity and the insane are left at large though protesting their madness.

Conolly, as he is represented in the *Household Words* article, is not an obvious target for Reade's satire: opposed to private speculation in the trade of lunacy, opposed to the unwarranted confinement of the insane, an elegant writer using experience and reading to support his arguments, he would seem a more likely model for Alfred than for Dr Wycherley. Hunter and MacAlpine, however, build up a convincing case for what they see as a cruel attack on Conolly, including in their evidence references to his *Study of Hamlet*, where he attempts to 'prove' Hamlet's madness and which was published in the same year as *Hard Cash*. It is still, though, difficult to understand the reason for the attack. Andrew Scull takes a rather more sceptical view of the career and writings of Conolly than do Hunter and MacAlpine, drawing attention to the way that the opinions he expressed in print seem to have altered according to the fluctuations in his career.[54]

Conolly began his career as an ordinary practitioner before moving to London in 1828 to become Professor of the Principles and Practice of Medicine at University College, and his writings at this stage, when he was still outside the asylum system, public and private, were critical of existing practices. In 1839 he succeeded to the post of resident physician at Hanwell Asylum on his second application and his ideas changed, so that from railing against the indiscriminate confinement of the insane, he became a supporter of institutional treatment. Disputes with the Middlesex magistrates led to his resignation of this position after only four years, and, after a short spell as visiting consultant, he devoted his remaining years to writing and acting as expert witness in legal cases where the question of sanity was in dispute, whilst making an income as proprietor and consultant in the private asylum business. His publications now expressed his faith in the private institutions he had earlier condemned. Whether this change of attitude was ideological or pragmatic it is difficult to say, but critical voices were heard even at the time, Reade's amongst them.[55]

By the time that Reade was writing *Hard Cash*, Conolly thus represented someone who not only relied on insanity for his income, but whose pronouncements were invested with considerable authority and influence. His 'reforms' at Hanwell had secured him a place in the limelight, so that in attacking him Reade was throwing darts at a recognisable public figure, not, however, for the work that had made him famous, but for the things he did and said thereafter. In *The Female Malady*, Elaine Showalter hints at an obsessional side even to Conolly's humanitarian work at Hanwell, saying that he developed 'a kind of driven identification' with the insane poor and, plagued by a chronic skin irritation, became an insomniac 'who prowled the wards restlessly at night'.[56] But more pertinent to Reade's enmity is Scull's exposure of the frighteningly wide range of behaviours that Conolly, as an official diagnostician, would define as insane, including 'excessive eccentricity', 'utter disregard of cleanliness and decency', 'perversions of the moral feelings and passions', and a disposition 'to give away sums of money which they cannot afford to lose'.[57]

Reade interrogates this last presumption in the courtroom scene. Under cross-examination, Wycherley is forced to admit that his diagnosis of Alfred's 'insanity' had been based on 'guess-work and hearsay', that he had intruded on a family disagreement and had himself provoked the 'very irritation that he had set down to madness' (p. 452). Most damaging of all, and another missile in the specific direction of Conolly, is the admission drawn from Wycherley that 'he received fifteen per cent from the asylum keepers for every patient he wrote insane' (p. 452). Conolly had been recently involved, to his discredit, in just such a case and sued for false imprisonment. But it is important to be clear that the legally trained and litigiously-minded Reade was not simply aiming his criticisms at the medical profession, but at the law and legal processes. In this scene both are condemned. Alfred's morally upright and generous gesture of signing his money away in favour of the Dodd family as reparation for his father's theft, a gesture that would for Conolly have been a symptom of madness, causes a similar reaction amongst the lawyers: 'All the lawyers present thought this looked really mad' (p. 453).

As a trained lawyer, it is not surprising to find that Reade interests himself in the litigious aspects of Alfred's plight, but references to legal processes enter into all the fictions examined in this chapter. In Collins's short story, Roland Cameron presents a petition to the Lord Chancellor, 'praying that the decision of the Lunacy Commission might be set aside' (p. 287). Despite the evidence of friends that he is 'perfectly quiet, harmless, and sane', a safe companion on sailing or shooting expeditions, the Lords Justices, on the assertion of one doctor, decide against him. The episode, however, stands not so much as an opportunity to expose the questionable processes of justice, as a representation of one more obstacle in the path of true love, and Cameron and his wife decide on flight to America. Since the first-person narrator of this story is not Cameron but his wife, he is put into a more passive position than Merivale adopts in his autobiographical account. Nevertheless, when it comes to the question of legal retribution, Merivale fights shy. Like Alfred in *Hard Cash*, he contemplates taking out an action for false imprisonment, but is advised against it, because he cannot give exact details of how he was 'imprisoned', or by whom.

Reade's fictional treatment of the same situation allows him to vilify legal processes and to show Alfred as not only entirely sane, but as a model of rationality. Alfred's suing of his father for false imprisonment in the asylums, like most adversarial cases, encounters many obstacles as his father's lawyers and his father himself play all the tricks that procedure allows. The question is finally one of Alfred's sanity, but as Colt QC puts it, 'in a case of this kind, it lies upon the defendant to prove the plaintiff's insanity' (p. 464), and this the defendant, Alfred's father, is unable to do. Alfred's lucid disquisition on insanity is in fact irrelevant, since the case relies on Mr Hardie's inability to prove that Alfred's allegations of embezzlement were the result of a delusion. In other words it has to be, and is shown that, although Alfred has acted with impetuosity and chivalry, he has not acted insanely; insanity is revealed as a convenient ploy at the service of the unscrupulous. Its convenience is the result of both the difficulty of definition and the enormous range of behaviours that could be subsumed under the heading of insanity. It is also dependent upon the belief, unquestioned even by Dr Sampson, the representative of enlightened medical practice, that the mad should be confined. But Reade's main point is that abuse of the system is inevitable so long as the care of the insane is a commercial operation. He has nothing to say about the public asylums; the weight of his invective falls upon the 'dark places' where patients too easily become victims, inadequately protected against self-interested parties. The 'protection' afforded by the Commissioners is exposed as a sham and the only route to fair play seems to be through the agency of those in national office, such as the Lord Chancellor, who are removed from the sway of private interest. At the end of the book, Frank Beverley, revivified by the (somewhat incredible) love of Mrs Archbold, in a proceeding that for brevity and fair-mindedness presents a marked contrast with all that Alfred has to endure, is examined by the Lord Chancellor and found perfectly capable of managing his own property.

Whereas Reade's protagonist conducts his case in a public arena, Maud Vernon, the female victim of wrongful confinement in *The Rose and the Key* has a more informal and entirely private experience. Her examination by the Commissioners and her later interview with the god-like Mr Damian are conducted within the precincts of the asylum, Glarewoods. This is a feminised version of the situation in *Hard Cash*, and Maud reacts with nervousness, unable to articulate answers to Dr Antomarchi's questions when forced to face up to his controlling gaze. Her terror and confusion are only assuaged when Mr Damian, 'not looking at her otherwise than a well-bred old gentleman might', talks to her 'encouragingly and kindly'.[58] The courtesy that is the conduit to her expression of her own sanity contrasts markedly with the aggressive situation through which Alfred displays his talents as well as his sanity. In the competitive jousting of the courtroom, which recalls the boat race earlier in the novel, he is the star of the show – and the winner. His masculinity has been threatened by his father's plot, by confinement and the loss of control, and by allegations of irrationality. But his physical prowess and courage, his capacity for self-control, and his unflagging capacity for rational reflection and argument have demonstrated his essential manliness. Moreover, there is no suggestion, as there is in *The Rose and the Key*, that the confinement is in any way deserved. In one

particularly horrific scene from this later novel, a refractory patient is subjected to a shower bath. This is no ordinary shower bath, but one lasting
for thirty-five minutes, in which the water falls with tremendous force on
a woman who is strapped into an iron chair, and which is followed by a
severe emetic. Maud is forced to witness the treatment. The narrator at this
point not only refers outside the fiction to a case of such treatment in 'fact',
but makes a moralistic comment: 'It is well when, even in after life, we can
see that our sufferings have made us better ... This awful time in Maud's
life will do good work in her ... These awful days, if they lead her to see
and to amend her faults, will not have passed in vain.'[59] Maud's fault has
been to defy her mother. The psychology of *The Rose and the Key* is, as is
usual in Le Fanu, complex, but it is clear that the female victim of wrongful confinement in this text is being accused of insanity because of behaviour that fails to satisfy a despotic and disturbed mother's standards of
docility and obedience. In the case of the male victims in Reade's and
Cockton's novels and in Collins's short story, the plot is generated more
mechanistically, powered by motives of financial greed.

Reade orientates his novel towards the male-dominated world of insti-
tutionalised medicine and law, making a stand against a society that prioritises money over individuals. His brand of sensationalism sets domestic
and private relationships within the context of these institutions and he is
loud in his criticism of cumbersome legal procedures and asylums where
such tortuous practices as 'tanking' are tolerated and even actively encouraged. But his aims and sympathies are limited. Since his case is fortified by
dwelling on the horrors of confining the sane with the 'truly' mad, his
depiction of madness draws on traditional concepts of the inhumanity of
the insane, emphasising the degree to which they are different from other
people. Conservative, then, in his belief that confinement is essential for
the truly mad and that there are 'positive indicia' of insanity, he nevertheless finds himself having to acknowledge the murky area where sanity and
insanity are not so clearly distinguished. The figure of his hero represents
a standard by which the sanity of others can be judged, and he himself
learns the means of assessing insanity. According to the text his knowledge
is acquired through observation, but, as I have indicated above, he has in
fact also experienced mental torments that allow him an insight into the
world of madness. By skating over the implications of these experiences,
Reade is able to present an argument for reform of the system that is apparently clear cut, but because it fudges the issue of diagnosis the practical
problems are still unresolved.

All the texts considered in this chapter contain themes familiar to the representation of madness: the wandering body that, in a version of synecdoche, stands for the wandering mind; the loss of control where, however dubious the loss of *self*-control, the individual loses autonomy; the association of madness with physical violence, and the animalistic connotations of madness. But the novels discussed here do not deal with the inner experience of madness; they are sensation novels in that they look primarily at externals, and plotting and secrets at the narrative level are more important than the uncovering of the secrets of the mind. Appearances are important and can be deceptive, whether it is the voices that appear to emanate from Valentine Vox or the books that are only painted iron. But deception is also a matter of action and plot. By showing how easily a man can be classified as mad on the basis of behaviour that deviates to the slightest degree from what is considered normal, doubt is thrown on the criteria by which a man's mental state is judged, on the difficulties of defining madness and on the dangers of unregulated commercialism. In *Hard Cash* the difficulties of defining madness operate at two different levels: they are shown at the level of action, where mistakes are made and deceptions are practised. But also the problems of definition are tackled at a conceptual level through narratorial comment and the trial scene, when Alfred offers his virtuosic performance in court. All these texts show how perilous a man's claim to sanity may be, and how, once classified as mad, a man can lose his autonomy and become as subject to the abuse of power as any woman. The imposition of physical restraint or confinement gives vivid expression to the impotence of a man whose state of mind is decided for him by others. At the same time, madness is seen as a social problem, not just in the possible threat an individual might present to society, but because society treats madness in an institutional way that is open to abuse, since it is either inadequate, where the provision is the responsibility of the local authority, or it has become an area of commercial speculation.

Notes

1 Daniel Defoe, *Augusta Triumphans* [1728], quoted in Roy Porter (ed.), *The Faber Book of Madness* (London: Faber & Faber, 1991), pp. 354-55.
2 John Conolly, *An Inquiry Concerning the Indication of Insanity* [1830], reprinted with an introduction by Richard Hunter and Ida MacAlpine (London: Dawsons of Pall Mall, 1964), p. 478.
3 Cockton, *Valentine Vox*, p. 15.

4 Cockton, *Valentine Vox*, p. 415.

5 Cockton, *Valentine Vox*, p. 451.

6 Cockton, Preface, *Valentine Vox*.

7 Porter, *Madness*, p. 355.

8 [Herman Charles Merivale], *My Experiences in a Lunatic Asylum by a Sane Patient* (London: Chatto & Windus, 1879).

9 [Merivale], *My Experiences*, p. 28.

10 [Merivale], *My Experiences*, p. 25.

11 Hypochondria and hypochondriasis are discussed by Janet Oppenheim in '*Shattered Nerves*', Shuttleworth in *Victorian Psychology*, Taylor in *Secret Theatre* and Jane Wood in *Victorian Fiction*.

12 [Merivale], *My Experiences*, p. 131.

13 [Merivale], *My Experiences*, p. 7.

14 Sheridan Le Fanu, *The Rose and the Key* [1871], unabridged republication of the 1895 edition (New York: Dover Publications, 1982).

15 [Merivale], *My Experiences*, p. 40.

16 [Merivale], *My Experiences*, p. 56.

17 [Merivale], *My Experiences*, p. 150.

18 [Merivale], *My Experiences*, pp. 58–59.

19 [Merivale], *My Experiences*, p. 112.

20 Peter McCandless, 'Liberty and Lunacy: The Victorians and Wrongful Confinement', in Andrew Scull (ed.), *Madhouses, Mad-Doctors, and Madmen: The Social History of Psychiatry in the Victorian Period* (London: Athlone Press, 1981), p. 356.

21 McCandless, 'Liberty and Lunacy', p. 357.

22 M.E. Braddon, *Taken at the Flood* [1874] (London: Simpkin, Marshall, Hamilton, Kent & Co., 1890).

23 Wilkie Collins, 'A Mad Marriage', in *Miss or Mrs.* (London: Chatto & Windus, 1875).

24 Collins, 'Mad Marriage', p. 276.

25 Collins, 'Mad Marriage', p. 288.

26 Collins, 'Mad Marriage', p. 293.

27 Collins, 'Mad Marriage', p. 262.

28 Collins, 'Mad Marriage', pp. 265–66.

29 See John Sutherland, 'Dickens, Reade and *Hard Cash*', *Dickensian*, 81 (1985), pp. 5–12, for details of the prolonged negotiations betwen Dickens (operating through Wills) and Reade.

30 Charles Reade, *Readiana* (London: Chatto & Windus, 1883); *idem, Hard Cash* (London: Chatto & Windus, 1880?). All references are to this edition and are incorporated into the text.

31 Reade, Preface, *Hard Cash*. Wayne Burns details the elaborate procedures Reade adopted to control the mass of information he had accumulated in '*Hard Cash*: "Uncomparably My Best Production"', *Literature and Psychology*, 8 (1958), pp. 34–43.

32 Quoted in Malcolm Elwin, *Charles Reade* (London: Jonathan Cape, 1934), p. 155.

33 Last sentence of Charles Reade, *Put Yourself in His Place* [1870], quoted in Elton Edward Smith, *Charles Reade* (London: George Prior Publishers, 1976), p. 104.

34 Wayne Burns, *Charles Reade: A Study in Victorian Authorship* (New York: Bookman Associates, 1961), p. 234.

35 Charles Reade, *A Terrible Temptation* [1871] (London: Chatto & Windus, 1880?), p. 154.
36 Reade, *Temptation*, p. 203.
37 Reade, *Temptation*, p. 205.
38 Elwin, *Charles Reade*, p. 155.
39 Documented in Elwin, *Charles Reade*, p. 166.
40 Hughes, *Maniac in the Cellar*.
41 Charles Dickens, 'The Sensational Williams', *All the Year Round*, 10 (1864), pp. 14–17 (14).
42 Dickens, 'Sensational Williams', p. 14.
43 Dickens, 'Sensational Williams', p. 14.
44 Thomas Laycock, 'On the Naming and Classification of Mental Diseases and Defects', *Journal of Mental Science*, 9 (1863), pp. 153–70 (154, 158).
45 Elwin, *Charles Reade*, p. 166.
46 Park, 'Biological Thought'.
47 Burrows and the *Lancet* are quoted in McCandless, 'Liberty and Lunacy', p. 348.
48 Reade, *Readiana*, p. 115.
49 Charles Reade, 'Very Hard Cash', *All the Year Round*, 10 (1863), pp. 121–28 (124).
50 Richard Hunter and Ida MacAlpine, 'Dickens and Conolly: An Embarrassed Editor's Apology', *Times Literary Supplement*, 11 August 1961, pp. 534–35.
51 Dickens with Wills, 'Idiots', pp. 313–17. The other institution visited was Essex Hall near Cochester.
52 'Things within Dr. Conolly's Remembrance', *Household Words*, 16 (1857), pp. 518–23 (518).
53 Anon., 'Dr. Conolly's Remembrance', p. 522.
54 Andrew Scull, 'A Victorian Alienist: John Conolly, F.R.C.P, D.C.L (1794–1866)', W.F. Bynum, Roy Porter and Michael Shepherd (eds), *The Anatomy of Madness: Essays in the History of Psychiatry*, vol. 1, *People and Ideas* (London: Tavistock, 1985), pp. 103–50.
55 Scull, 'Victorian Alienist', p. 135, mentions, for instance, the opinion of John Bucknill.
56 Showalter, *Female Malady*, p. 47.
57 John Conolly, *A Remonstrance with the Lord Chief Baron Touching the Case Nottidge versus Ripley*, quoted in Scull, 'Victorian Alienist', p. 129.
58 Le Fanu, *Rose and the Key*, p. 417.
59 Le Fanu, *Rose and the Key*, p. 360.

4

Madness and Marriage

In 1858 Robert and Charlotte Bostock appealed to the new Divorce Court for judicial separation, one of the first cases to be heard after the Divorce Act of 1857. The differences between them derived from problems in negotiating a course between authority and its abuse on the part of the husband, and between defiance and submission on the part of the wife. At one stage of their quarrels, surgeons who had been called in by Charlotte advised her that her husband should be tended by a 'keeper' because of the danger of sudden attack. There were signs that Robert was suffering from mental disturbance and his determination to protect his authority in the home could put her in danger. In another case heard that year, John and Frances Curtis brought to the court a litany of marital wrongs that had led to John's suffering a breakdown, characteristically diagnosed as 'brain fever' in 1850.[1] Brain fever in this case was clearly considered a mental rather than a physical affliction, since John was confined in an institution and put in a straitjacket. He was released, but, after several years of dispute in which he tried to discipline his wife by refusing to let her manage their children, and by humiliating her in front of the servants, suffered another attack of 'brain fever' and was again confined. After his release, he tried to persuade Frances to return to him. When she refused and retreated with the children to her sister's, he sought out her address and tried to drag away the youngest child. In a letter written to her mother, Frances complained that her husband 'carries the idea of his authority to a mania'.[2] In yet another case, heard in 1869 and 1870, James Kelly, Anglican vicar of St George's Church in Liverpool, insisted on his marital authority with a zeal that left him open to the charge of obsession. To punish his wife for what he perceived to be her plotting against him, he entirely deposed her from her position as manager of the household, treating her, in the words of the judge, 'like a child or lunatic'.[3] Although Kelly was never diagnosed as mad, there are strong suggestions in his behaviour that his obsessional paranoia and determination to exert his authority as a husband took him beyond the bounds of sanity. These and other cases are discussed in *Cruelty and Companionship*, James Hammerton's study of marital discord. The first part of the book, dealing with working-class marriages, shows an overwhelming focus on the issue of violent physical abuse, but the second part, on middle-class marriages, raises a greater variety of concerns to do with power and the exercise of authority. Hammerton summarises the tendency of the three cases described above as hinting 'at the regular propensity for men's obsession with control to skirt the borders, at least, of mental illness'. However, he continues, the main significance of these cases is that 'the object of each husband's obsession was his sense of his own unlimited authority expressed in the desire for mastery, determination to control outside influences like doctors, and the illegitimacy of his wife's defiance, sometimes extending over many years'.[4]

The Victorian period witnessed a great deal of controversy and – eventually – legislation concerning marriage. The issues of divorce, property and a wife's earnings, custody of children, and the thorny question of marriage to a deceased wife's sister or deceased husband's brother were all thoroughly aired in the newspapers and journals of the time. The implications of the legal position and the consequences in terms of human relationships were explored in many novels of the Victorian period, several of which concern the way in which madness develops in response to stresses in the marital relationship. Much has been written about the 'separate spheres' thesis, exposing the extent to which the preservation of Christian values in a fiercely competitive commercial society depended on the artificial assumption that women would preserve moral standards in the privacy of the home, whilst men provided economic security by their performance in the ruthless market place. Some men, however, did not need to work in this sense, since they had a private income, and for others, those with land, the place of work was the home and its associated property. The separation of spheres is less clearly demarcated in such instances, and more recently historians have questioned in other ways the extent to which the lives of men and women were predicated on a separation of interests and activities.[5] Nevertheless, within marriage it was generally recognised, and enshrined in the words of the marriage service, that women would obey their lord and master. Since for most of the nineteenth century married women had no legal existence apart from their husbands and, unless they were protected by a trust, no financial rights, much depended on the balance of mastery and obedience that was achieved within individual relationships. A woman may have been her husband's chattel, but not all husbands were tyrannical in exercising their rights, and not all wives were submissive in performing their duties. It is the interplay of personalities and of emotional needs and demands that, despite the interesting work that is now being done using diaries, journals and letters, is so hard for the historian to chronicle – but which is the stuff of novelists. In this chapter I shall be concentrating particularly on those novels where it is the husband that goes mad: *Griffith Gaunt* (1866), *He Knew He Was Right* (1867–68), *Sowing the Wind* (1867) and *The Fatal Three* (1888), but I shall also be referring to one novel that concerns female madness, *St Martin's Eve* (1866).

It has been suggested by P.D. Edwards that Trollope may have been spurred to write *He Knew He Was Right* by an article in the *Spectator*, 'Madness in Novels', which in discussing the sensation fiction of Mary Braddon, Ellen (Mrs Henry) Wood, and James Payne, wonders what a realist writer like Trollope would do with the theme of madness.[6] In this article, Braddon is credited with 'restoring the lost sensational effect to character 'by making her most notorious heroine, Lady Audley, mad'.[7] In fact, Lady Audley's madness is arguable, and the equivocal stance adopted by the narrator takes advantage of the ingrained confusion between madness and badness. Lady Audley's attempted murder of her first husband is an attempt to protect her second (bigamous) marriage; it offers a rational solution to a problem, and it is not her fault that it fails.[8] James Payne's novel, *The Clyffards of Clyffe*, similarly concerns an unscrupulous heroine who is spurred to extraordinary activities by her desire for possession of the property to which she has only the entitlement of residence after the death of her husband. Despite a prefatory avowal that the novel is intended as 'a Romance' and not a sensation novel, the idea of madness as an inherited curse is only one of many sensational features.[9] *St Martin's Eve* by Mrs Henry Wood similarly concerns the fate of an ambitious young woman who marries better than she deserves socially speaking.[10] Although this is also a second marriage, there is no suggestion of bigamy, for it is the husband who has been married before and whose wife has tragically died. Wood's heroine, Charlotte, is torn apart by jealousy, not of her husband's first wife, but of this wife's child, Benja, the child who is heir to the estate. When Charlotte herself gives birth to a son, Georgie, she is tormented by the constant reminders of his inferior status. After the death of her husband, prey to an inherited constitutional weakness, her distress at her own son's secondary position develops into an obsession, which drives her, it is widely suspected though never fully proved, to murder the older boy. Unfortunately, her own son, bereft at the loss of a much-loved companion, fails in health, and for the rest of the book she roams restlessly round Europe, ostensibly for the sake of his health, but, it is also suggested, in search of peace of mind for herself. She is unsuccessful in restoring Georgie to health and after his death returns to England to live with a branch of her husband's family.

Throughout the earlier part of the novel there are hints of a secret in her background, and her mother appears both unduly solicitous and unduly respectful of Charlotte's imperious demands. After there have been several explosive outbursts of temper on Charlotte's part, focusing on the hapless Benja, it is revealed that there is a suspicion that she might have inherited the madness in which her father died. She is said to have lapsed into a fit of insanity after the death of her son, and by the end of the book, the insanity having been confirmed, is locked in a private asylum. It is in a fit of madness, we are finally to assume, that she has caused or suffered Benja to die in a raging fire. In a moment of dramatic irony, as Charlotte talks to her doctor who is attending Georgie in his last hours, she exclaims: 'What right had George St John to marry? If people know themselves liable to any disease that cuts off life, they should keep single; and so let the curse die out,' and she expresses her wish that her little boy had inherited her own constitution.[11] Unlike the physician ('A very peculiar expression momentarily crossed the surgeon's face'), she appears oblivious of the possibility that Georgie might have inherited from her the curse of insanity. In this novel, then, insanity is part of a larger interest in inheritance, whether of property, wealth and position, or of physical and psychological disposition, and acts as a signifier of Charlotte's exclusion. Condemned finally, like Lady Audley, to end her days in an asylum, she becomes a recognisably marginal and, in the terms of the novel, best-forgotten member of society; her younger sister, herself settling into a happy marriage, is advised that she had better not visit her sister in the asylum. *St Martin's Eve*, again like *Lady Audley's Secret*, seems to bear the message that incarceration in an asylum is an alternative to prison. For it is strongly suspected that she is guilty of setting Benja on fire, or at least of allowing him to burn to death. Furthermore there is evidence of guilt in the descriptions of Charlotte's troubled conscience, and her fit on St Martin's Eve amounts almost to a confession of guilt.

The complaint of the writer of the *Spectator* article is that madness is too easy a device to make a story sensational, that madness can in a fairly mechanical way allow a novelist to expose passionate jealousy without going to the trouble of detailed psychological analysis. According to this

author, Wood has not the skill 'to create Othello', and therefore must resort
to madness as a way of making 'natural' the improbabilities of her tale.[12]
Another novel dealing with madness within marriage from the same year
as *St Martin's Eve* (1866), but not referred to in the *Spectator* article, is
Charles Reade's *Griffith Gaunt*.[13] Here the comparison with *Othello*, the
benchmark of marital jealousy, is explicit and, given that the comparison
is with a male character, more appropriate. The story is given two novel
twists, however: the Iago figure is a female, and the jealousy is given a foundation in religion. Catherine (Kate) Peyton marries Griffith Gaunt after
inheriting two estates which he might reasonably have expected to inherit
himself. Unlike him, she is a staunch Catholic, and an important role is
played in her life by her spiritual adviser. When the elderly Father Frances
retires from his post, his place is taken by the young, mesmerically fervent
Father Leonard. There is undoubtedly an attraction between him and
Kate, and the seeds of jealousy are sown and cultivated by Kate's maid,
Caroline Ryder, who is herself in love with Griffith, and who is explicitly
described as a 'female Iago' (p. 200). When Caroline finally convinces him
that his wife and her adviser are meeting in secret, Griffith falls down in an
epileptic fit. Reade does not devote much time to analysing Griffith's state
of mind. Indeed, the text declares its aesthetic as being concerned with
externals. Talking about Kate after Father Leonard has confessed to her
that he is jealous of her husband, the narrator has this to say:

> Her mind was in a whirl; and, were I to imitate those writers who undertake
> to dissect and analyse the heart at such moments, and put the exact result on
> paper, I should be apt to sacrifice truth to precision; I must stick to my old
> plan, and tell you what she did: that will surely be some index to her mind,
> especially with my female readers. (p. 194)

Accordingly, the description of Griffith's state of mind is limited to the
statement that he is 'gnawed mad by the three vultures of the mind –
doubt, jealousy, and suspense'. Despite the suggestion of the melancholic
in his wasting away, he is described as a maniac: 'His clothes hung loose
on his wasted frame; his face was one of uniform sallow tint, like a
maniac's; and he sat silent for hours beside his wife, eyeing her askant from
time to time like a surly mastiff guarding some treasure' (p. 204). The animalistic imagery presages violent behaviour: when he discovers Kate and
her adviser in what turns out to be an innocent meeting, he attacks Father
Leonard and then rides off 'with the face, the eyes, the gestures, the inco-
herent mutterings of a raving Bedlamite' (p. 208). Madness in this case

turns into fever and delirium, as it does with Basil in Collins's novel. But, unlike Collins, Reade forbears to describe Griffith's fantasies. Just as he is concerned with showing characters through direct speech, and the description of physical appearance and behaviour, rather than through psychological analysis, so his concept of insanity is delivered in physical rather than psychological terms, as it also is in *Hard Cash*.

This emphasis on physicality relates to Reade's concept of masculinity, which is based on the muscularity if not the Christianity of Kingsley and Hughes. As in *Hard Cash* physical prowess is valorised, and although Griffith is criticised for his drinking and his lack of sensitivity towards his wife, it is made clear that this is partly her fault for paying more attention to her religion than her husband. Reade's emphasis on the importance of the physical is given a curious twist towards the end of a complicated plot at the point when Griffith and Catherine are reunited though still not in a close affectionate relationship. She is dangerously close to dying, having just given birth to their son, and the young doctor, saying that only a blood transfusion will save her, prepares to donate the blood himself. Griffith will have none of it:

> Griffith tore off his coat and waistcoat, and bared his arm to the elbow. 'Take every drop I have. No man's blood shall enter her veins but mine.' And the creature seemed to swell to double his size, as with flushed cheek and sparkling eyes he held out a bare arm corded like a blacksmith's, and white as a duchess's. (p. 399).

It is this transfusion of Griffith's 'bright red blood smoking hot' into Kate's body that not only revivifies *her*, but revives their love and gives him 'a fascinating power over her'. There is a curious foreshadowing of the sexual connotations of blood transfusion that is a feature of *Dracula*. In the earlier novel, though, the mesmeric power with which the vampire first transfixes his or her victims is consequent upon, rather than antecedent to the transference of blood. The emphasis is on the association of male power with the physical rather than the spiritual or psychical. By the end of the novel, however, after Griffith has been re-united with his wife, the Christian element has been re-incorporated into his life, as the marital plot is resolved. Griffith acquiesces in the inclusion of an elderly religious adviser as part of the household and builds a chapel to the house. Madness in this novel is not used to explain a crime, or to absolve the sufferer from responsibility, since Griffith's bigamous marriage is contracted only after his recovery; instead it signifies the nadir of a state of mind and of a relationship. It provides a convenient shorthand for indicating extreme mental disturbance in an appropriately, for this writer, physical semiotic.

It is unlikely that Reade's painting of jealousy 'in its extreme forms' would have satisfied the writer of the article in the *Spectator* any more than Ellen Wood's did. The writer that he suggests *would* have 'the art to paint ... the morbid passion [jealousy] in its naturalistic nineteenth-century dress' was Anthony Trollope.[14] And indeed, in accordance with his aesthetic of 'truth of description, truth of character, human truth as to men and women', it is detailed psychological analysis of characters in a contemporary context that is Trollope's aim in *He Knew He Was Right*.[15] As he says in the *Autobiography*, he wanted to create sympathy for the character of a man who is driven mad through jealousy. And whether or not he took his lead from the *Spectator* article, his references to *Othello* are overt in this story of a man whose jealous suspicions of his wife are fanned by an Iago figure in the shape of a private detective, Bozzle. So, on the one hand, through the implicit comparisons with *Othello*, Trollope creates an emotional situation that is timeless, where the entanglement is the result of human nature; on the other hand, the novel is set firmly in the middle of the nineteenth century, in the period after the Divorce Act of 1857. The Iago figure, Bozzle, is after all a private detective, a member of a profession that was becoming increasingly significant as a result of the dramatic increase in the number of matrimonial disputes where adultery needed to be proved in a court of law.

The spectacular break-up of this marriage is set in the context of other people's attempts to make marriages. Emily's sister, Nora, and the French sisters, Arabella and Camilla, are all in the throes of finding partners. Marriage is thus a central concern of the novel. In the case of the Trevelyans, the making of the marriage is described almost perfunctorily, as if it is a business operation. There is no romantic wooing as in *Othello*; apart from the statement that Louis 'fell in love with Emily', there is no mention of the emotional basis of the marriage. And there is no parental opposition, for Emily's father, like Mr Bennet in *Pride and Prejudice*, has too many daughters and too little money to allow any of them to refuse a reasonable offer. The only suggestion of opposition comes from Emily's mother, who fears that her daughter's obstinacy may wreck the marriage. Unlike *Othello*, where jealousy is represented as a poignant consequence of love, in this novel jealousy is a consequence of possessiveness. Trollope's starting point is the characters of the two protagonists; both Louis Trevelyan and his wife, Emily, are described as people who liked to have their own way, and her mother is worried from the beginning that Emily's obstinacy may wreck the marriage. When this is set against the making of the other marriages in the novel, and in particular Emily's sister Nora's refusal (with many misgivings and backward looks) of the advantageous offer from the Honourable Mr Glascock, it does seem as though Trollope is saying that a marriage that is entered into for material reasons rather than for love, is doomed. This conclusion is confirmed by the humorous subplot that ends with Mr Gibson's capture by Arabella French: 'Poor Mr. Gibson, – we hardly know whether most to pity him, or the unfortunate, poor woman who ultimately became Mrs. Gibson' (p. 784). For the French sisters any marriage seems to be better than no marriage, but by the end of the novel Camilla seems to be reconciled to the situation of unmarried sister. A more independent attitude is evinced by Priscilla Stanbury, who absolutely refuses to consider marriage, since she knows herself well enough to realise that she is better off living a single existence.

But although it is suggested that marriage must have a secure loving foundation if it is to survive, it is also made clear through these various intrigues and manoeuvres that for women without an independent income, marriage is an important if not the only route to financial security. Nora Rowley's reflections sum up the position for many women: 'The lot of a woman, as she often told herself, was wretched, unfortunate, almost degrading. For a woman such as herself there was no path open to her energy, other than that of getting a husband' (p. 30). The alternative, as she sees it, is to be 'poor alone, to have to live without a husband, to look forward to a life in which there would be nothing of a career, almost nothing to do, to await the vacuity of an existence in which she would be useful to no one' (p. 30). In the marriages of this book it is not the women who bring financial resource to their husbands; so there is emphasis on the role of husbands as providers of financial support. Louis Trevelyan has £3,000, 'arising from various perfectly secure investments', with which to launch his marriage (p. 1). Since Louis does not have the labour of maintaining property in order to ensure his income, there is no clear definition of how he should spend his time, and various alternatives are presented. He has published a book of poems and is now, thinking that he is not yet ready to try for a seat in Parliament, travelling 'that he might see men and know the world' (p. 3). After his marriage we hear that he spends time among his books and is writing an article for a scientific quarterly review. This desultory career as a man of letters in fact leaves him in the economic position of a middle-class woman, a non-competitor in the marketplace.

When, therefore, the seed of jealousy is sown, he is free to brood, aware at the same time that both the jealousy and the brooding is unmanly behaviour: 'He spent his time in thinking of his wife, and of the disgrace which she had brought upon him. Such a life as this, he knew, was unmanly and shameful' (p. 255). Like the speaker of *Maud* he becomes prey to morbid introspection; he has the self-awareness, but not the self-control necessary to prevent his brooding from becoming obsessional.

Throughout the text there are indications, both in narratorial comment and in the behaviour of other characters, as to some of the positive characteristics of manliness. It is manly to be assertive, to speak out where necessary; it is certainly manly to honour one's wife. A negative example is provided by the comic character Mr Gibson, who is tossed between the French sisters, and initially bestowed by Miss Stanbury on her niece, Dorothy, as if he were her gift. Feeling himself to be deprived of the masculine right of deciding his own fate, there are several references to his fear of going mad. Such references need not be taken too seriously since they draw on colloquial usage of the term, but, in a text which focuses on the more literal move towards insanity of the protagonist, they do take on more meaning than they might in another context, and reflect something of Louis Trevelyan's dilemma. Like the husbands in the legal cases cited at the beginning of the chapter, Trevelyan is seriously committed to the conventional view of marital relations which featured the husband as the source of authority and control within the family. Having retreated to the barren seclusion of the villa at Casalunga, he reflects on the possibility that, should he yield in any way to his wife, he would run the risk of being 'shut up in dark rooms' and, even worse than losing his liberty, would thus 'lose his power as a man' (p. 742). Trevelyan expresses the view later to be voiced by the twentieth-century critic Herbert Sussman, that the opposite of manliness is madness; but he lives out the alternative, that *excessive* masculinity is also madness. The descriptions of his state of mind as he draws closer to insanity read like a caricature of the Victorian male's desire for mastery, but the situation described between him and Emily bears great resemblance to the actual marital conflicts described in the cases I mentioned at the beginning of the chapter. Acting in her role as observer and commentator, Nora expresses the opinion that 'such perversity on the part of a man made it almost unwise in any woman to trust herself to the power of a husband' (p. 366).

What was new after the Matrimonial Causes Act of 1857 was the publicity given to cases where the power of the husband came under public scrutiny in the divorce court and, almost inevitably, in the press. As the cases that Hammerton discusses show, there could indeed be great difficulty in deciding whether a husband's treatment of his wife was unreasonable because he was mad, or simply because he was excessively unreasonable. In a passage that adopts the tone of a newspaper article, Trollope considers the difficulty of drawing a dividing line between sanity and insanity:

> There is perhaps no great social question so imperfectly understood among us at the present day as that which refers to the line which divides sanity from insanity. That this man is sane and that other unfortunately mad we do know well enough; and we know that one man may be subject to various hallucinations ... and yet be in such a condition of mind as to call for no intervention either on behalf of his friends, or of the law; while another may be in possession of intellectual faculties capable of lucid exertion for the highest purposes, and yet be so mad that bodily restraint upon him is indispensable. We know that the sane man is responsible for what he does, and that the insane man is irresponsible; but we do not know, – we can only guess wildly, at the state of mind of those, who now and again act like madmen, though no court or council of experts has declared them to be mad ... Now Trevelyan was, in truth, mad on the subject of his wife's alleged infidelity. (p. 361)

There is a similar passage in *Lady Audley's Secret*, where the narrator reflects on the ease with which anyone might topple over the precipice into insanity. For Trollope, though, as it is for Andrew Wynter in *The Borderlands of Insanity*,[16] the emphasis is rather on the difficulty of diagnosing one man's state of mind when he is neither obviously sane or obviously insane. The chapter in which this passage occurs is headed 'Verdict of the Jury – "Mad, My Lord"'; Trevelyan has, as it were, been put in a court of law, but he has not actually committed a crime. For all the textual comparisons with Othello, he does not smother his wife in her bed; in fact he never threatens her with physical harm. Instead, like Frankford in Thomas Heywood's *A Woman Killed with Kindness* (a play written about the same time as *Othello*) he sends her away to live, suitably chaperoned, in the country. Even when he kidnaps their son, he has done nothing absolutely illegal, and the wife's right to custody of the child could not be taken for granted in the particular circumstances described here. Whereas Lady Audley and Charlotte Carleton St John escape the processes of the law by being declared insane and hustled into madhouses, Louis Trevelyan escapes the law by, in fact, not acting illegally. Nevertheless, he is subject to moral condemnation both by other characters and by the narrator. Sir Marmaduke, in his role as outraged father and, incidentally, an example of an indifferent colonial governor, expresses his opinion in characteristically intemperate terms: 'Trevelyan should either be thrashed within an inch of his life, or else locked up in a mad-house' (p. 588). And the narrator concludes that he has misused his power as a husband 'grossly and cruelly' (p. 919). The long passage quoted above makes it clear, moreover, that Trevelyan should face some sort of judgement. As John Sutherland suggests, in holding up Trevelyan for forensic judgement, Trollope may have had in mind the case of Daniel Macnaughton, who assassinated Peel's private secretary and was acquitted in 1843 on grounds of insanity, and more recent controversy concerning the difficulty of determining insanity in criminal cases (p. 943 n. 361). Since Trevelyan has not actually committed a crime, however, and there can be no question of legal guilt, the use of judicial imagery and language focuses attention on the extent to which he can be held to be responsible for his actions, and therefore the extent to which he is morally culpable.

The narrator tries to exculpate Trevelyan on the grounds of insanity: 'Now Trevelyan was, in truth, mad on the subject of his wife's alleged infidelity' (p. 361). He is, in fact, diagnosing monomania, a partial insanity. In *A Treatise on Insanity*, published in 1835, James Prichard, following Esquirol, had described the individual suffering from monomania as being 'rendered incapable of thinking correctly on subjects connected with the particular illusion, while in other respects he betrays no palpable disorder of mind'.[17] This term passed from medical literature into common parlance as a way of describing an obsessional state of mind, or patterns of behaviour that strayed beyond the limits of the socially acceptable, and was in popular use throughout most of the nineteenth century. For the narrator partial insanity is a way of explaining behaviour that must otherwise be evil: 'Had he not been mad he must have been a fiend, – or he could not have tortured, as he had done, the woman to whom he owed the closest protection which one human being can give to another' (p. 925). However, although he is adamant about the question of madness, it is not the narrator, but the doctor who uses the particular clinical term. Interestingly, though, the doctor is reluctant to diagnose actual insanity:

> He admitted that his patient's thoughts had been forced to dwell on one subject till they had become distorted, untrue, jaundiced, and perhaps monomaniacal; but he seemed to doubt whether there had ever been a time at which it could have been decided that Trevelyan was so mad as to make it necessary that the law should interfere to take care of him. (p. 900)

The Victorian recognition of borderline states may have created difficulties in deciding about criminal responsibility, but it could be convenient for those physicians who did not, for one reason or another, want to label their patients as insane and certify them for confinement. The diagnosis of a mental breakdown, with its suggestion of an underlying somatic disorder, was socially more acceptable and more likely to be applied to someone of Trevelyan's class. The doctor's hesitancy in diagnosing insanity and his preferred opinion that 'weakness of the mind has been consequent upon the weakness of the body' (p. 924) allows Trevalyan to escape social stigma as well as the madhouse. However, the diagnosis of a somatic failing which has mental consequences is contradicted by the text, which has shown Trevelyan's physical debility as, rather, consequent upon his mental derangement. Furthermore, a narratorial comment a little later flatly contradicts the doctor's diagnosis: 'And he was mad; – mad though every doctor in England had called him sane' (p. 925). It seems that the text is struggling between a medical opinion that exonerates Trevelyan on grounds of physical illness, and a moral judgement that exonerates him on grounds of diminished responsibility.

Trollope writes in *An Autobiography*: 'It was my purpose to create sympathy for an unfortunate man who, while endeavouring to do his duty to all around him, should be led constantly astray by his unwillingness to submit his own judgement to the opinion of others.'[18] One way in which he does this is by making it clear that the blame for the marital situation does not rest entirely on the husband's shoulders; as I noted earlier, Emily is represented as exacerbating the situation. Furthermore, the reader is encouraged to see Trevelyan's point of view in the long passages of painstaking internal analysis. Despite Emily's protest that her husband's mind is a mystery to her, there is no mystery for the reader; Trevelyan's mind is laid open for inspection, and Trollope shows that, however tyrannous his behaviour, the man is suffering mental torment.

As so often in the literature of madness, Trevelyan's deranged mind is represented in his aimless wanderings through Europe. Unlike Charles Merivale, who is brought home from his continental roaming, Trevelyan is never officially confined, but he does confine himself in an Italian villa at Casalunga. The description of this place suggests both its function as a place of confinement, however voluntary ('a huge entrance ... seemed to have been constructed with the intention of defying any intruders not provided with warlike ammunition'), and its aesthetic function as a metaphor for Louis's current state: 'its look of desolation was extreme'

(p. 732). The eccentricity of his choice of abode is also reflected in his physical appearance:

He wore an old red English dressing-gown, which came down to his feet, and a small braided Italian cap on his head. His beard had been allowed to grow, and he had neither collar nor cravat. His trousers were unbraced, and he shuffled in with a pair of slippers, which would hardly cling to his feet. He was paler and still thinner than when he had been visited at Willesden, and his eyes seemed to be larger, and shone almost with a brighter brilliancy. (p. 734)

Despite the suggestion of fever in the description of his eyes, the rest of the description is close allied to the iconography of melancholy, and the illustration that accompanies the scene slightly later when he sits by the brook to reflect on his fate shows clearly the traditional pose of melancholic.[19] In the scene that follows when Emily comes to see him and their child, the narrator maintains the focalisation through Trevelyan, representing the psychological complexities of his determination to keep the child in his possession. In the later scene when Hugh Stanbury arrives at Casalunga to persuade his friend to allow himself to be taken back to England, Trevelyan's increasing physical deterioration is again represented in his appearance: he is dirty, his hair is long and dishevelled and his beard covers his face, and beneath his dressing gown he now wears night-shirt and drawers (p. 868). And it is a measure of his increasing mental alienation that the narrator no longer represents his point of view; he is shown in terms of outward appearance only, as if the point of contact between a sane and an insane mind has been lost.

By the end of the book he has crumbled into a patient, and is treated like a child by the physician. His extreme debility makes him the centre of other people's consideration, and finally gives him the right to have his own way. The penultimate chapter resumes the metaphor of legal processes with its heading, 'Acquitted'. The reference this time, however, is not to Trevelyan, but to his wife, who has been writhing under her husband's unspoken but clearly implied accusation of infidelity. A final rite – not of forgiveness (she says there is nothing to forgive) – but withdrawing the charge of infidelity is crucially important to her, as 'an act of justice' (p. 927). He must give some sign that he knows that she is not a 'harlot', and in an unconscious parody of Othello, as he lies dying, she asks him to kiss her hand. In a sophisticated discussion of the semiotics of *He Knew He Was Right*, Chris Wiesenthal analyses the ambiguity of the sign that Louis actually gives, which is interpreted by his wife as reparation for all the 'evil he that he had done' (p. 928).[20] It is uncertain, though, that this is Louis's intention. Although he is forgiven by his wife, who treats him, despite her conviction of his madness, as a reasonable human being, that this not quite how he is treated in the text. That final sign is not represented naturalistically as a kiss, nor as words, but as the movement of his lips against her hand and 'the sound of his tongue within' (p. 927). His gesture seems less the voluntary expression of a considered response than the random movements of a man who is reduced to body parts. It is a synecdoche that aligns him with the feverish movement of the lizards that were 'glancing in and out of the broken walls' in the scene of his decline at Casalunga (p. 867), and it is his wife who chooses to interpret the sign as an act of mercy as well as of justice, thus conferring on Louis the humanity of a reasonable man: 'To her mind the acquittal was perfect; but she never explained to human ears ... the manner in which it had been given' (p. 928).

Trollope's *donné* is a particular trait of personality, and the consequences when two people with the same trait get married. As Trollope painstakingly traces the growth of the disagreement between the Trevelyans, he preserves a balance between free will and determinism by continually indicating how things could have turned out otherwise. Responsibility is shared between the predatory Colonel, who rather too freely allows himself to enjoy the society of attractive women who are married to other men, Emily, and Louis himself. It is not only narratorial comment, but Nora's commentary on the disagreement, her persuasion of her sister to act otherwise, that ensures the reader is made aware of the possibilities for alternative courses of action. At the same time the omniscient narrator provides the reader with access to the internal reasoning and self-justification of the three characters of the jealousy triangle, which implies that they have the free will to choose what they will do. Once Louis has slipped into madness, however, the implication is that he is no longer responsible for his actions. There is a sense of relief in the narratorial statement that opens the final chapter: 'At last the maniac was dead' (p. 928), but as I have been arguing, up to this point there has been equivocation about the assessment of Trevelyan as bad or as mad, and consequently about how he should be judged.

There is less uncertainty in *Sowing the Wind*, Eliza Lynn Linton's dissection of a marriage and a mind that disintegrates under an extreme desire for control.[21] In this novel, the husband, St John Aylott, is jealous of *all* intrusions into the intimacy of his marriage and expects total control over his wife, Isola: 'Her husband ruled her life, without a question of divided authority rising between them ... He ordered her daily life as if she had

been a child without reason or free will' (p. 4). There are, however, intruders: Isola's only aunt, Mrs Osborn, and her feminist daughter, Jane, in particular, and the shadowy figure of Harriet Grant. As a way, therefore, of
preserving the hermetic seal of his marriage, St John decides to leave
London for Newfield, depicted as a conventional idyllic village. The move
proves useless as a way of avoiding company, since they are now thrown
into a new set of acquaintances, and their increasing marital discord is
exacerbated by the dramatic intrusion of a past that St John steadfastly
refuses to accept.

As in *He Knew He Was Right* jealousy is the disturbing factor in the marriage; St John is jealous of any friendships that Isola forms, but particularly
those with the journalist, Harvey Wyndham, which is short-lived, and
with the explorer Gilbert Holmes. The latter is an important relationship,
but it is made clear that Isola is not unfaithful to her husband. St John, like
Trevelyan, is jealous because he is unreasonably possessive and unreasonably proud. Harriet Grant turns out to be the sister he has disowned
because of her disreputable marriage with a travelling circus-rider, so when
she dies and leaves her baby for him to look after he absolutely refuses.
Such inhumanity is attacked by Isola, who insists that they take the child
(there is no-one else), and who becomes a loving adoptive mother. St John
is further condemned by his exorbitant jealousy of the child. The situation
is not unlike that in *St Martin's Eve*, but whereas Charlotte Carleton St
John's jealousy of her stepson is given some justification in that her jealousy is on behalf of her own son, for St John Aylott there is no justification. He regards the child as the usurper of his own position as the prime,
indeed the sole object of Isola's affections and attentions, and it is made
clear in the text that this is a shamefully unmanly attitude.

St John is represented as lacking the qualities associated with masculinity in his unreasonable behaviour towards his wife, his accusations of infidelity, and in his failure to rescue Isola from a fire at an inn where they are
staying. He fails both in his domestic role, and in his economic role. In an
attempt to prove his masculinity and salve his emotional wounds after Isola
has insisted they must look after the child, St John moves back to London,
and throws himself into speculation on the stock market. He is as unsuccessful in the competitive environment of commerce as he is in the
affective environment of home. Having lost his fortune, he is reduced
to accepting accommodation with the despised Osborns, and work as a
clerk in Gilbert's business, whilst Isola makes a small income from 'fancy
work'. From the outset St John is shown to fall short of true masculinity

of appearance: 'He was tall and slightly built, but his shoulders were too narrow and drooping for the finer kind of manly beauty ... his face had a curiously Spanish look, but without the Spanish masculinity of expression' (p. 2). His habit of never standing 'square, face to face and chest broadside' (p. 2) is contrasted, in retrospect, with the later description of Gilbert, 'who stood ... square and firm on his own feet' (p. 65). Gilbert stands as an example of true manliness; he has the qualities of 'courage, power, unselfishness, honour' (p. 59). It is he who rescues Isola from the fire. Appearances are important in this novel and the spiritual affinity they recognise is mirrored in a physical similarity: 'It was easy for an ethnologist to see that they both belonged to the fair-haired, strong-limbed Scandinavian race' (p. 102). But, although at one point they are compared with Othello and Desdemona as he tells her of his exotic voyages, there is never any suggestion of sexual attraction. The ambiguity that has characterised their relationship throughout the novel is confirmed rather than resolved at the end of it, when he clasps her to his breast: ' "Brother Gilbert!" she cried ... "My sister! ... I have come to take care of you, Isola!" ' (p. 316). There is an uncomfortable discrepancy between the close physical embrace and the suggestion of a non-marital relationship, whether that of siblings or that of religious colleagues, but whatever relationship Linton is recommending is a union in which the male partner takes responsibility for looking after the female.

As in so many of the novels I have discussed, St John's madness is depicted in terms of its external manifestation in appearance and behaviour, and is categorised as a violent mania growing out of his jealousy of the child, Reg. In one of several melodramatic scenes in this novel, Isola finds her husband trying to suffocate the child with his hands:

> The tangled hair was falling thick before his brow. The bloodshot eyes seemed like a darkened line of flame behind the lashes ... the lips were parted and drawn back from the clenched teeth. The lines round the mouth and dilated nostrils were as deep as if dug out with a graver. (p. 282)

Physical appearance is an important signifier of madness, as it is in the image of Trevelyan sunk in melancholy; here and in other places in the novel, Linton draws on the traditional iconography of mania. St John's mental deterioration is also caught, like Griffith's, in bestial imagery. After his climactic attack with a knife on Gilbert, he falls to the floor in abject contrition: 'It was some moments before St. John could rise from the floor where he was writhing, weeping, praying like a creature possessed – or, if not possessed, then loathsome in his unmanliness' (p. 305) This picture of reptilian abasement represents moral condemnation of a man who has lost all self-control and self-respect, and recalls older conceptions of madness in terms of a reduction to animal status. However, after his attempt to suffocate Reg, Isola assesses his mental state in terms that are close to Prichard's classification of madness. Prichard had divided insanity into 'moral' insanity, on the one hand, and 'intellectual' insanity, on the other hand. Intellectual insanity was in turn subdivided into 'monomania', 'mania' and 'incoherence or dementia'. As I have said, the appearance St John presents is that of mania, but Isola considers that 'he was not mad to the point of ignorance of what he did ... If mad at all, it was from pride and jealousy and a wayward will too long unchecked.' His madness, she concludes, is madness 'in the spiritual sense of an unsound soul ... not madness intellectually' (p. 283). The narrator, aligned with Isola throughout the novel, says nothing to contradict her assessment, and the implication, therefore, is that St John is behaving in a morally reprehensible fashion, for which he must be held accountable. Such a position is necessary for the polemic of the text, which is based on outrage at the unequal distribution of responsibility and control in marriage. But it is undercut by the suggestion of hereditary madness, since, it turns out, St John's mother died mad. St John finally loses his wits after a visit offering help from his despised, peasant grandfather: 'It had come ... the man whom she [Isola] held in her arms and clasped to her heart as his last place of refuge, was mad; and his human life was over now for ever' (p. 309). He dies in an asylum, redeeming himself only by telling Isola at last that he loves her. Whereas Trollope attempts to apportion responsibility for the breakdown of their marriage between Louis and Emily, Linton throws the blame squarely at St John. In this text, which juxtaposes disapproved models of femininity against equally disapproved models of masculinity, Isola and Gilbert stand out as exemplars of what a woman and a man should be, and madness reads as a punishment for lack of noble masculinity, unwarranted pride and incapacity in forming valid relationships.

Questions of responsibility, free will and determinism run through another, later novel that deals with marriage, jealousy and madness, Mary Braddon's *The Fatal Three* (1888).[22] The fatal three of the title could be identified as the three main characters, George and his two wives, Mildred and Fay. But more obviously the fatal three are the three Greek fates, identified in the titles of the three parts of the novel: 'Clotho; or spinning the thread'; 'Lachesis; or the meter of destiny'; 'Atropos; or, that which must be'. One of the tensions in the novel is between Christian belief and recognition of the forces of blind fate. In the original edition, a prefatory 'Key-Note' contrasts those who 'fashion their lives with their own thoughts and their own actions' and those who are 'the sport of Fate, and who move unconsciously towards darkest doom'.[23] The idea of characters who move towards a 'mysterious destiny' and the idea that they are 'a pre-ordained sacrifice to the powers of evil' encourages the reader to expect a sensation novel where, in the words of E.S. Dallas, 'man is represented as made and ruled by circumstance'.[24] But as I shall be arguing, the novel's interest in internal analysis and in the particular way it relates the present to what has happened in the past undermines the presumption of fatalism in favour of a more contemporary mode of psychological determinism, even as it cultivates the sensational element.

At the centre of the novel is the marriage of George Gresham and Mildred Fausset. It is depicted as one of idyllic harmony with George as the ideal husband and father. Their home is 'one of those ideal homes which adorn the facade of England and sustain its reputation as the native soil of domestic virtues, the country in which good wives and good mothers are indigenous' (p. 36). The centre of their life is their daughter, Lola, and George is the beneficent ruler of this little world. Like Louis Trevelyan, George has a private income, but he occupies himself in a less desultory way. Emphasis is laid on his conscientious fulfilment of the duties of a land-owner, maintaining and improving his property and caring for his tenants, as well as his whole-hearted involvement in the life of his wife and daughter. Emphasising its ideality, this marriage is contrasted with two others, that of her parents, who are shown to be in unequal partnership and lacking in devotion to home, and that of George with his first wife, Vivian Faux. This marriage, which is shown retrospectively, is one of unequal affection; it has been an unhappy mistake, a union of two displaced persons, in which George's sense of duty towards his wife is shown as sadly inadequate to her needs. After a year the marriage collapses under the pressure of Vivian's unreasonable jealousy, and she commits suicide. The marriage of George and Mildred is also threatened in two ways. In the first place, they have to face the tragic death of their daughter, Lola, who contracts typhoid fever as a result of contaminated water being used in her father's dairy. Since George has prided himself on his husbandry and on his paternal devotion to Lola, her death seems to show his dismal deficiency in both respects, he becomes emotionally withdrawn, and Mildred finds it impossible to reach him for mutual consolation.

Thus far, the novel analyses the marriage in terms of psychological realism. But there is a second threat, which is based on a contemporary controversy, but which is treated in consonance with the theme of fatalism. The threat derives from a number of coincidences focusing on the figure of Vivian Faux. This is the assumed name of Fay Fausset. The alliterative and assonantal links between these names lead to a further link between Fay and fate, as well as signalling the falseness of her identity. Fausset is also Mildred's family name, and for a period of her childhood Fay has come to live with Mildred and her parents, introduced as the ward and distant relative of her father. She has to leave, however, once Mildred's mother has become convinced that the girl is in fact Mr Fausset's illegitimate daughter, and the two girls lose contact. It is the workings of fate, or a sensational coincidence, that Mildred should marry the man who has earlier married the woman she believes to be her half-sister. Again it is pure coincidence or fate that Mildred, after many trials and much suffering, should come across letters from her father to his sister that reveal that Miss Fausset, the austere and religious spinster, is the mother of Fay, and that Fay and Mildred are, therefore, not half-sisters, but cousins. The relationship between the women is important because at the time marriage with a deceased wife's sister was a matter of considerable controversy. It fell within the prohibited degrees of marriage and was consequently illegal, but from the middle of the nineteenth century there was continual discussion about repeal. The prohibition was based on passages in the Old Testament (Leviticus 18; Genesis 38; Deuteronomy 25), but the meaning of these passages was much disputed, and feelings ran high in the conflict between traditionalists who opposed repeal and moderates who could see no reason in theology or morality for the ban.[25] Once Mildred realises, as she thinks, that she is married to the husband of her dead half-sister, she feels she must abandon the relationship and wanders abroad with a favourite niece.

Cutting across the interpretative modes of fatalism and psychological realism is the opposition of paganism and religion. George has been introduced as the father and husband in a devout Christian marriage, on a Sunday, having just returned from church, but as tragedy envelops his family he is overpowered by a 'sense of fatality – of undeserved evil' (p. 46). The narrator tells us: 'Upon one side of his character he was a Pagan, seeing in this affliction [the death of his daughter] the hand of Nemesis, the blind Avenger' (p. 59). And as cracks and fissures begin to appear in the marriage under the strain of loss and mourning, George becomes a more mysterious figure. He is afflicted with nightmares and he refuses to reveal to

Mildred the secret sorrows of his past. Whereas the mystery that Trevelyan's mind presents to his wife is no mystery to the reader, in George's case the mystery is preserved. When Mildred finds him by Lola's monument groaning and calling out, 'Judgment! … judgment!' (p. 62), the reader has no more idea than she does what it is all about. Mildred, on the other hand, remains steadfast in her religious faith, but this is not shown as particularly commendable. As it happens her religious education has been in the hands of Mr Cancellor, 'an ecclesiastic after the antique pattern'; 'he was generous, he was merciful, gentle, self-sacrificing, pure in spirit; but he was not liberal-minded' (p. 101). Mr Cancellor is not, therefore, a supporter of the movement to repeal the prohibition on marriage to a deceased wife's sister. It is under his influence that Mildred is so intransigent in her view that it would be wrong to continue in a marriage that has been falsely contracted. For her, as for him, the dictates of conscience based on holy scripture are above any considerations of the law. Both Mildred and George, then, come to see Lola's death fatalistically as punishment for the errors or wrongs of the past. Mildred is tempted to see it as 'God's judgment upon iniquity' (p. 155); what George thinks he is being judged for only becomes clear towards the end of the book.

In the second phase of the narrative Mildred travels on the Continent, in effect echoing the aimless wandering of her husband both before and after his marriage with Fay/Vivian, and at the same time uncovering the secrets of his past, including the ambiguous matter of Fay's death falling from a cliff and his own descent into madness. The onset of George's insanity is comparatively sudden. He is arrested on suspicion of causing Fay's death, and his mind gradually gives way when he is confined in a police cell between sessions with the French *juge d'instruction*. As in *Griffith Gaunt*, insanity is represented as a response to intolerable psychological strain, a form of escape from the nightmare situation into which his wife's jealousy has plunged him. Unlike Reade, however, Braddon analyses George's state of mind in some detail; in his hallucinations he sees himself as a political dissident, plotting against Victor Emmanuel to create a Republic of Italy and become its President. Not only does this represent an escape from the tyranny of his domestic life, but it is an imaginary compensation for the lack of power he has experienced within his marriage. Madness, therefore, does not enter the text in a way that is either psychologically or aesthetically arbitrary. Nor is it simply used as motivation for a crime. George is held on suspicion of murder, but there is no evidence, nor are there witnesses to prove either murder or suicide, and, as Mildred's friend, Lady Lochinvar, points out, 'It is a case of not proven' (p. 213). Lady Lochinvar's evaluation, however, is only an informal one, for the legal situation is fudged. It is confirmed by a doctor during the second questioning by the magistrate that George has lost his reason and the legal proceedings are described no further: no specific legal judgement is passed.

The question of judgement, though, still hangs in the text. Judicial judgement is in fact irrelevant, since the fact that George is not guilty of Fay's death has already been made clear by the narrator, who has shown the moment of death and has told us quite categorically that Fay died by flinging herself off a cliff. So there is no question of George's responsibility, diminished or otherwise – at least in the immediate sense. However, his conviction that Lola's death is some sort of judgement indicates that he does feel himself to be indirectly responsible for Fay's death. This is confirmed in the description of the immediate psychological aftermath, a flashback focalised mainly through George, in which it is clear that he does hold himself responsible, since her suicide is a response to 'one hard speech': 'I own that when you torment me, as you are doing to-day, I have sometimes thought of death – yours or mine – as the only escape from mutual misery' (p. 250), and he reflects on 'the wild revenge of a woman's passionate heart which made him a murderer' (p. 251). An alternative way of interpreting his insanity, then, is that it is a self-inflicted punishment, and his confinement in an asylum is the equivalent to confinement in prison. But that is not how it seems in the text. Internal analysis has favoured George rather than Fay, and he has been shown as making every effort to preserve the marriage. At the same time the degree of interest shown in the early lives of all three characters, the influence of their home and family background reduces responsibility not by making them victims of fate so much as people whose lives are determined by their disposition and childhood experiences. The chronology of the novel, unlike the sequential structure that Trollope adopts, is disjointed, jumping backwards and forwards, so that instead of the painstaking tracing of psychological processes, there is a gradual uncovering of secrets. This narrative strategy is characteristic of sensation and gothic fiction, but instead of creating a sense that the characters are ruled by circumstances in the blatant, plot-directed fashion that would validate the novel's apparent claim of fatalism, the interest in psychological processes means that the revelations of the text importantly include those of the formative influences on the lives of the characters. Whereas Trevelyan's madness is seen as the result of an intractable mind overcome by jealousy, George's madness is seen as a response to circumstances, a sort of amnesia that allows him to escape psychologically from an insupportable situation.

As John Tosh puts it, 'The belief in the household as a microcosm of the political order ... underlined the importance of the man being master in his own home' (p. 185).[26] For the men who go mad in the novels discussed above home is the focus of their lives. What the novels show is how easily the ideal of a safe haven, wisely governed by the husband, can degenerate into a tormenting hell. Madness may result from deficient masculinity or manliness, but it can also result from an excess of masculinity. Or, to put it another way, the incidence of madness in these novels highlights the problems and the dangers of living up to the ideals of masculine behaviour, of understanding the limits, for instance, of a husband's authority over his wife, or the extent to which he can exercise power without becoming a tyrant. What they also show is that it cannot be so easily assumed that the responsibility for the deterioration belongs solely to a husband who abuses his authority. All the wives featured here have strong ideas, preoccupations, or minds of their own, and the novels document the painful process of negotiation between husband and wife, with jealousy as the focal point. The perilous nature of these negotiations is made evident in the madness and death which is the fate of all the husbands except Griffith Gaunt. With such endings to the novels, it is masculinity, or the abuse of masculine powers that is criticised and the stereotypical view of male–female relations that is queried. The texts discussed in this chapter adopt different narrative strategies, but as in all the novels covered by this study, where the representation of madness focuses on external appearances, there is it seems an almost inevitable turning to the iconographic: the traditional appearances, poses or actions of the melancholic or the maniac, the aimless wandering, the animalistic associations. Madness is conceived in the case of Griffith Gaunt and St John Aylott as the loss of self-control which can result in violence, but in the cases of Louis Trevelyan and George Gresham it is, rather, a loss of mental rather than physical control where the husband finds that he is powerless to control his wife. In one case the desire to dominate spirals into an obsession; in the other the failure to control leads to a total divorce from reality. What is unusual in the novels by Trollope and Braddon is the careful psychological analysis, the probing into the mind of the mad man, and the way this interacts with other narratorial features to engage with the troubling issue of free will and responsibility. The next chapter will show how this issue is absorbed by concerns about the pathological egoism of the individual, and the way in which society is degenerating.

Notes

1 See Chapter 2 for further discussion of brain fever.
2 A. James Hammerton, *Cruelty and Companionship: Conflict in Nineteenth-Century Married Life* (London: Routledge, 1992), p. 92.
3 Hammerton, *Cruelty*, p. 98.
4 Hammerton, *Cruelty*, p. 100.
5 I am thinking in particular of L. Davidoff and C. Hall, *Family Fortunes: Men and Women of the English Middle-Class, 1780–1850* (London: Hutchinson, 1987), and Amanda Vickery, 'Golden Age to Separate Spheres? A Review of the Categories and Chronology of English Women's History', *Historiographical Review*, XXXVI (1993), pp. 383–414.
6 P.D. Edwards, 'Trollope and the Reviewers: Three Notes', *Notes and Queries*, November 1968, pp. 418–20.
7 Anon., 'Madness in Novels', p. 135.
8 Braddon, *Lady Audley's Secret*.
9 James Payne, *The Clyffards of Clyffe* (London: Hurst & Blackett, 1866).
10 Mrs Henry Wood, *St. Martin's Eve* [1866] (London: Ward, Locke & Co., 1916?).
11 Wood, *St. Martin's Eve*, p. 326.
12 Anon., 'Madness in Novels', p. 135.
13 Charles Reader, *Griffith Gaunt: or Jealousy* [1866] (London: Chatto & Windus, no date). All subsequent references are to this edition and are incorporated into the text.
14 Anon., 'Madness in Novels', p. 135.
15 Trollope, *Autobiography*, p. 147; *idem, He Knew He Was Right* [1869], ed. John Sutherland, The World's Classics (Oxford: Oxford University Press, 1985). All subsequent references are to this edition and are incorporated into the text.
16 See Introduction for further discussion.
17 James Cowles Prichard, *A Treatise on Insanity and Other Disorders Affecting the Mind* (London: Sherwood, Gilbert & Piper, 1835), p. 26.
18 Trollope, *Autobiography*, p. 204.
19 Chris Wiesenthal, *Figuring Madness*, ch. 4, gives a detailed and illuminating account of the association between monomania and melancholy, situating Trevelyan's disorder in an 'anatomy of melancholy'.
20 Wiesenthal, *Figuring Madness*, pp. 90–91.
21 Eliza Lynn Linton, *Sowing the Wind* [1867] (London: Chatto & Windus, 1890). All subsequent references are to this edition and are incorporated into the text.
22 M.E. Braddon, *The Fatal Three* [1888] (Stroud: Sutton Publishing Ltd, 1997).
23 M.E. Braddon, *The Fatal Three* (Simpkin, Marshall & Co., no date). Subsequent references are to the Sutton edition and are incorporated into the text.
24 Dallas, *Gay Science*, vol. II, p. 293.
25 In fact the ban on marriage with a deceased wife's sister was not lifted until 1907, and marriage to a deceased husband's brother was not permitted until 1961.
26 Tosh, 'What Should Historians Do?', pp. 179–202.

5

The Zoophagous Maniac: Madness and Degeneracy in *Dracula*

But however silly a term *fin-de-siècle* may be, the mental constitution which it indicates is actually present in influential circles. The disposition of the times is curiously confused, a compound of feverish restlessness and blunted discouragement, of fearful presage and hang-dog renunciation. The prevalent feeling is that of imminent perdition and extinction. *Fin-de-siècle* is at once a confession and a complaint. The old Northern faith contained the fearsome doctrine of the Dusk of the Gods. In our days there have arisen in more highly-developed minds vague qualms of a Dusk of the Nations, in which all suns and all stars are gradually waning, and mankind with all its institutions and creations is perishing in the midst of a dying world.[1]

Max Nordau's evocation of the spirit of the age at the end of the nineteenth century caused a sensation when it was first published. He tapped into a rich vein of commentary in which cultural and moral criticism were intertwined, as the trial of Oscar Wilde so poignantly demonstrates. Nordau's journalistic flamboyance feeds off the very culture it attacks. For Nordau, inspired by the work of Lombroso and Morel, the period was one of degeneration, which he defines as a disease affiliated with hysteria. Both are associated with the nervousness that is part of life in modern industrial society. Like his precursors, Nordau believes that degeneracy is recognised by physical 'stigmata': 'Science, however, has found, together with these physical stigmata, others of a mental order, which betoken degeneracy quite as clearly as the former.'[2] Such degenerates occupy a 'borderland between reason and pronounced madness', and like all degenerates 'lack a sense of morality and of right and wrong'.[3] Following the lead of the psychologist, Henry Maudsley, Nordau characterises the extreme position as one of moral insanity, which shared with degeneracy the characteristics of 'egoism' and 'impulsiveness', or lack of self-control.

Although the idea of degeneration was originally a biological concept, it adapted easily to more figurative usage, providing a scientific foundation for the moral panic at the end of the century. In the deviations from and perversions of what was seen as normal, society seemed to be no longer progressing, but regressing; it was both hurtling forward to disintegration and retreating into primitivism. As Jonathan Dollimore has put it, 'this was evolution simultaneously accelerating forward out of control and regressing backward out of control; a terrifying forward *and* backward unbinding of the arduously achieved higher forms of civilization and biology'.[4] In *The Pathology of Mind* Maudsley makes explicit the comparison between insanity and primitivism:

> The former [primitive] lacks by nature that which the latter [insane] has lost by disease when he is the outcome of a morbid degeneration of kind and, sunk to a congenital idiocy by reason of defective nervous plexuses, is less capable of ordinary intellectual and moral culture than the low savage.[5]

That madness has moral connotations is made quite clear: '... if insanity be on the increase among civilized peoples the increase is due more to their pleasures than their pains – to idleness, luxury, and self-indulgence more than to work, thrift, and self-denial.'[6] On the other hand, Maudsley is influenced by the work of those who were showing that mental states had a physiological basis. He enumerates the traditional causes of insanity: grief, remorse, disappointed love, domestic cares and anxieties, jealousy, pride, and asks whether madness is associated with particular religious sects, with certain nations or occupations, with one sex rather than the other, only to conclude that such questions are 'too vague and general, too wanting in precision, to admit of instructive answers'.[7] The only safe conclusion is that 'all moral commotions and mental overstrains which cause insanities ... do it by straining or breaking the molecular ties of the nervous structure and so injuring or destroying its vital elasticity'.[8]

There is a tension underlying Maudsley's work between the explanation of insanity in terms of physiological processes, for which the individual can hardly be morally accountable, and the association of madness with reprehensible styles of living, for which the individual *is* responsible and can therefore be held morally culpable. This tension is implicit also in the concept of degeneration, for if, as William Greenslade says in *Degeneration, Culture and the Novel, 1880–1940*, 'the nature of human evil can be explained as organic anomaly', then the reverse is also true and organic anomaly can be explained as evil.[9] Greenslade points out that the idea of degeneration was a fruitful source of myth in the post-Darwinian world, and it will be the aim of this chapter to show how notions of degeneration enter into that most potent of late nineteenth-century myths, *Dracula*.

When Bram Stoker wrote *Dracula* in 1897 he added a number of new features to the established tradition of vampiric literature, including the lunatic asylum, the madman and the doctor. The working notes for the novel show that the idea of madness was present from an early stage; a cast list dating from the spring of 1890 includes a mad doctor and a mad patient who has 'a theory of perpetual life'.[10] In the chapter outline dated 14 March 1890 Dr Seward's diary in Book 1 includes mention of 'the fly patient' who is in love with death, and two years later, as the 'Fly man', he figures in Seward's diary as a herald of Harker's arrival at Castle Dracula rather than of Dracula's arrival at Carfax. It would seem, then, that the idea of insanity was an integral part of the Stoker's conception, but his reading of clinical literature does not appear to have been extensive. Christopher Frayling's list of books in Stoker's library relevant to the writing of *Dracula* mentions only Lavater's *Essays on Physiognomy.* But Clive Leatherdale notes that Stoker's source material, as revealed in the papers held by the Rosenbach Foundation, included books by Herbert Mayo (*On the Truths contained in Popular Superstitions, with an Account of Mesmerism,* 1851) and Thomas Pettigrew (*On Superstitions connected with the History and Practice of Medicine and Surgery,* 1844).[11] Also three of Stoker's brothers were medical men and could no doubt provide information. It is not the purpose of this chapter, however, to trace a one-to-one correspondence between Stoker's representation of madness and that of any particular clinical source, but to see what conception of insanity informs his writing, what part it plays in the novel as a whole, and how it relates to the novel's ideas about masculinity. In so doing I shall be concerned with the complex interplay of realism and fantasy, and with the progressive dissolution of the demarcation between sanity and madness.

Although, as has been well noted, *Dracula,* like *The Woman in White,* is constructed from diary entries, letters and newspaper reports; unlike the earlier novel, the assemblage does not appear as the work of one individual operating as an author/editor and there is greater emphasis on the recording of events, impressions and thoughts almost as they happen rather than submitting formal reports afterwards. This is particularly the case before those having some sort of contact with Dracula have joined forces and pooled their information. Apparently disparate phenomena are recorded, for which causes have to be discovered and between which links are gradually revealed. One of the chief narrators is John Seward, the doctor of the asylum in the grounds of Carfax, Dracula's first London residence, and the phenomena that he records are the symptoms of madness exhibited by Renfield, his 'pet' lunatic. Dr Seward's diary, with its comment '*Kept in phonograph*', which accompanies the first entry, is one of several reminders that we are in the mechanised world of the late nineteenth century, but there are features of the text's rhetoric that reduce its contemporaneity. For instance, Seward's position as one of three suitors who all propose to Lucy Westenra on the same day puts him in a fairy-tale situation, and the parallels with the earlier journal of Jonathan Harker add further allusions which strengthen the suggestion of fantasy. In his determination to find consolation in work and in particular to understand the unusual lunatic, Renfield, Seward follows in his own way the pattern set by Harker, for whom keeping a journal 'becomes a therapeutic act of self-preservation'.[12] For both it is a means of exerting some control in circumstances that highlight their vulnerability.

In this first outlining of the mystery presented by the madman, Seward draws on the terms conventionally employed in the discourse of madness, but without noticeable coherence. He remarks on the need to make himself 'master of the facts of his [Renfield's] hallucination', describes him as being of a 'sanguine temperament' and then gives details of his swings of mood from morbid excitability to periods of gloom.[13] Hallucinations had long been established as one of the standard symptoms of insanity, but the concept is not particularly pertinent to Renfield's madness and is not mentioned again in connection with him, though, as I shall later discuss, it is of relevance to the text more generally. The reference to a 'sanguine temperament', on the other hand, recalls the ancient humours-based theory of personality, which usefully introduces the motif of blood, and this is combined with more contemporary ideas of mood and the notion of manic-depression.[14] Already the text gives signs of swinging between old wisdom and superstition, on the one hand, and, on the other, late nineteenth-century rationality and positivism. This is in fact a key feature of the text and madness becomes a crucial arena for the interplay of the two modes of interpretation and understanding, just as it does for the oscillation between realism and fantasy. Seward presumes that Renfield's madness is the result of some 'disturbing influence' on the sanguine temperament, the two together giving 'a mentally-accomplished finish' (p. 61). Just what this means is unclear, but it does give the impression that once all the operative factors have been determined, the case of Renfield will become comprehensible. As a case study, then, Renfield has an analogous position in the text to that of Dracula. Both represent phenomena underlying which, it is assumed, there is a coherent pattern to be discovered, provided one follows the correct procedure of sharp observation, meticulous record keeping and logical deduction.

Renfield's scheme of collecting and eating flies, then spiders, then sparrows, which has culminated in a request for a kitten leads Seward to the hypothesis that he is an undeveloped homicidal maniac who, like the old lady in the nursery rhyme, is working his way up a hierarchy of consumption in the interests of absorbing as many lives as he can through a cumulative process. Having confirmed this hypothesis by offering Renfield a cat as a preferable, because more vivacious (that is, containing more life) alternative to a kitten, Seward invents a new classification for the lunatic and calls him 'a zoophagous (life-eating) maniac' (p. 70). This term was not part of nineteenth-century nosology, but is borrowed from natural science, and the transference underlines the degree to which Renfield is seen as an animal, a specimen for the scientist to observe and catalogue, a not unusual attitude in Victorian medicine. Renfield's blood lust thus establishes him as a ready-made acolyte for Dracula. For neither is the absorption of blood necessary to sustain life, since the vampire is immortal, and the lunatic, being alive, still has access to more normal means of sustenance. In Renfield's case his zoophagy is an attempt to eat his way up the Great Chain of Being, in the hope that by absorbing other lives he will indefinitely prolong his own; it takes the rationale of food to an illogical conclusion, by assuming that 'life' is a quantifiable commodity, capable of indefinite prolongation. Taboos, though frequently validated in terms of religion, are a matter of social expedience. The taboo that Renfield is breaking focuses attention on the subject of food and the distinction between the eating of flesh purely for the purposes of sustaining life and the drinking of blood for the purposes of increasing power: 'I don't want souls, indeed, indeed! I don't. I couldn't use them if I had them! they would be no manner of use to me. I couldn't eat them ...' (p. 269). His repeated cry, 'The blood is the life' is in fact taken from Deuteronomy 12.23–25 and is an invocation of the Judaic belief, shared by other races, that blood literally is the source of life. Renfield thus breaks the taboo which the Old Testament imposes on the eating of flesh unless it has been properly drained, but his desire for blood, together with his worship of the Master also parallels the figurative reincarnation of the belief in the Christian Eucharist. Since, however, the Catholic doctrine of transubstantiation holds that in receiving communion wine the communicant is drinking the blood of Christ, Renfield's abstention from lower life forms in the promise of something better (Seward deduces that Dracula has promised him a human life) seems *parodic* of conventional religious beliefs only to the extent that his drinking necessitates a preliminary killing for that specific purpose. Renfield's madness, in fact, returns to literality what has become a figurative practice.

Dracula, similarly, gives literal substance to the Christian belief in resurrection, but thereby inverts religious values, as David Punter points out, since his soul has failed to find God.[15] His vampirism, unlike Renfield's, has no regard for souls; it is his insistence on living at a purely physical level, his transgression of all social and moral laws that makes him such a formidable opponent, for he is limited by none of the qualms that affect even a lunatic. As Punter notes, he represents pure desire. Dracula's aim is not simply to prolong his own life, which is already endless, but to colonise the world with his own kind. His encounters, with their heavy sexual overtones, represent blood-sucking as a form of mating, the progeny of which is the women themselves, transmogrified into vampires; mating, therefore, seems more like infecting. In addition, the comparison with Renfield, whose 'cause' is defined as insane solipsism, has the effect of pathologising Dracula's equally solipsistic mission. Through the excessive egoism of the figures of both Dracula and Renfield, then, the novel articulates symbolically the fears of degeneracy that were so prevalent in the last quarter of the nineteenth century. Daniel Pick has discussed the contribution *Dracula* makes to the debates about degeneracy, drawing attention to their moralistic dimension:

> The novel provided a metaphor for current political and sexual political discourses on morality and society, representing the price of selfish pursuits and criminal depravity. The family and the nation, it seemed to many, were beleaguered by syphilitics, alcoholics, cretins, the insane, the feeble-minded, prostitutes and a perceived 'alien invasion' of Jews from the east who, in the view of many alarmists, were feeding off and 'poisoning' the blood of the Londoner.[16]

By insisting on his involvement with the natural world and his regulation by 'natural' laws, the novel might seem to be relegating the vampire to a sphere outside human responsibility, but Van Helsing does place great emphasis on Dracula's previous life as a warrior who is good and strong: '... it is not the least of its terrors that this evil thing is rooted deep in all good; in soil barren of holy memories it cannot rest' (p. 241). Dracula is, in fact, an example of 'a great and noble race' who is thought to have had dealings with 'the Evil One' and those very qualities that are necessary to preserve and aggrandise a race have been perverted. In addition, by externalising the source of degeneracy on to the parasitical figure of Dracula, Stoker protects bourgeois society from charges of immorality and reinforces the claims of conventional restraints, though the justification for them is not well substantiated. Responsibility for the degeneracy is placed on the shoulders of an outsider, who becomes a scapegoat for the ills of modern society. David Punter has commented on the function performed by old legends in establishing a connection between aristocracy and immortality, and in this particular case how the myth created by Stoker, by exploring the connotations of lineage and nobility that are contained within the word 'blood', combines ideas of aristocratic immortality with fears of invasion and the threat to bourgeois values and beliefs imposed by a degenerate aristocracy. Providing further substance for the parallel between Dracula and Renfield, Renfield's periods of sanity are important in establishing his good birth and education; he, too, is in fact a gentleman who has degenerated.

The possibility that medical science might stem degeneracy are explored through the relationship of Dr Seward and his patient. In Francis Ford Coppola's 1992 film, Renfield's madness is explained by his having been Harker's predecessor at Castle Dracula and thus learning his vampiricism at first hand. This actually makes sense and is consistent with the madness that Harker feels is threatening and the brain fever he does in fact suffer, but it is not written into the text, where the aetiology of Renfield's madness is not discussed. Nina Auerbach interestingly links *Dracula* with both *Trilby* and with Freud's *Studies on Hysteria*, which were published between 1893 and 1895. But she also suggests that 'Dr. Seward's relentless attempt to make sense of his patient Renfield's "zoophagy" is a weird forecast of the later Freud rationalizing the obsession of his Wolf Man and Rat Man'.[17] In a more recent article, Stephanie Moss argues that Stoker was extremely likely to have been introduced to Freud's ideas through his wide circle of acquaintances.[18] One of his friends was Frederic Myers, who, with Henry Sidgwick, convened the Society for Psychical Research in 1882. The aim of the Society was to investigate 'that large body of debatable phenomena designated by such terms as mesmeric, psychical and spiritualistic', and to do so 'in the same spirit of exact and unimpassioned inquiry which has enabled Science to solve so many problems'.[19] By 1887, the Society included such luminaries as William Ewart Gladstone, Alfred Lord Tennyson, John Ruskin and Charles Lutwidge Dodgson (Lewis Carroll), and in the following years Myers's serious interest in psychology included his reading of Freud and the introduction of Freud's work to the Society in 1893. There is no evidence that Stoker was a member, but it does seem likely that he would have known of the Society's work through his acquaintance with Myers and with other men who were active in it.[20]

However much Stoker may owe to the interest in and practice of hypnosis amongst Freud and his contemporaries, I would suggest that the case study he presents in Renfield bears few signs of psychoanalytic understanding on the part of the 'therapist'. A Freudian approach is classically retrospective, aimed at uncovering causes; here, on the other hand, there is no mention of a history to the disorder, no attempt to detect causes; the trajectory is forward, and the object of understanding not so much the patient but a situation and the means of bringing that situation under control. Before it has become clear that Renfield is a piece in a jigsaw, Seward's aim has been to 'master' the facts, and there is something almost Faustian about his desire for knowledge. In this first diary entry he indicates his awareness that there is an element of cruelty in his pressing Renfield with questions: 'In my manner of doing it there was, I now see, something of cruelty. I seemed to wish to keep him to the point of his madness – a thing which I avoid with the patients as I would the mouth of hell' (p. 60). His following comments are cryptic to the point of obscurity: '(*Mem.*, under what circumstances would I *not* avoid the pit of hell?) *Omnia Romae vernalia sunt.* Hell has its price! *verb. sap.*' (pp. 60–61). Translating the Latin as 'everything in Rome was up for sale', what he seems to be saying is that there might be something he would go to hell for and that if everything can be bought still everything must be paid for. Like Faust, Seward, it appears, could be tempted to sell his soul for knowledge. His next entry provides further evidence of his ambition:

> Why not advance science in its most difficult and vital aspect – the knowledge of the brain? Had I even the secret of one such mind – did I hold the key to the fancy of even one lunatic – I might advance my own branch of science to a pitch compared with which Burdon-Sanderson's physiology or Ferrier's brain knowledge would be as nothing. If only there were a sufficient cause! I must not think too much of this, or I may be tempted; a good cause might turn the scale with me, for may not I too be of an exceptional brain, congenitally? (p. 71)

Unlike George Eliot's Lydgate, the motivation underlying professional ambition is not the alleviation of human suffering but personal aggrandisement, and these reflections are reminiscent of Macbeth's attempts to avoid temptation. Burdon Sanderson was the author of the standard text on vivisectional methodology, and David Ferrier caused a sensation with his experiments in the West Riding Lunatic Asylum and later with monkeys at King's College, London.[21] He was in fact prosecuted by the anti-vivisectionists, though the case failed to hold. Sir James Crichton Brown, who ran the asylum, allowed him to use the resources of the pathology laboratory, which included 'a liberal supply of pigeons, fowls, guinea-pigs, rabbits, cats, dogs' on which he performed the experiments reported in 1873 that proved that particular movements could be related to specific parts of the brain.[22] It was probably a later report in which he applies some of his ideas to cases at the asylum that lies behind Seward's musings. In 1874, Ferrier examined the case notes and post-mortem reports relating to five patients who had died at the West Riding Asylum.[23] He was particularly anxious to see if there was any relationship between the symptoms described and particular lesions of the brain and to compare his findings with the results of his experiments on animals. It is noticeable that in all cases there were physical symptoms that would not now be associated with insanity. Two patients suffered from epileptic fits, a third had a tumour on the brain, the fourth suffered from aphasia following apoplectic fits (and heavy drinking). The fifth case, the only woman to be discussed, was described as suffering from 'melancholia', a standard category of madness, but the case notes indicate that she had also had fits and strokes. In no case, therefore, was there a psychological condition without an associated physical condition, but although Ferrier concludes that on the whole a relationship can be seen between 'the symptoms during life and lesions of the hemispheres which were revealed after death',[24] nevertheless he has to admit that there are mental conditions which are 'more difficult of exact explanation'.[25] In *Functions of the Brain* Ferrier distinguishes between the sensory and motor functions of the brain;[26] in the West Riding report of 1874 he adds the psychical function, which he is optimistic might also one day be elucidated by physiological experimentation and pathological obser-vation. Seward, it would appear, has ambitions to pursue such elucidation. The mad-doctor recognises the possibility that he is using his pet lunatic as an object of experimental inquiry rather than as a patient for treatment, and he recognises, too, the danger of his own ambitions. His desire for a great 'cause' and his *using* of Renfield are sinister signs that the doctor is aligned with Dracula; and the lunatic is one locus of their struggle for mastery

 Dracula does not, as does *Hard Cash* or even *The Rose and the Key*, offer an explicit condemnation of the medical profession, but there seems to be implicit criticism, not only in this depiction of the medical scientist risking human cruelty in the course of advancing knowledge, but also in the failure of Seward (and Van Helsing) to recognise and respond to the urgency of Renfield's pleas to be removed from the asylum. As Reade had done, Stoker testifies to the stranglehold that the label of madness exerts; Renfield's vehemence in pleading not even for release, but simply to be moved elsewhere, is seen, partly because he is unable to advance a reason, as further evidence of insanity rather than as a legitimate response to circumstances. In his introduction to *A Social History of Madness*, Roy Porter writes of the difficulties of communication faced by people who have been designated mad, since their protests 'have been interpreted as symptoms of their madness'.[27] Yet, he maintains, the stories of the mad *do* relate to the world around them, and should not be ignored: 'The writings of the mad challenge the discourse of the normal [and] the assumption that there exist definitive and unitary standards of truth and falsehood, reality and delusion, is put to the test.'[28] As a zoophagous maniac, Renfield's every utterance and movement is a clue to happenings in the larger world of Dracula's invasion and significance is thus attached to him even before it is quite realised what he signifies. 'If normality condemns madness as irrational, subhuman, perverse', as Porter puts it, then the subhuman, perverse world that Dracula inhabits is similarly condemned as madness.[29] Ironically, it is only when Renfield is speaking with apparent rationality that he is distrusted, since his alignment with the vampire has been taken for granted. Stoker thus stresses the fact that it is precisely madness that enables Dracula to make an ally of Renfield.

It is established in the text that similarities exist between the lunatic and the vampire, and between the vampire and the doctor, but it is also established subtextually that there are points of identification between the lunatic and his doctor. Both, for instance, keep meticulous records, Seward in words, Renfield in figures, and Seward might, figuratively, be said to be preying on Renfield, whom he sees as a distraction from his disappointed love, as Renfield preys on insect and animal life. Seward does, indeed, at one point wonder if the lunatic might think they have something in common as he reflects on the implications of Renfield's scorn of the attendants' fear that he might attack the doctor (p. 107), but the fact that he *is* attacked would seem to indicate that the alternative hypothesis (that Renfield is using him) is more likely. Nevertheless both are implicated in the theme of egoism that is not only so prevalent in Victorian literature, but is, by the end of the century associated with degeneracy. Seward's first diary entry ends with some reflections on this subject. He hypothesises that Renfield is probably more dangerous if unselfish:

> In selfish men caution is as secure an armour for their foes as for themselves ... when self is the fixed point the centripetal force is balanced with the centrifugal: when duty, a cause, etc., is the fixed point, the latter force is paramount, and only accident or a series of accidents can balance it. (p. 61)

In the second entry he records his envy of the lunatic whom he sees as having a strong cause to give purpose to his life, his aim being to absorb many lives as possible. He seems to be unaware at this stage that such a cause is as selfish as any could be and also as dangerous to others, and longs for similar motivation: 'If I only could have as strong a cause as my poor mad friend there, a good, unselfish cause to make me work' (p. 71). Seward's more speculative ruminations are certainly difficult to make sense of and raise the suspicion that he is following his patient into the realm of madness, but once he has enlisted in the chivalric 'cause' against the vampire, his entries become less speculative and consequently less obscure. Before being persuaded of the nature of the cause, however, he has to overcome his own resistance to Van Helsing's suggestion of vampirism and, interestingly, he compares his position to that of 'a mad man, and not a sane one' (p. 193). For him madness lies in 'going in my mind from point to point' without the coherence of an underlying thesis, and he further compares this position to that of 'a novice blundering through a bog in a mist' (p. 193). The imagery here links Seward's state of mind with the 'cloudiness' of Renfield's insanity and the mist of the protean Dracula, but there is a further association with the narrative method of the text, where it is only the reader's preliminary witnessing of the events at Dracula's castle that enable some sort of sense to be made of the fragmentary evidence that comprises the rest of the novel.

Presented with the thesis he demands, Seward still finds difficulty, because, as a representative of science and rationality, he is ill-equipped to understand the alternative world of superstition and the senses, and again he seeks an explanation in the conveniently capacious and ill-defined concept of madness As a doubting Thomas, he is singularly resistant to Van Helsing's theory that Lucy has been rendered Un-Dead through Dracula's attacks: 'Yesterday I was almost willing to accept Van Helsing's monstrous ideas; but now they seem to start out lurid before me as outrages on common sense' (p. 204). The emotive language, though, indicates that it is not just rationality that is offended but the sense of decency, of what is socially acceptable. Against the need to find '*some* rational explanation of all these mysterious things' he balances the possibility that Van Helsing is mad and has done the mysterious things himself, only to find that 'almost as great a marvel' as the vampire theory (p. 204). Yet Van Helsing, too, comes close to doubting his sanity. Clive Leatherdale, in his book *Dracula: The Novel and the Legend*, commenting on the way various characters in the novel come to doubt their sanity, points out that this was not uncommon in nineteenth-century literature.[30] I would certainly agree with this, but I would not agree with the suggestion he then makes 'that Stoker seems almost to be saying that madness is nothing to be afraid of'.[31] Leatherdale quotes an exchange between Seward and Van Helsing in support of this view: ' "Dr. Van Helsing, are you mad?"..."Would I were! ... Madness were easy to bear compared with truth like this" ' (p. 194). But later there is evidence that the contrary opinion is held. Van Helsing and Mina stop at the foot of Dracula's castle at twilight and are there visited by the vampire women. It is this incident that causes him to question his sanity, or at least to fear that others will:

> Let me be accurate in everything, for though you and I have seen some strange things together, you may at the first think that I, Van Helsing, am mad – that the many horrors and the so long strain on nerves has at the last turn [*sic*] my brain. (p. 365)

The stress on accurate reportage recurs throughout this text, frequently being associated with the need to establish the veracity of an individual's experience, as if the ability to record it in detail is proof of sanity. Van Helsing, however, proves his sanity by proving the hypothesis that his vision is not just the result of his memories of Harker's experience 'befooling' (p. 366) him, but has substance. Having completed the 'butcher work' (p. 371) of driving the stake into the bodies of the three women, he can exclaim: 'I am at least sane. Thank God for that mercy at all events, though the proving it has been dreadful' (p. 369). Compared with the greater weight of this instance, the exchange quoted by Leatherdale treats madness as a colloquial hyperbole to stress the awfulness of Lucy's vampirism. The languorous sexuality of the temptation scene and the brutal sexuality of Van Helsing's revenge, however, suggests that sanity for him is equated with potency or virility, or at any rate with the ability to take control of the situation.

Stoker was writing at a time when gender relations were under intense scrutiny, and when many people felt that the traditional roles of both men and women were being threatened. The suffragette movement and the 'New Woman' debate challenged what had seemed to many to be the sacred role of women as 'angels in the house'. At the same time, a number of scandals – in particular the sensational trial and conviction of Oscar Wilde in 1895 – focused on male homosexuality as an undermining of traditional masculinity. Elaine Showalter (1995) has called the *fin de siècle* a period of sexual anarchy. It is not surprising, then, to find that *Dracula* is riddled with fears about gender that are not always very precisely articulated. What I am suggesting here is that the narrative strategy of *Dracula* is an attempt to control the fears revealed in the text. The narrative is largely in the hands of those whom Stoker sees as taking the lead in the society of the future – the young professionals, Seward and Harker, under the tutelage of the magus, Van Helsing. Thus, the sharing of experiences and the collating of evidence is the textual equivalent of the bonding in a common onslaught against the threat of Dracula. To the extent that the novel is also an adventure story (and the final, rather drawn-out, chase back to Transylvania after Dracula does follow the model of an adventure story), it is a tale of male courage and comradeship, of fighting and resourcefulness – the qualities, in fact, of manliness. But both Seward and Harker reveal apprehensions and fears that show how unstable are the boundaries of self-definition. These are particularly acute in the case of Harker.

In the first part of the novel, Harker's situation and the experiences he endures threaten his sense of manhood. Not only is he in the power of a tyrannical older man, but the visitation of the three vampires puts him in a feminised position; they take the lead in sexual advance, while he lies quiet, 'looking out under [his] eyelashes in an agony of delightful anticipation' (p. 38). At the end of the scene, overcome with the horror of what the women might do with Dracula's donation of the child in the bag, like any Victorian heroine, he sinks down unconscious. It is in a feminised position, sitting at the 'little oak table where in old times possibly some fair lady sat to pen ... her ill-spelt love-letter' (p. 36), that Jonathan turns to his journal. At the beginning, he explains that his diary will be a useful aide-mémoire when he comes to tell Mina about his experiences; later, it will become important as a way of recording facts in an increasingly bewildering situation (p. 25). After his encounter with the three vampire women, entering things in his journal is no less than a desperate attempt to preserve his sanity: '... feeling as though my own brain was unhinged or as if the shock had come which must end in its undoing, I turn to my diary for repose. The habit of entering accurately must help to soothe me'

(p. 36). Whatever the temporary relief afforded by the diary-writing, in the end Harker suffers a total breakdown and loses his place as narrator until after Lucy's death. When he resumes, in Chapter 14, his comments are interesting. Mina has shown his Transylvanian diary to Van Helsing, who has written to her to vouch for its truth. This validation of his experiences has, he then writes, 'made a new man of me. It was the doubt as to the reality of the whole thing that knocked me over. I felt impotent, and in the dark, and distrustful' (pp. 187–88). A connection is thus made between having experiences that are verified by a third party, masculinisation and writing; once Harker can be sure that he was not simply hallucinating, he can be confident of his manhood, and can again write and therefore take an active role as a narrator.

There is a second threat to Harker's masculinity through the way in which he is drawn into closer and closer identification with the Count – or rather in the way that they seem to change places in a grotesque sort of doubling that is characteristic of Gothic writing. In the first section of the novel, Dracula, with vampiric appetite, sucks information out of the young lawyer before stealing the clothes he has worn on his journey to the castle, and, carrying 'the terrible bag' that has contained the child-victim, allows people to believe not only that Harker has left the castle, but that he is responsible for the child's disappearance. Harker is horrified when he sees the non-human way in which the Count crawls, head first, down the wall, but nevertheless imitates him when it seems to be the only way of getting out of the castle. Furthermore, after commenting on the Count's assiduous letter-writing, he himself is put to that activity by the Count before being left alone in the castle with 'those awful women' (p. 40). Later it appears that Dracula is adopting Harker's persona in an even more inti- mate context. When Seward describes the scene in which Dracula visits Mina for the first time, the scene that the men interrupt, it is as though he is describing a tableau. Tableaux vivants –moments or scenes in which the action is 'frozen' for dramatic effect – were very popular in the theatre of the time, and Stoker's own theatrical background clearly influences his writing in this scene. Since there is so little movement, Seward can dwell on the details of Harker's position, of the pose held by Dracula and Mina, of Dracula's expression of fury at the interruption, and of Mina's state after his disappearance – all of which intensifies the horror of the situation and makes a great impact. He incorporates an image to convey more dramati- cally the effect of the Count's forcing Mina to suck the blood from his chest, comparing the action with that of a child forcing a kitten to drink from a saucer of milk. Other comparisons can be made, however. Not only does the relation between them mimic that of a mother suckling her child, but, given that this is a woman sucking a man, it is impossible to avoid the suggestion that this is an act of *fellatio*, and that Mina's scream, 'so wild, so ear-piercing, so despairing', is in fact the cry of an anguished, frustrated woman.

Seward's abbreviated retelling of the episode for Harker's benefit is very brief, containing none of the gory details, and, naturally enough, leaving out the description of Harker himself lying on the bed, either asleep or in some sleeplike state, flushed and breathing heavily. Instead, he describes how Harker, comforting Mina in his arms, is himself listening to this account. In 'The Vampire in the Looking-Glass', Philip Martin (1988) discusses the implications of the differences in detail between these two accounts, and I should like to compare my interpretation with his, because I think that something rather suggestive emerges out of the conjunction.[32] The crucial passage from the second account is this:

> I told him exactly what had happened, and he listened with seeming impassiveness; but his nostrils twitched and his eyes blazed as I told how the ruthless hands of the Count had held his wife in that terrible and horrid position, with her mouth to the open wound in his breast. It interested me, even at that moment, to see that whilst the face of white set passion worked convulsively over the bowed head, the hands tenderly and lovingly stroked the ruffled hair.
> (p. 284)

Martin is particularly concerned with the second sentence quoted above, and, assuming that the face and the hands referred to here belong to Dracula, sees it as evidence of some tenderness in Dracula's dealings with women. But I think there is an ambiguity as to whose face and hands are being referred to, and an alternative explanation can be offered. As Martin (1988) acknowledges, it is physiologically impossible for Dracula to have one hand holding Mina's hands away from their bodies, the other on her neck (as has been described in the first account of the scene), *and* at the same time to be stroking her hair. Mina's account, which comes later, corroborates Seward's first description of their position, so Martin, adopting a psychoanalytical approach, puts forward the idea that Seward is experiencing the confusion of a child who interrupts its parents during intercourse and cannot be sure whether the father is giving the mother pleasure or pain. Rather more straightforwardly, however, I would suggest that the face and the hands are those of Harker, since the lead-up to the passage

I have just quoted says: 'He [Harker] put out his arms and folded her to his breast … He looked at us over her bowed head … his mouth was set as steel' (p. 284). It is Harker's face whose twitching nostrils and blazing eyes betray his passion, and contrast with the tenderness of his loving hands, so different from the 'ruthless' hands of Dracula. By slipping so easily from one tableau (Dracula forcing Mina to drink blood from his chest) to the other (Harker holding his wife to his breast and comforting her by stroking her hair), Seward unconsciously coalesces the two male figures. Dracula has usurped Harker's marital position, and Seward's accounts emphasise that usurpation by allowing one figure to stand so easily for the other.

The scene is described for yet a third time, this time from the point of view of the female participant. Seward, of course, has not been able to say anything about Mina's feelings; he has described simply what is before his eyes. Mina has already related one of the vampire's earlier visits; ignorant of what was really happening, she was aware, like Lucy, only of two red eyes emerging out of a strange, invasive mist, while she 'lay still and endured' (p. 258). When Dracula arrives for this, the third climactic visit, she remembers again how he materialised out of mist in her room. She describes no longing or sexual fascination, as Harker and Van Helsing do, but this time her paralysis is not simply a matter of endurance; she emphasises her bewilderment, but says that 'strangely enough, I did not want to hinder him' (p. 287). Furthermore, her horrified way of leaving her sentence unfinished ('I must either suffocate or swallow some of the—', p. 288) allows the reader to substitute 'blood', 'milk' or 'semen' for the missing word. This is one of the few occasions on which we have Dracula's words. His statement that she is now 'flesh of my flesh' both parodies the statement in the marriage service that husband and wife 'shall be one flesh' and underlines the sexual nature of his attack. Furthermore, his assumption of a conjugal role is suggested in his assurance that she will henceforth be his 'companion and helper' (p. 288), a role she has hitherto been playing as Mrs Harker. Mina's account of the scene, then, provides further evidence of Dracula's usurpation of Harker's marital role.

David Punter maintains that Dracula attacks 'the whole concept of morality by preying upon and liberating aspects of the personality which are not under moral control'.[33] I would argue, however, that it is not so much a matter of Dracula taking advantage of insufficient moral control, but of actually breaking down the barriers of bourgeois socialisation through his hypnotic skills. Like a snake, the vampire is able to fascinate his victims into paralysis and compliance by a sort of mesmeric or hypnotic

process that was itself a matter of intense interest and debate in the nineteenth century. Mesmerism, or 'animal magnetism' was a theory and practice that had been promoted by Franz Anton Mesmer in pre-revolutionary
France and was based on the idea of a universal energy that manifested
itself in a fluid or force that flowed between people and the cosmos. It was
popularised in Britain by Dickens's friend John Elliotson, whose position
as a scientist helped to confer respectability on a theory that was attractive
to cranks.[34] Elliotson, however, was also partly responsible for the disre-
pute into which mesmerism fell, since he was in the habit of giving public
displays, and his career at University College ended with the scandal
aroused by the case of the Okey sisters, which involved charges of sexual
manipulation. The popularity of mesmerism in the 1830s, '40s and '50s
gradually waned as hypnotism gained favour owing to the work of James
Braid in England and Charcot in France. Abandoning the notion of mesmeric fluid, hypnotism emphasised the importance of the subject's psychological state, the 'suggestibility' that governed the hypnotist's chance of
exerting power, and thus also aroused distrust since it could be equated
with mental despotism.[35]

That Stoker was familiar with the work of Charcot is evident from the
text. In an important scene, Van Helsing tries to combat Seward's scientific arrogance:

> 'Do you not think that there are things which you cannot understand, and yet
> which are; that some people see things that others cannot? ... I suppose now you
> do not believe in corporeal transference. No? Nor in materialization. No? Nor
> in astral bodies. No? Nor in the reading of thought. No? Nor in hypnotism –'
> 'Yes,' I said. 'Charcot has proved that pretty well.' (p. 191)

Van Helsing here includes hypnotism in a list of concepts belonging to the
paranormal, yet it proves, from Seward's acceptance, to be a process that
has acquired at least partial scientific respectability. As Jenny Bourne Taylor
points out, mesmerism was a peculiarly fruitful subject for the nineteenth
century novelist:

> Mesmerism ... made up an extraordinarily rich and flexible discourse, provid-
> ing a set of terms and references that could invoke, in a simultaneously realis-
> tic and figurative way, processes of dominance and subordination, hidden
> forces within the self, secret traces of the past, links between the body and the
> surrounding world and the psychic and the physical, correspondences and
> modes of transference between self and other.[36]

The mythic approach of *Dracula* draws on all these aspects of a process that, as the quotation above shows, is seen as both scientific and mysterious, but I shall concentrate on its significance in the structuring of power relations in the book.

Mesmerism or hypnosis is exerted in some degree by three different characters, linked always with the establishing of dominance and subordination. Least explicit are the references to the power of Seward's eye. Commenting on the doctor in generally favourable terms, Lucy considers 'what a wonderful power he must have over his patients' (p. 55). Like Antomarchi in *The Rose and the Key*, Seward possesses an unflinching gaze: 'He has a curious habit of looking one straight in the face, as if trying to read one's thoughts' (p. 55). But Seward's power extends only to his patients; although he tells Lucy that she affords him 'a curious psychological study' (p. 55), his behaviour towards her implicitly acknowledges her power over him, and, like Renfield, he makes obeisance to a higher authority. His power over his patient is limited too, because he is in contest with Dracula who is stronger.

When first the lunatic tries to resist him, Dracula subdues Renfield by a sort of mesmeric process combined with the tempting offer of lives:

> He held up His hand, and they all [the rats] stopped; and I thought He seemed to be saying: 'All these lives will I give you, ay, and many more and greater … if you will fall down and worship me!' And then a red cloud, like the colour of blood, seemed to close over my eyes; and before I knew what I was doing, I found myself opening the sash and saying to Him: 'Come in, Lord and Master!' (p. 279)

In fact, despite the physical trappings, which might seem to suggest mesmerism rather than hypnotism, I would suggest that what is essential here is Renfield's psychological state, which, it has already been established in the text, is eminently susceptible to Dracula's persuasion. His reference to the voice is so tentative ('I thought He seemed to be saying') that it might be read as merely the externalisation of his own desire, and the cloud 'the colour of blood', which seems to close over his eyes, might be seen to represent his own obsession with blood. 'Cloudiness' is indeed a word that is attached to insanity by Seward (p. 269). In addition, the clear reference to the tempting of Christ as described in Luke 4.5–7 superimposes a spiritual coding through which the mesmerist acquires satanic overtones, as do those other fictional mesmerists, Antomarchi and Svengali.

Dracula appears to have easy access also to the volition of Lucy, who,

like Renfield, has shown a susceptibility to Dracula's attentions in her som-
nambulism. She, too, describes the feeling of powerlessness: 'I tried to stir,
but there was some spell upon me ...' (p. 43). In neither of her accounts
of Dracula's attacks is she able to remember what has actually happened in
terms of person-to-person contact. The Whitby encounter is rendered in
mystical terms and elemental imagery with Dracula's presence indicated
solely through the red eyes and the howling of dogs. This allows for a flex-
ibility of interpretation, but the parallel with Renfield lends weight to the
suggestion that Dracula is in fact offering a temptation and that by submitting to his desires, Lucy is following the dictates of her subconscious.
Furthermore the earliest, quite explicit, instance of vampiric hypnotism in
the text shows Jonathan Harker on the point of succumbing to primitive
desires: 'I felt myself struggling to awake to some call of my instincts; nay,
my very soul was struggling and my half-remembered sensibilities were
striving to answer the call. I was becoming hypnotized!' (p. 44). It is interesting that he expresses the process as one of struggling to awake, when the
usual image is of being put to sleep, as if the life the three women offer him
is one of greater awareness and activity. His earlier encounter with them
has left no doubt as to his 'wicked, burning desire' for their kisses (p. 37).
The novel seems, then, so far as the male victim is concerned, to be com-
municating anxieties about the relaxation of conscious self-control which
can lead to the unleashing of instincts inimical to the respectability and
order of society, but it also seems to reflect current fears about the possibility of sexual manipulation of the hypnotised female subject, in the
course of which she is infected with a predatory sexuality that threatens the
most cherished values of Victorian society.

Mina, too, has suffered the Count's hypnotic attentions and, like
Harker, discovered that his quasi-sexual advances were not entirely unwel-
come: 'strangely enough, I did not want to hinder him' (p. 287). The cry
with which she responds to Dracula's disappearance after he has been discovered *in flagrante delicto* is ambiguous; it seems to be interpreted by the
men as an agonised awareness of her contamination, but, as I have already
said, it could equally well represent the frustration of interrupted sex.
Dracula's gross physical abuse secures him partial psychological mastery of
Mina who then, in effect, offers herself as a traumatised (hysterical) subject
to the hypnotic attentions of the physician/magician, Van Helsing.
Oscillating between allegiance to the vampire and obedience to the
vampire hunter, Mina is put into a position analogous with Renfield's, who
has been the locus of a struggle between Dracula and Seward. Van Helsing

thus takes over Seward's place as Dracula's opponent, but, since he is forced to fight according to the rules of superstition and folklore, the professor is no more a representative of scientific procedure than is Dracula himself. His ability to hypnotise Mina, for instance, is limited by the laws that determine the vampire's cycle of power, and his entry into her mind is governed by a similar condition to that ruling a vampire's first entry anywhere, which must be by invitation.

Peter Keating puts *Dracula* in a tradition of literature which sees facts and science as obscuring rather than revealing the truth about life; in fiction of this kind 'true knowledge is attained not by marching doggedly forward with each scientific discovery, but by moving further and further back to a point where the mind is no longer corrupted by modern scientific reasoning'.[37] There is, however, a binary opposition informing this approach that the text of *Dracula* questions. Scientific fact is not established purely through reasoning, but, particularly in the nineteenth century, on the basis of empiricism. The recording, collating and comparison that leads to the deduction of vampirism at work in the 1890s amounts to the establishment by scientific methods of facts that folklore and superstition had long recognised without feeling the need of proof. Where the problem lies in this case is in the apparent uncovering of facts that contradict customary experience and expectations; what defies belief is the insistence that the dead will not necessarily lie down, and this is as likely to be resisted by the reader as it is by the characters in the novel. Lacking direct sensory experience, then, the reader must needs see what the book has to say as 'real' on a different basis – if indeed it is seen a real at all – and interpret the text as allegorical, poetic, mythic, at any rate symbolic in one way or another. In her volume on fantasy literature, Rosemary Jackson, working on a basis of Todorov's formulation, describes the fantastic mode as confounding 'elements of both the marvellous and the mimetic'. She goes on: 'They [fantastic narratives] assert that what they are telling is real – relying upon all the conventions of realistic fiction to do so – and then they proceed to break that assumption of realism by introducing what – within those terms – is manifestly unreal'.[38] Situated between the marvellous and the mimetic, fantasy borrows 'the extravagance of one and the ordinariness of the other' (p. 35). Since fantasy bears a problematic relationship with 'reality', then, it raises questions about the nature of reality and truth which cannot be answered in as straightforward a way as they can be in, say, allegory, where a meaning can be 'read off' from the story. Nor can the ambiguities of fantasy be interpreted in terms of the metaphorical constuctions of poetry, since in the former the vehicle has actually *become* the tenor. As Jackson says, 'the fantastic cannot be placed alongside allegory nor poetry, for it resists both the conceptualizations of the first and the metaphorical structures of the second' (p. 41). Fantasy's concern with the unseen and the unsaid, and its dislocation of the 'normal' lead to a characteristic preoccupation with certain themes including insanity. Through the concept of hallucination, insanity offers the possibility of reconciling fantasy with reality by pathologising the power of the imagination, hence, in *Dracula*, the frequent references to insanity on the part of characters who are unable to assimilate otherwise experiences that so radically subvert their expectations.

On the other hand, the one character who is, as far as the text is concerned, indubitably mad, is not, after the very first diary entry, accused of suffering from delusions; what particularly interests his doctor is, first, his 'zoophagous' habits and, second, his swings of mood. Like Bersicker, the wolf that escapes from London zoo only to return 'in a sort of penitent mood' to be 'received and petted like a sort of vulpine prodigal son' (p. 140), Renfield is seen as a phenomenon of nature, another of the indices of Dracula's whereabouts. The wolf's name, with its connotations of frenzy, and the degree to which he is personified brings him close in status to Renfield, who is represented as animalistic, as is also, of course, Dracula. Underlining the association between the wolf and Dracula is its name. The *Oxford English Dictionary* attributes the word 'berserk' to 'a wild Norse warrior, who fought on the battle-field with a frenzied fury known as the "berserker rage" ', and Van Helsing refers to such a 'berserker Icelander' in his long disquisition on vampirism (p. 239). The vampirism which is, as Van Helsing points out, part and parcel of the animal kingdom, enters into the human world by means of the fantastic category of being, the 'Un-Dead', but also through a madman's distorted understanding of scriptural teaching. These two characters might seem to stand for opposed ways of thinking, since Dracula represents what can only be understood in terms of ancient beliefs and folkloric values and Renfield represents an object for scientific scrutiny, but the polarity is obscured by a conceptual framework that owes as much to outmoded conventions as it does to the theories of contemporary medical science.

It is partly through the ambiguous figure of the lunatic that Dracula's behaviour is interpreted so as to secure a relevance that cannot be simply dismissed as fantasy. If through the text's rhetoric vampiric behaviour is both naturalised (blood is their 'pabulum') and pathologised (they are parasites who spread disease), Dracula's relationship with Renfield extends still further the pathological implications of his behaviour. Their shared obsession with blood and with the colonising of lives that is categorised as mania on the part of Renfield extends the label of madness and its connotations of immorality to Dracula also. But the comparison works both ways, and if the taint of madness paradoxically reduces the vampire to a kind of normality, so the symbiotic relationship with Dracula extends the range of implications contained in the idea of insanity. When he describes his last encounter with the vampire, Renfield shows a peculiar self-awareness that amounts almost to double identity. Drawing on the conventional attributes of the mad, he says: 'I had heard that madmen have unnatural strength; and as I knew I was a madman – at times anyhow – I resolved to use my power' (p. 280). Renfield's strength is nothing, however, compared with Dracula's greater psychic and, it turns out, physical power and he is literally smashed up. Although some moral remnants are salvaged that procure him an undeniable humanity and allow him to be the narrator of the last episode in his own story, he is seen, finally, as the weakness in the defences surrounding Mina, the representative of virtue.

But if madness seems to be an endemic degeneracy through which foreign influences of a far more dangerous degeneracy can attack civilised society, there is a range of comparisons that still further undermines the relative security that is apparently offered by confinement in a lunatic asylum, for not all insanity is so confined. By allowing most of the characters to doubt their sanity at one time or another and by hinting at an affinity between the lunatic and his doctor, the novel questions the possibility of any easy distinction between sanity and madness, just as it blurs the boundaries between science and superstition, and the final disposal of both Dracula and Renfield is no sure guarantee that the dangers they represent will not return. Dracula is disposed of satisfactorily on the level of explicit action, thus removing the threat to the social and moral order, but the implications of the earlier responses of the other characters and the mixed blood of Mina's child allow for doubts as to whether the threat is entirely dispelled.

Dracula is a novel of ambiguities and contradictions, in which the generic mixture of realism and fantasy is mirrored in the two modes of understanding and interpretation: the folkloric or superstitious, and the scientific. It presents a vision of a society in which the attempt to live according to traditional Christian or chivalric moral codes is likely to be defeated by the inexorable workings of biological determinism. Madness is a focal point. Its representation in this novel incorporates the customary conception of insanity as the loss of self-control which can lead, if unrestrained, to violent behaviour, thus relating the human to the animal. Although the lunatic is seen almost entirely from the outside, with no attempt to penetrate his mind, the emphasis is on his patterns of behaviour; there is little description of his physical appearance and thus no reference to traditional visual iconography. However, traditional ways of understanding are incorporated in the references to ancient humoral theories of personality. At the same time the attempts by the physician to understand the lunatic employ the concepts of contemporary medical discourse, and the novel as a whole draws on the most up-to-date ideas relating to hypnosis, on the one hand, and, on the other hand, cerebral physiology. This can be related to the opposition running through the whole novel between the mind as a mystery and the mind as a locus for scientific experimentation and research. Madness is seen as a threat to masculinity because it leads to a diminution of autonomy, as in so many of the novels I have discussed. The madman is a subject for study, a problem to be solved; he is not regarded as a suffering individual to be cured. In the solipsism of his lunacy he is vulnerable to psychic invasion, just as a society that is fragmented, weak and confused is prey to malign alien influence, against which the only defence is unselfish cooperation.

Notes

1 Max Nordau, *Degeneration* [1895] (Nebraska: University of Nebraska, 1993), p. 2.
2 Nordau, *Degeneration*, p. 17.
3 Nordau, *Degeneration*, p. 18.
4 Jonathan Dollimore, 'Perversion, Degeneration, and the Death Drive', in Andrew H. Miller and James Eli Adams (eds), *Sexualities in Victorian Britain*, (Bloomington, IN: Indiana University Press, 1996), p. 96.
5 Maudsley, *Pathology of Mind*, p. 12.
6 Maudsley, *Pathology of Mind*, p. 32.
7 Maudsley, *Pathology of Mind*, p. 85.
8 Maudsley, *Pathology of Mind*, p. 85.
9 William Greenslade, *Degeneration, Culture and the Novel, 1880–1940* (Cambridge: Cambridge University Press, 1994), p. 25.
10 Christopher Frayling, *Vampyres: Lord Byron to Count Dracula* (London: Faber & Faber, 1991), p. 35. Frayling's discussion of Stoker's working and research papers for *Dracula* shows that Stoker started preparing for the novel in March 1890.
11 Clive Leatherdale, *The Origins of Dracula* (London: William Kimber, 1987), mentions

particularly Pettigrew's *On Superstitions Connected with the History and Practice of Medicine and Surgery.*

12 David Seed, 'The Narrative Method of *Dracula*', *Nineteenth-Century Fiction*, 40 (1985), pp. 61–75 (65).

13 Bram Stoker, *Dracula* [1897], ed. Maud Ellman (Oxford: Oxford University Press, 1998), p. 61. All subsequent references are to this edition and are incorporated in the text.

14 The term 'manic-depression' was not yet in general currency. Daniel Hack, *Tuke's A Dictionary of Psychological Medicine*, 2 vols (London: J. & A. Churchill, 1892) does not include it amongst the other manic disorders.

15 David Punter, *The Literature of Terror: A History of Gothic Fictions from 1765 to the Present Day* (London: Longman, 1980), p. 261.

16 Daniel Pick, ' "Terrors of the Night": *Dracula* and "Degeneration" in the Late Nineteenth Century', *Critical Quarterly*, 30 (1988), pp. 71–87 (80).

17 Nina Auerbach, 'Magi and Maidens: The Romance of the Victorian Freud', *Critical Inquiry*, 8 (1981–82), pp. 281–300 (290).

18 Stephanie Moss, 'Bram Stoker and the Society for Psychical Research', in Elizabeth Miller (ed.), *Dracula: The Shade and the Shadow* (Westcliffe-on-Sea: Desert Island Books, 1998), pp. 82–92.

19 Moss, 'Bram Stoker', p. 85.

20 Barbara Belford, *Bram Stoker: A Biography of the Author of 'Dracula'* (London: Weidenfeld & Nicolson, 1996), pp. 212–13, makes the unsupported statement that Stoker attended the meeting at which Freud's work was introduced.

21 For information about Burdon Sanderson, David Ferrier and the anti-vivisection movement, I am indebted to Robert Maxwell Young, *Mind, Brain and Adaptation in the Nineteenth Century: Cerebral Localization and Its Biological Context from Gall to Ferrier* (Oxford: Clarendon Press, 1970), Richard D. French, *Antivivisection and Medical Science in Victorian Society* (Princeton, NJ: Princeton University Press, 1975), and Nicolaas A. Rupke (ed.), *Vivisection in Historical Perspective* (London: Croom Helm, 1987).

22 David Ferrier, 'Experimental Researches in Cerebral Physiology and Pathology', in *The West Riding Lunatic Asylum Reports*, ed. J. Crichton Brown, vol. 3, 1873, pp. 30–96 (30).

23 Ferrier, *Reports*, vol. 4, 1874, pp. 30–62.

24 Ferrier, *Reports*, vol. 4, 1874, p. 61.

25 Ferrier, *Reports*, vol. 4, 1874, p. 59.

26 David Ferrier, *Functions of the Brain* [1876], facsimile of 2nd edition (London: Routledge/Thoemmes Press, 2000).

27 Roy Porter, *A Social History of Madness: Stories of the Insane* (London: Weidenfeld & Nicolson, 1987), p. 5.

28 Porter, *History of Madness*, p. 3.

29 Porter, *History of Madness*, p. 3.

30 Guy de Maupassant's short story 'The Horla' (1887) is a disturbing dramatisation of the quandary in which not only the sufferer but the observer is placed when faced with invisible persecution.

31 Clive Leatherdale, *Dracula: The Novel and the Legend* (Wellingborough: Aquarian

Press, 1985), p. 170.

32 Philip Martin, 'The Vampire in the Looking-Glass: Reflection and Projection in Bram
    Stoker's *Dracula*', in C. Bloom, B. Docherty, I. Gibb and K. Shand (eds), *Nineteenth-
    Century Suspense: From Poe to C. Doyle* (London: Macmillan, 1988), pp. 80–92.

33 Punter, *Literature of Terror*, p. 263.

34 The case of James Tilley Matthews (see Porter, *History of Madness*, pp. 55–59) illustrates
    the ease with which belief in mesmeric rays could be taken as a symptom of insanity.

35 Fred Kaplan, *Dickens and Mesmerism: The Hidden Springs of Fiction* (Princeton, NJ:
    Princeton University Press, 1975), gives a general account of mesmerism in England.
    Michael J. Clark, 'The Rejection of Psychological Approaches to Mental Disorder in
    Late Nineteenth-Century British Psychiatry', in Andrew Scull (ed.), *Madhouses, Mad-
    Doctors and Madmen* (London: Athlone Press, 1981), pp. 271–312, summarises atti-
    tudes to hypnosis as a method of mental treatment in the latter part of the century.
    Taylor, *Secret Theatre*, offers a comprehensive and interesting overview, indicating the
    relevance of the mesmerism/hypnotism debate for fictional writing. The most exten-
    sive study, however, is by Alison Winter, *Mesmerized: Powers of Mind in Victorian
    Britain* (Chicago: University of Chicago Press, 1998).

36 Taylor, *Secret Theatre*, p. 58.

37 Peter Keating, *The Haunted Study: A Social History of the English Novel, 1875–1914*
    (London: Fontana Press, 1991), p. 350.

38 Jackson, *Fantasy*, p. 34.

Conclusion

It is now twenty years since Elaine Showalter's ground-breaking study *The Female Malady* was published. This wonderfully rich and suggestive book advances the thesis that 'madness, even when experienced by men, is metaphorically and symbolically represented as feminine: a female malady' (p. 4). Showalter's study of the cultural history of madness as a female malady covers the representation of madwomen in literary, clinical and legal texts, and in visual media. I have confined my area of research to the nineteenth century and furthermore to literary representations of mad men, in an attempt to investigate her claim that madness is a female malady. In choosing which texts to discuss, I decided on a wide coverage that would combine some familiar novels and a well-known poem, as well as lesser-known texts. I did not aim for a comprehensive survey of the literature, since I wanted to be able to analyse the texts in some detail. Madness is implied or suggested in many nineteenth-century novels, and occurs in others as a passing feature. In the texts discussed here the madness is explicit and it is a significant feature of the narrative. I have looked at the way mad men are represented and at the way that madness functions in the texts with the aim of seeing if the onset of madness does indeed threaten a man's masculinity, whether it is the result of effeminacy, whether madness puts men into a feminised position. I was also interested to see what the treatment of men's madness in fiction might say more generally about masculinity and a man's role in society.

In his study of insanity, *On Obscure Diseases of the Brain*, Forbes Winslow is scathing about the accuracy of literary depictions of insanity, with the honourable and not entirely unexpected exception of Shakespeare. What I hope my study has shown, however, is that clinical accuracy is not necessarily the – or the only – aim of literary representations of madness. Certain categories, such as monomania, brain fever, idiocy or moral insanity; or belief in the hereditary nature of insanity, or in degeneration, did indeed enter into imaginative writing as they did into general currency. However, the business of creative writers is not simply documentary accuracy, so although standard medical terms may be employed, depictions of insanity are also influenced by older conventions of showing madness and by themes running through the texts. Elaine Showalter draws attention to the fashion for photographing mad women from the middle of the nineteenth century. But it was not only mad women who were the object of a portraying gaze; there was a long tradition of the visual representation of madness which was interested in both men and women. In most of the novels discussed here that have a third-person narrator, in which therefore the mad man can be objectified, physical appearance is important, and usually draws on a traditional iconography of madness. Thus, for instance, the representation of Barnaby Rudge is in many ways congruent with nineteenth-century documentary descriptions of idiots, but in other respects his portrayal draws on iconographic features of mania or melancholy. The exception is Renfield in *Dracula*, who is seen less in terms of appearance than of behavioural patterns, and whose physician refers to the long-established humoral theory. Renfield is exceptional in another way, since his behaviour so defeats understanding in terms of contemporary nosology that a new category of madness has to be coined, and this of course is related to the wider concerns of the novel. Also prevalent in imaginative writing right up to the end of the century is the image of the mad man as an animal or wild beast. This was an idea that nineteenth-century commentators on madness and its treatment saw as characteristic of the unenlightened eighteenth century, contrasting it with the more humane attitude of their own times, but we see it persisting in more imaginative representations of madness, because of its association with the main conception of madness that runs through both imaginative and documentary literature, whether it concerns mad men or mad women: that of madness as the loss of self-control.

There are two other themes that are recurrent in the depictions of madness I have discussed, both again linked with the issue of control. Early writers about hysteria wrote about the wandering womb. In the novels studied here it is the men themselves who wander, whether on the Continent or about the streets of London. As the sufferer loses control of his mind, the image of his wandering body is the physical expression of the psychological disturbance, and at the same time, because so often the wanderer is dislocated from his surroundings, articulates in visual terms the idea of alienation. *Maud* is the only text studied in this book where madness is not reflected in straying; it is confined within the limits of the

form which so closely correlates with the intense inwardness of the obsessive mind. Renfield, too, is confined rather more conventionally in an
asylum, but in this novel the wandering of insanity is transferred onto
his fantastical counterpart, the aberrant figure of Dracula himself.
Confinement is the other recurrent theme. Whether in the asylum or not,
it is seen as one way of containing or restraining the man who has lost
control. The speaker of *Maud*, George Fausset, St John Aylott and Renfield
are all confined in asylums, and Barnaby is confined in prison. Trevelyan
puts himself in voluntary confinement in Casalunga, and Basil is confined
through physical weakness in his own home. In all these cases confinement
is a way of limiting a man's autonomy and of course his sphere of action;
he is, in fact, in a feminised position where others take control. The
extreme case of depriving a man of independence is represented through
the issue of wrongful confinement, where the man loses his power of deciding his own fate, not because he is mad, but because of machinations on
the part of relatives, usually for financial reasons.

Writing about madness, whether in fiction or non-fiction, whether the
commentators come from a medical, a religious or a philosophical background, hovers between a medical and an ethical approach, within which
the recommendation of self-control as a prophylactic sits easily. Self-
control facilitates the adjustment between the individual and the rest of
society, counteracting the natural human tendency towards egoism. It is
particularly important in a man, because he was expected to control others,
both in the domestic sphere and in the wider social context. *Barnaby Rudge*
expresses fears about the loss of social control which results when political
leaders are not capable of exercising their power properly, and are themselves manipulated by others who are self-interested. *Dracula* expresses
fears about the degeneration of society unless excessive egoism is counter-
attacked by the control of personal interest and by collaboration. But
although *Barnaby Rudge* is an historical novel, it is also a novel about family
relations and heredity. Through the figure of an idiot Dickens dramatises
the tyranny of the past over the present at the personal level. Fathers and
indeed family life are notably absent from *Dracula*, but a metaphorical
transformation takes place whereby Van Helsing becomes the surrogate
father, and the band of crusaders become brothers with Mina as their
'mother'. In all the other texts, however, madness is shown as rooted in the
domestic context. I have referred to John Tosh's work in establishing the
importance of domesticity in establishing a young man's sense of masculinity, and later in defining his role as householder, husband and father.

What these novels and the poem demonstrate is the potential for tension and conflict in domestic relationships and the consequent madness when a man fails to acquire or maintain the appropriate control.

Although these novels are interested in the feminine qualities of men, and the degree to which the possession of such qualities may compromise their masculinity, I would suggest that it is too limiting, at least so far as literary representations are concerned, to suggest that when they become mad they are succumbing to a female malady. Certainly there are situations, associated with the loss of control, when men find themselves in a feminised position, but madness in the texts discussed here is shown as being inherently linked with a man's sense of his own masculinity. In this way the representation of madness in imaginative writing exposes and explores some of the fears, ambiguities and hazards of achieving and maintaining masculinity in a patriarchal society.

Bibliography

Primary sources

A Constant Observer, *Sketches in Bedlam; or Characteristic Traits of Insanity* (London: Sherwood, Jones & Co., 1824).

Anon., 'The Cure of Sick Minds', *Household Words*, 19 (1859), pp. 415–18.

——, 'Idiots Again', *Household Words*, 10 (1854), pp. 197–200.

——, 'Insanity and Madhouses', *Quarterly Review*, 15 (1816), pp. 388–417.

——, 'Madness in Novels', *The Spectator*, 3 February 1866, pp. 134–35.

——, 'The Star of Bethlehem', *Household Words*, 16 (1857), pp. 145–50.

——, 'Things within Dr.Conolly's Remembrance', *Household Words*, 16 (1857), pp. 518–23.

——, 'The Treatment of the Insane', *Household Words*, 3 (1851), pp. 572–76.

Ainsworth, Harrison W., *Jack Sheppard, a Romance* (London: Richard Bentley, 1839).

Allen, Matthew, *Essay on the Classification of the Insane* (London: John Taylor, 1838).

Arnold, Thomas, *Observations on the Nature, Kinds, Causes and Prevention of Insanity*, 2 vols (London: Richard Phillips, 1806).

Braddon, Mary Elizabeth, *The Fatal Three* [1888] (Stroud: Sutton Publishing Ltd, 1997).

——, *The Fatal Three* (Simpkin, Marshall & Co., no date).

——, *Lady Audley's Secret* [1862], ed. David Skilton, The World's Classics (Oxford: Oxford University Press, 1987).

——, *Taken at the Flood* [1874], (London: Simpkin, Marshall, Hamilton, Kent & Co., 1890).

——, *The Trail of the Serpent* [1861] (New York: The Modern Library, 2003).

Brontë, Charlotte, *Jane Eyre* [1847], ed. Margaret Smith, The World's Classics (Oxford: Oxford University Press, 2000).

Browne, W.A.F, *What Asylums Were, Are and Ought to Be* (Edinburgh: A. & C. Black, 1837).

Browning, Robert, *The Poems*, vol. 1, ed. John Pettigrew, supplemented and completed by Thomas J. Collins (Harmondsworth: Penguin, 1981).

Cockton, Henry, *The Life and Adventures of Valentine Vox, the Ventriloquist* (London: Robert Tyas, 1840).

Collins, Wilkie, *Armadale* [1866], The World's Classics (Oxford: Oxford University Press, 1989).

——, *Basil* [1852], The World's Classics (Oxford: Oxford University Press, 1990).

——, *The Critical Heritage*, ed. Norman Page (London: Routledge & Kegan Paul, 1974).

——, *The Dead Secret* [1857], Pocket Classics (Gloucester: Alan Sutton Publishing Ltd, 1986).

——, *Jezebel's Daughter* [1888], Pocket Classics (Gloucester: Alan Sutton Publishing Ltd, 1995).

——, *The Law and the Lady* [1875], ed. David Skilton (Harmondsworth: Penguin, 1998).

——, 'A Mad Marriage', in *Miss or Mrs* (London: Chatto & Windus, 1875), pp. 253–98.

——, 'Mad Monkton', in *The Queen of Hearts* (London: Chatto & Windus, 1875), pp. 106–63.

——, *The Woman in White* [1860], ed. John Sutherland, The World's Classics (Oxford: Oxford University Press, 1996).

Conolly, John, *The Construction and Government of Lunatic Asylums* [1847], (London: Dawsons of Pall Mall, 1968).

——, *An Inquiry Concerning the Indications of Insanity* [1830] (London: Dawsons of Pall Mall, 1964).

Dallas, E.S., *The Gay Science*, 2 vols (London: Chapman & Hall, 1866).

Dickens, Charles, *American Notes* [1842] (Harmondsworth: Penguin, 1972).

——, *Barnaby Rudge* [1841], ed. Gordon Spence (Harmondsworth: Penguin, 1973).

——, *David Copperfield* [1850] (Harmondsworth: Penguin, 1984).

——, *Sketches by Boz* [1836], The New Oxford Illustrated Dickens (London: Oxford University Press, 1957).

——, with Wills, W.H., 'A Curious Dance Round the Christmas Tree', *Household Words*, 4 (1852), pp. 385–89.

——, 'The Sensational Williams', *All The Year Round*, 10 (1864), pp. 14–17.

Dickens, Charles, with Wills, W.H., 'Idiots', *Household Words*, 7 (1853), pp. 313–17.

Ellis, Havelock, *Man and Woman* (London: Walter Scott Publishing Co. Ltd, 1894).

Esquirol, Jean Etienne, *Mental Maladies: A Treatise on Insanity*, trans. by E.K. Hunt (Philadelphia: Lea & Blanchard, 1845).

Ferrier, David, *Functions of the Brain* [1876], facsimile of 2nd edition (London: Routledge/Thoemmes Press, 2000).

——, 'Experimental Researches in Cerebral Physiology and Pathology', in *The West Riding Lunatic Asylum Reports*, ed. J. Crichton Brown, vol. 3, 1873, pp. 30–96.

——, untitled article, in *The West Riding Lunatic Asylum Reports*, ed. J. Crichton Brown, vol. 4, 1874, pp. 30–62.

Foucault, Michel, *Madness and Civilization*, trans. by R. Howard (London: Tavistock, 1967).

Gerard, Emily, 'Transylvanian Superstitions', *The Nineteenth Century*, 18 (1885), pp. 130–50.

[Gilbert, William], *Shirley Hall Asylum; or, the Memoirs of a Monomaniac* (London, 1863).

Hack, Daniel, *Tuke's A Dictionary of Psychological Medicine*, 2 vols (London: J. & A. Churchill, 1892).

Haslam, John, *Observations on Madness and Melancholy* (London: J. Callow, 1809).

Hobbes, Thomas, *Leviathan* [1651] (Harmondsworth: Penguin, 1985).

Hughes, Thomas, *The Manliness of Christ* (London: Macmillan, 1879).

Knight, Paul Slade, *Observations on the Causes, Symptoms, and Treatment of Derangement of the Mind* (London, Manchester, 1827).

Laycock, Thomas, 'On the Naming and Classification of Mental Diseases and Defects', *Journal of Mental Science*, 9 (1863), pp. 153–70.

Le Fanu, Sheridan, *The Rose and the Key* [1871] (New York: Dover Publications, 1982).

Linton, Eliza Lynn, *Sowing the Wind* [1867] (London: Chatto& Windus, 1890).

McCarthy, Justin, 'Charles Reade', *The Galaxy*, 14 (1872), pp. 437–46.

Mackenzie, Henry, *The Man of Feeling* [1771], Oxford English Novels (Oxford: Oxford University Press, 1967).

Mansel, Henry, 'Sensation Novels', *Quarterly Review*, 113 (1863), pp. 482–514.

Maudsley, Henry, 'Memoir of the Late John Conolly, M.D.', *Journal of Mental Science*, 12 (1866), pp. 151–74.

Henry Maudsley, *The Pathology of Mind: A Study of Its Distempers, Deformities and Disorders* [1895], intro. Sir Aubrey Lewis (London: Friedman, 1979).

Mayo, Thomas, *An Essay on the Relation of the Theory of Morals to Insanity* (London, 1834).

[Merivale, Herman Charles], *My Experiences in a Lunatic Asylum* (London: Chatto & Windus, 1879).

Morison, Alexander, *Cases of Mental Disease* (London, Edinburgh, 1828).

——, *Outlines of Lectures on Mental Diseases* (Edinburgh, 1825).

Müller, Max, *Comparative Mythology* (London: Routledge, 1909).

——, *The Science of Language*, 2 vols (London: Longmans, 1891).

Neville, William B., *On Insanity, Its Nature, Causes and Cure* (London, 1836).

Nordau, Max, *Degeneration* [1895] (Nebraska: University of Nebraksa, 1993).

Oliphant, Margaret, 'Sensation Novels', *Blackwood's Edinburgh Magazine*, 91 (1862), pp. 564–84.

Payne, James, *The Clyffards of Clyffe* (London: Hurst & Blackett, 1866).

Perceval John, *A Narrative of the treatment experienced by a gentleman during a state of mental derangement; designed to explain the causes and the nature of insanity, and to expose the injudicious conduct pursued towards many unfortunate sufferers under that calamity* (London: Effingham Wilson, 1840).

Philippe Pinel, *A Treatise on Insanity* [1806], trans. D.D. Davis (New York: Hafner Publishing Co., 1962).

Prichard, James Cowles, *A Treatise on Insanity and Other Disorders Affecting the Mind* (London: Sherwood, Gilbert & Piper, 1835).

Reade, Charles, *Griffith Gaunt: or Jealousy* [1866] (London: Chatto & Windus, no date).

——, *Hard Cash* [1863] (London: Chatto & Windus, 1880?).

——, *It Is Never Too Late to Mend* [1856], (London: Chatto & Windus, 1887).

Plays by Charles Reade, ed. Michael Hammet (Cambridge: Cambridge University Press, 1986).

Reade, Charles, *Readiana* (London: Chatto & Windus, 1883).

——, *A Simpleton* [1872] (London: Chatto & Windus, 1896).

——, *A Terrible Temptation* [1871], (London: Chatto & Windus, 1880?).

——, 'Very Hard Cash', *All the Year Round*, 10 (1863), pp. 121–28.

Ricks, Christopher, *Tennyson* (London: Macmillan, 1972).

Spofford, H.P., 'Charles Reade', *The Atlantic Monthly*, 14 (1864), pp. 137–49.

Spurzheim, Johann Gaspar, *Observations on the Deranged Manifestations of the Mind, or Insanity* (London, 1817).

Stoker, Bram, *Dracula* [1897], ed. Maud Ellman, The World's Classics (Oxford: Oxford University Press, 1996).

Swinburne, Algernon Charles, *Studies in Prose and Poetry* (London: Chatto & Windus, 1897).

Tennyson, Alfred, *The Poems of Tennyson*, ed. Christopher Ricks, Longmans Annotated English Poets (London: Longman, 1969).

Trollope, Anthony, *An Autobiography* [1883] (Harmondsworth: Penguin, 1996).

——, *He Knew He Was Right* [1869], ed. John Sutherland, The World's Classics (Oxford: Oxford University Press, 1985).

——, *Kept in the Dark* [1882], Pocket Classics (Gloucester: Alan Sutton Publishing Ltd, 1987).

Tuke, Daniel Hack, *A Dictionary of Psychological Medicine*, 2 vols (London: J. & A. Churchill, 1892).

Tuke, Samuel, *Description of the Retreat* (York: Alexander, 1813).

Winslow, Forbes B., *On Obscure Diseases of the Brain and Disorders of the Mind* (London: John Churchill, 1860).

Wood, Mrs Henry, *St. Martin's Eve* [1866] (London: Ward, Locke & Co., 1916?).

Wordsworth, William, 'The Idiot Boy', in *The Poems*, vol. 1, ed. John O. Hayden (New Haven, CT, and London, Yale University Press, 1977), pp. 281–95.

Wynter, Andrew, *The Borderlands of Insanity* (London: Robert Hardwicke, 1875).

Secondary sources

Alexander, G., and Selesnick, Sheldon I., *The History of Psychiatry* (New York: Harper & Row, 1966).

Altick, Richard D., *Victorian Studies in Scarlet* (London: Dent, 1970).

Ashley, Robert P., *Wilkie Collins* (London: Arthur Barker, 1952).

Auerbach, Nina, 'Magi and Maidens: The Romance of the Victorian Freud', *Critical Inquiry*, 8 (1981–82), pp. 281–300.

——, *Woman and the Demon: The Life of a Victorian Myth* (Cambridge, MA: Harvard University Press, 1982).

Bakhtin, M.M., *The Dialogic Imagination*, trans. Caryl Emerson and Michael Holquist (Austin, TX: University of Texas Press, 1981).

Bareham, Tony (ed.), *Anthony Trollope* (London: Vision Press, 1980).

X   Barickman, Richard, MacDonald, Susan, and Stark, Myra (eds), *Corrupt Relations* (New York: Columbia University Press, 1992).

Belford, Barbara, *Bram Stoker: A Biography of the Author of 'Dracula'* (London: Weidenfeld & Nicolson, 1996).

Boyle, Thomas, *Black Swine in the Sewers of Hampstead: Beneath the Surface of Victorian Sensationalism* (London: Hodder & Stoughton, 1989).

Boyle, Thomas F., ' "Fishy Extremities": Subversion of Orthodoxy in the Victorian Sensation Novel', *Literature and History*, 9 (1983), pp. 92–96.

Brantlinger, Patrick, 'What is "Sensational" about the "Sensation Novel"?', *Nineteenth Century Fiction*, 37 (1992), pp. 1–28.

X   Brooks, Peter, *The Melodramatic Imagination* (London: Yale University Press, 1976).

Burns, Wayne, *Charles Reade: A Study in Victorian Authorship* (New York: Bookman Associates, 1961).

——, 'Charles Reade's *Hard Cash*: "Uncomparably My Best Production" ', *Literature and Psychology*, 8 (1958), pp. 34–43.

Bynum, William F., 'Rationales for Therapy in British Psychiatry, 1780–1835', in Andrew Scull (ed.), *Madhouses, Mad-Doctors and Madmen* (London: Athlone Press, 1981), pp. 35–57.

Byrd, Max, *Visits to Bedlam* (Columbia, SC: University of South Carolina Press, 1974).

Carlson, Eric T., and Dain, Norman, 'The Meaning of Moral Insanity', *Bulletin of the History of Medicine*, 36 (1962), pp. 130–40.

——, 'The Psychotherapy That Was Moral Treatment', *American Journal of Psychotherapy*, 117 (1960–61), pp. 519–24.

X Chesler, Phyllis, *Women and Madness* (London: Allen Lane, 1972).

X   Christ, Carol, 'Victorian Masculinity and the Angel in the House', in Martha Vicinus (ed.), *A Widening Sphere: Changing Roles of Victorian Women* (Bloomington, IN: Indiana University Press, 1977), pp. 146–62.

Clark, Michael J., ' "Morbid Introspection", Unsoundness of Mind, and British Psychological Medicine, c.1830–c.1900', in W.F. Bynum, Roy Porter and Michael Shepherd (eds), *The Anatomy of Madness: Essays in the History of Psychiatry*, vol. III, *The Asylum and Its Psychiatry* (London: Tavistock, 1985), pp. 71–101.

——, 'The Rejection of Psychological Approaches to Mental Disorder in Late Nineteenth-Century British Psychiatry', in Andrew Scull (ed.), *Madhouses, Mad-Doctors and Madmen* (London: Athlone Press, 1981), pp. 271–312.

Clarke, William M., *The Secret Life of Wilkie Collins* (London: Allison & Busby, 1988).

Colley, Ann C., *Tennyson and Madness* (Atlanta, GA: University of Georgia Press, 1983).

Cooter, Roger, 'Phrenology and British Alienists, ca. 1825–1845', in Andrew Scull (ed.), *Madhouses, Mad-Doctors and Madmen* (London: Athlone Press, 1981), pp. 58–104.

Crawford, Iain, ' "Nature...Drenched in Blood": *Barnaby Rudge* and Wordsworth's "Idiot Boy" ', *Dickens Quarterly*, 8 (1991), pp. 38–47.

Dain, Norman, *Concepts of Insanity in the United States, 1789–1865* (New Brunswick: Rutgers University Press, 1964).

Davidoff, L., and Hall, Catherine, *Family Fortunes: Men and Women of the English Middle-Class, 1780–1850* (London: Hutchinson, 1987).

Davis, Nuel Pharr, *The Life of Wilkie Collins* (Urbana, IL: University of Illinois Press, 1956).

DePorte, Michael V., *Nightmares and Hobbyhorses* (San Marino, CA: Huntington Library, 1974).

Dollimore, Jonathan, 'Perversion, Degeneration, and the Sex Drive', in Andrew H. Miller and James Eli Adams (eds), *Sexualities in Victorian Britain* (Bloomington, IN: Indiana University Press, 1996), pp. 96–117.

Donnelly, Michael, *Managing the Mind: A Study of Medical Psychology in Early Nineteenth-Century Britain* (London: Tavistock, 1983).

Doob, Penelope B.K., *Nebuchadnezzar's Children: Conventions of Madness in Middle English Literature* (New Haven, CT: Yale University Press, 1974).

Dyson, A.E., *The Inimitable Dickens: A Reading of the Novels* (London: Macmillan, 1970).

Eagleton, Terry, *Myths of Power* (London: Macmillan, 1975).

Edwards, P.D., *Anthony Trollope, His Art and Scope* (Brighton: Harvester, 1978).

——, 'Trollope and the Reviewers: Three Notes', *Notes and Queries*, November 1968, pp. 418–20.

Eliot, T.S., *Selected Essays* (London: Faber & Faber, 1932).

Elwin, Malcolm, *Charles Reade* (London: Jonathan Cape, 1934).

Farson, Daniel, *The Man Who Wrote 'Dracula': A Biography of Bram Stoker* (London: Michael Joseph, 1975).

Feder, Lillian, *Madness in Literature* (Princeton, NJ: Princeton University Press, 1980).

Foucault, Michel, *Madness and Civilization: A History of Insanity in the Age of Reason*, trans. R. Howard (London: Tavistock, 1967).

Frayling, Christopher, *Vampyres: Lord Byron to Count Dracula* (London: Faber & Faber, 1991).

French, Richard D., *Antivivisection and Medical Science in Victorian Society* (Princeton, NJ: Princeton University Press, 1975).

Freud, Sigmund, 'The "Uncanny"', in *The Standard Edition of the Complete Works of Sigmund Freud*, vol. XVII (1917–1919), trans. James Strachey (London: Hogarth Press, 1955), pp. 218–53.

Fullinwider, S.P., 'Insanity as the Loss of Self: the Moral Insanity Controversy Revisited', *Bulletin of the History of Medicine*, 49 (1975), pp. 87–101.

Genette, Gérard, *Narrative Discourse*, trans. Jane E. Lewin (London: Blackwell, 1980).

Gilbert, Sandra M., and Gubar, Susan, *The Madwoman in the Attic: The Woman Writer and the Nineteenth-Century Literary Imagination* (New Haven, CT, and London: Yale University Press, 1979).

Gilman, Sander, *Seeing the Insane* (New York: John Wiley & Sons, 1982).

Gilman, Sander L., *Difference and Pathology: Stereotypes of Sexuality, Race and Madness* (London: Cornell, 1985).

Goldberg, Michael, *Carlyle and Dickens* (Athens, GA: University of Georgia Press, 1972).

Goffman, Erving, *Asylums* (Harmondsworth: Penguin, 1968).

Gombrich, Ernst, *Art and Illusion: A Study in the Psychology of Pictorial Representation* (London: Phaidon Press, 1960).

Greenslade, William, *Degeneration, Culture and the Novel, 1880–1940*, (Cambridge: Cambridge University Press, 1994).

Grove, Thelma, 'Barnaby Rudge: A Case Study in Autism', *Dickension*, 83 (1987), pp. 139–48.

Hall, Donald E. (ed.), *Muscular Christianity: Embodying the Victorian Age* (Cambridge: Cambridge University Press, 1994).

Hammerton, James A., *Cruelty and Companionship: Conflict in Nineteenth-Century Married Life* (London: Routledge, 1992).

Hayter, Alethea, *Opium and the Romantic Imagination* (London: Faber & Faber, 1968).

Heller, Tamar, *Dead Secrets: Wilkie Collins and the Female Gothic* (New Haven, CT, and London: Yale University Press, 1992).

Hoeldtke, Robert, 'The History of Associationism and British Medical Psychology', *Medical History*, 11 (1967), pp. 46–65.

Hollington, Michael, *Dicken and the Grotesque* (London: Croom Helm, 1984).

Hollington, Michael, 'Monstrous Faces: Physiognomy in *Barnaby Rudge*', *Dickens Quarterly*, 9 (1991), pp. 6–15.

Howell, Colin, 'Asylums, Psychiatry and the History of Madness', *Queens Quarterly*, 93 (1986), pp. 19–24.

Hughes, Winifred, *The Maniac in the Cellar: Sensation Novels of the 1860s* (Princeton, NJ: Princeton University Press, 1980).

Hume, Kathryn, *Fantasy and Mimesis: Responses to Reality in Western Literature* (London: Methuen, 1984).

Hunter, Richard, and MacAlpine, Ida, *Three Hundred Years of Psychiatry, 1555–1860: A History Presented in Selected English Texts* (Oxford: Oxford University Press, 1963).

——, 'Dickens and Conolly: An Embarrassed Editor's Apology', *Times Literary Supplement*, 11 August 1961, pp. 534–35.

Hyder, Clyde K., 'Wilkie Collins and *The Woman in White*', *PMLA*, 54 (1939), pp. 297–303.

Jackson, Rosemary, *Fantasy: The Literature of Subversion* (London: Methuen, 1984).

James, Henry, *Notes and Reviews* [1921] (New York: Dunster House, 1968).

Jones, Kathleen, *Lunacy, Law and Conscience, 1744–1845* (London: Routledge & Kegan Paul, 1955).

Jordanova, Ludmilla, *Sexual Visions: Images of Gender in Science and Medicine between the Eighteenth and Twentieth Centuries* (Brighton: Harvester, 1989).

Kaplan, Fred, *Dickens and Mesmerism: The Hidden Springs of Fiction* (Princeton, NJ: Princeton University Press, 1975).

Keating, Peter, *The Haunted Study: A Social History of the English Novel, 1875–1914* (London: Fontana Press, 1989).

Kendrick, Walter M., 'The Sensationalism of the Woman in White', *Nineteenth-Century Fiction*, 32 (1977), pp. 18–35.

Knoepflmacher, U.C., 'The Counterworld of Victorian Fiction', in Jerome H. Buckley (ed.), *The Worlds of Victorian Fiction*, Harvard Studies 6 (Cambridge, MA: Harvard University Press, 1975).

Leary, Barbara Fass, 'Wilkie Collins's Cinderella: The History of Psychology and *The Woman in White*', *Dickens Studies Annual*, 10 (1982), pp. 91–141.

Leatherdale, Clive, *Dracula: The Novel and the Legend* (Wellingborough: Aquarian Press, 1985).

——, *The Origins of Dracula* (London: William Kimber, 1987).

Leavis, F.R., and Leavis, Q.D., *Dickens the Novelist* (Harmondsworth: Penguin, 1972).

Lindsay, Jack, 'Barnaby Rudge', in John Gross and Gabriel Pearson (eds), *Dickens and the Twentieth Century* (London: Routledge & Kegan Paul, 1962), pp. 91–106.

Lodge, David, *Language of Fiction: Essays in Criticism and Verbal Analysis of the English Novel*, 2nd edition (London: Routledge & Kegan Paul, 1984).

Loesberg, Jonathan, 'The Ideology of Narrative Form in Sensation Fiction', *Representations*, 13 (1986), pp. 115–38.

Lovejoy, Arthur O, *The Great Chain of Being: A Study of the History of an Idea* (Cambridge, MA: Harvard University Press, 1961).

Lucas, John, *The Melancholy Man: A Study of Dickens's Novels* (London: Methuen, 1970).

Ludlum, Harry, *A Biography of Bram Stoker, Creator of Dracula* (London: New English Library, 1977).

Lukács, Georg, *The Historical Novel*, trans. Hannah Mitchell and Stanley Mitchell (London: Merlin Press, 1962).

MacAlpine, Ida, and Hunter, Richard, *George III: The Mad Business* (London: Allen Lane, 1969).

MacAndrew, Elizabeth, *The Gothic Tradition in Fiction* (New York: Columbia Press, 1979).

McCandless, Peter, 'Liberty and Lunacy: The Victorians and Wrongful Confinement' in Andrew Scull (ed.), *Madhouses, Mad-Doctors, and Madmen: The Social History of Psychiatry in the Victorian Period* (London: Athlone Press, 1981), pp. 339–62.

McKnight, Natalie, *Idiots, Madmen, and Other Prisoners in Dickens* (London: Macmillan, 1993).

MacLeod, John A., 'The Personality of Barnaby Rudge', *Dickensian*, 10 (1909), pp. 262–66 and 291–93.

McMaster, Juliet, ' "Better to be Silly": From Vision to Reality in Barnaby Rudge', *Dickens Studies Annual*, 13 (1984), pp. 1–17.

McNally, Raymond, and Florescu, Radu, *The Essential Dracula* (New York: Mayflower Books, 1979).

Magnet, Myron, *Dickens and the Social Order* (Philadelphia, PA: University of Pennsylvania Press, 1985).

Mangan, J.A., and Walvin, James (eds), *Manliness and Morality: Middle-Class Masculinity in Britain and America 1800–1940* (Manchester, Manchester University Press, 1987).

Marcus, Steven, *Dickens: From Pickwick to Dombey* (London: Chatto & Windus, 1965).

Martin, Philip W., *Mad Women in Romantic Writing* (Brighton: Harvester, 1987).

Martin, Philip, 'The Vampire in the Looking-Glass: Reflection and Projection in Bram Stoker's *Dracula*', in C. Bloom, B. Docherty, J. Gibb and K. Shand (eds), *Nineteenth-Century Suspense: From Poe to C. Doyle* (London: Macmillan, 1988), pp. 80–92.

Masson, Jeffrey, *Against Therapy* (London: Collins, 1989).

Masters, Anthony, *Bedlam* (London: Michael Joseph, 1977).

Micale, Mark S., 'Charcot and the Idea of Hysteria in the Male: Gender, Mental Science, and Medical Diagnosis in Late Nineteenth-Century France', *Medical History*, 34 (1990), pp. 363–411.

——, 'Hysteria Male/Hysteria Female: Reflections on Comparative Gender Construction in Nineteenth-Century France and Britain', in Marina Benjamin (ed.), *Science and Sensibility: Gender and Scientific Enquiry, 1780–1945* (Oxford: Basil Blackwell, 1991), pp. 200–39.

Moss, Stephanie, 'Bram Stoker and the Society for Psychical Research', in Elizabeth Miller (ed.), *Dracula: The Shade and the Shadow* (Westcliffe-on-Sea: Desert Island Books, 1998), pp. 82–92.

Newman, Stephen J., *Dickens at Play* (London: Macmillan, 1981).

Oddie, William, *Dickens and Carlyle: The Question of Influence* (London: The Centenary Press, 1972).

O'Neill, Philip, *Wilkie Collins: Women, Property and Propriety* (London, 1988).

Oppenheim, Janet, '*Shattered Nerves*': *Doctors, Patients, and Depression in Victorian England* (Oxford: Oxford University Press, 1991).

Park, Roberta J., 'Biological Thought, Athletics and the Formation of a "Man of Character": 1830–1900', in J.A. Mangan and James Walvin (eds), *Manliness and Morality: Middle-Class Masculinity in Britain and America, 1800–1940* (Manchester: Manchester University Press, 1987).

Parry-Jones, William, *The Trade in Lunacy* (London, 1972).

Peterson, Audrey, 'Brain Fever in Nineteenth-Century Literature: Fiction and Fact', *Victorian Studies*, 19 (1976), pp. 445–64.

Phillips, Walter C., *Dickens, Reade and Collins, Sensation Novelists* (New York: Columbia University Press, 1919).

Pick, Daniel, ' "Terrors of the Night": *Dracula* and "Degeneration" in the Late Nineteenth Century', *Critical Quarterly*, 30 (1988), pp. 71–87.

Polack, Ernest E., 'Was Barnaby Rudge Mad?', *Dickensian*, 12 (1911), pp. 298–99.

Poovey, Mary, 'Speaking of the Body: Mid-Victorian Construction of Female Desire', in Mary Jacobus, Evelyn Fox Keller and Sally Shuttleworth (eds), *Body/Politics: Women and the Discourse of Science* (London: Routledge, 1990), pp. 29–46.

Porter, Roy, *The Faber Book of Madness* (London: Faber & Faber, 1991).

——, *Mind-Forg'd Manacles: A History of Madness in England from the Restoration to the Regency* (Harmondsworth: Penguin, 1990).

——, *A Social History of Madness: Stories of the Insane* (London: Weidenfeld & Nicolson, 1987).

Punter, David, *The Literature of Terror: A History of Gothic Fictions from 1765 to the Present Day* (London: Longman, 1980).

Pykett, Lyn, *The Sensation Novel from 'The Woman in White' to 'The Moonstone'*, Writers and the Work (Plymouth: Northcote House, 1994).

Reed, John R., *Victorian Conventions* (Athens, OH: Ohio University Press, 1975).

Rice, Thomas J., 'The Politics of *Barnaby Rudge*', in Robert Giddings (ed.), *The Changing World of Charles Dickens* (Totowa, NJ: Vision and Barnes & Noble, 1983), pp. 51–74.

Ricks, Christopher, *Tennyson* (London: Macmillan, 1972).

Robinson, Kenneth, *Wilkie Collins* (London: Bodley Head, 1951).

Rupke, Nicolaas A. (ed.), *Vivisection in Historical Perspective* (London: Croom Helm, 1987).

Sadleir, Michael, *Things Past* (London: Constable, 1944).

Sage, Victor, *Horror Fiction in the Protestant Tradition* (London: Macmillan, 1988).

Scull, Andrew, 'The Domestication of Madness', *Medical History*, 27 (1983), 233–48.

——, 'Moral Treatment Reconsidered: Some Sociological Comments on an Episode in the History of British Psychiatry', in Andrew Scull (ed.), *Madhouses, Mad-Doctors and Madmen* (London: Athlone Press, 1981), pp. 105–18.

——, 'A Victorian Alienist: John Conolly, F.R.C.P., D.C.L. (1794–1866)', in W.F. Bynum, Roy Porter and Michael Shepherd (eds), *The Anatomy of Madness: Essays in the History of Psychiatry*, vol. 1, *People and Ideas* (London: Tavistock, 1985), pp. 103–50.

Scull, Andrew T., *Museums of Madness. The Social Organization of Insanity in Nineteenth-Century England* (Harmondsworth: Penguin, 1982).

Sedgwick, Eve Kosofsky, *The Coherence of Gothic Conventions*, (London: Methuen, 1986).

Seed, David, 'The Narrative Method of *Dracula*', *Nineteenth-Century Fiction*, 40 (1985), pp. 61–75.

Showalter Elaine, *The Female Malady: Women, Madness and English Culture, 1830–1930* (London: Virago, 1987).

——, *A Literature of Their Own: British Women Novelists from Brontë to Lessing* (London: Virago, 1988).

——, 'Victorian Women and Insanity', in Andrew Scull (ed.), *Madhouses, Mad-Doctors and Madmen*l (London: Athlone Press, 1981), pp. 313–36.

Shuttleworth, Sally, *Charlotte Bronte and Victorian Psychology* (Cambridge: Cambridge University Press, 1996).

Skultans, Vieda, *English Madness: Ideas on Insanity, 1580–1890* (London: Routledge & Kegan Paul, 1979).

——, *Madness and Morals* (London: Routledge & Kegan Paul, 1975).

Small, Helen, *Love's Madness: Medicine, the Novel, and Female Insanity, 1800–1865* (Oxford: Clarendon Press, 1996).

Smalley, Donald (ed.), *Trollope: The Critical Heritage* (London: Routledge & Kegan Paul, 1969).

Smith, Elton Edward, *Charles Reade* (London: George Prior Publishers, 1976).

Stallybrass, Peter, and White, Allon, *The Politics and Poetics of Transgression* (London: Methuen, 1986).

Steig, Michael, *Dickens and Phiz* (Bloomington, IN: Indiana University Press, 1978).

Stevens, Joan, ' "Woodcuts dropped into the text": The Illustations in *The Old Curiosity Shop* and *Barnaby Rudge*', *Studies in Bibliography*, 20 (1967), pp. 113–34.

Stignant, Paul and Widdowson, Peter, '*Barnaby Rudge* – a Historical Novel?', *Literature and History*, 2 (1975), pp. 2–44.

Summers, Montague, *The Vampire: His Kith and Kin* (London: Kegan Paul, 1928).

——, *The Vampire in Europe* (London: Kegal Paul, 1929).

——, *Victorian Ghost Stories* (London: Fortune Press, 1933).

Sussman, Herbert, 'The Study of Victorian Masculinities', *Victorian Literature and Culture*, 20 (1992), pp. 366–77.

——, *Victorian Masculinities: Manhood and Masculine Politics in Early Victorian Literature and Art* (Cambridge: Cambridge University Press, 1995).

Sutcliffe, Emerson Grant, 'Plotting in Reade's Novels', *PMLA*, 47 (1932), pp. 834–63.

Sutherland, John, 'Dickens, Reade and *Hard Cash*', *Dickensian*, 81 (1985), pp. 5–12.

Taylor, Jenny Bourne, *In the Secret Theatre of Home: Wilkie Collins, Sensation Narrative and Nineteenth-Century Psychology* (London: Routledge, 1988).

Taylor, Jenny Bourne, and Shuttleworth, Sally (eds), *Embodied Selves: An Anthology of Psychological Texts, 1830–1890* (Oxford: Clarendon Press, 1998).

Tosh, John, 'What Should Historians Do with Masculinity? Reflections on Nineteenth-Century Britain', *History Workshop Journal*, 38 (Autumn 1994), pp. 179–202.

——, *A Man's Place: Masculinity and the Middle-Class Home in Victorian England* (New Haven, CT, and London: Yale University Press, 1999).

Ussher, Jane, *Women's Madness: Misogyny or Mental Illness* (Hemel Hempstead: Harvester Wheatsheaf, 1991).

Vance, Norman, *The Sinews of the Spirit: The Ideal of Christian Manliness in Victorian Literature and Religious Thought* (Cambridge: Cambridge University Press, 1985).

Vicinus, Martha, '"Helpless and Unfriended": Nineteenth-Century Domestic Melodrama', *New Literature History*, 13 (1981–82), pp. 127–43.

Vickery, Amanda, 'Golden Age to Separate Spheres? A Review of the Categories and Chronology of English Women's History', *Historiographical Review*, XXXVI (1993), pp. 383–414.

Walk, Alex, 'Some Aspects of the "Moral Treatment" of the Insane up to 1854', *Journal of Mental Science*, 100 (1954), pp. 807–37.

Wall, Stephen, *Trollope and Character* (London: Faber & Faber, 1988).

Wiesenthal, Chris, *Figuring Madness in Nineteenth-Century Fiction* (Basingstoke: Macmillan, 1997).

Winter, Alison, *Mesmerized: Powers of Mind in Victorian Britain* (Chicago, IL: University of Chicago Press, 1998).

Wolff, Robert Lee, 'Devoted Disciple: The Letters of Mary Elizabeth Braddon to Sir Edward Bulwer-Lytton 1862–1873', *Harvard Library Bulletin*, 22 (1974), pp. 5–35 and 129–61.

Wood, Jane, *Passion and Pathology in Victorian Fiction* (Oxford: Oxford University Press, 2001).

Wright, David, *Mental Disability in Victorian England: The Earlswood Asylum, 1847–1901* (Oxford: Oxford University Press, 2001).

Wynter, Andrew, *The Borderlands of Insanity* (London: Robert Hardwicke, 1875).

Young, Robert Maxwell, *Mind, Brain and Adaptation in the Nineteenth Century: Cerebral Localization and Its Biological Context from Gall to Ferrier* (Oxford: Clarendon Press, 1970).

Index